Fagin

THE JEW

BY

Will Eisner

DOUBLEDAY

New York   London   Toronto   Sydney   Auckland

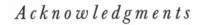

Acknowledgments

I am most grateful for the research assistance provided by Benjamin Herzberg, which went beyond my expectations.

To Dave Schreiner, my thanks for his keen insight and reliable editing.

And as always, I acknowledge my dependence on the patient, wise, and enduring encouragement from my dear wife, Ann.

PUBLISHED BY DOUBLEDAY
a division of Random House, Inc.

DOUBLEDAY and the portrayal of an anchor with a dolphin
are registered trademarks of Random House, Inc.

Book design by Will Eisner

Library of Congress Cataloging-in-Publication Data
Eisner, Will.
Fagin the Jew / by Will Eisner.— 1st ed.
p. cm
I. Title.

PN6727.E35F34 2003
741.5'973—dc21
2003048931
ISBN 0-385-51009-8

PRINTED IN THE UNITED STATES OF AMERICA

October 2003
First Edition
1 3 5 7 9 10 8 6 4 2

In June of 1940, I began a syndicated newspaper comic book insert called *The Spirit*, about a masked crime fighter. It featured a young African American boy, Ebony, as a humorous counterfoil. This was hardly innovative; Jack Benny had Rochester, the movies had Stepin Fetchit, and radio had Amos and Andy. These were accepted stereotypical caricatures of the time. It was an era in our cultural history when the misuse of English based on ethnic origin was fashionable humor. Ebony spoke with the classic "Negro" dialect and delivered a gentle humor that gave warmth to balance the coldness of crime stories. In my eagerness for readership, I thought I was on to a good thing.

In 1945, after an interruption for military service, I returned to the feature. By then, I had become more aware of the social implications of racial stereotypes, and I began to treat Ebony with greater insight. As often happens with cartoonists, I became very fond of him and sought to make him as real as I imagined him. As the rising civil rights movement became more prominent, I introduced a well-spoken black detective and treated my hero's black assistant in a more sensitive manner.

One day, I received a letter from an old high school classmate who had become a civil rights activist, chiding me for abandoning the "liberal" views we shared back in school. That same day, I got a letter from the editor of a Baltimore Afro-American newspaper commending me on my "fine treatment" of Ebony in my comic strip. These letters alerted me to the reality that, while my stories were designed as entertainment, I was nonetheless feeding a racial prejudice with this stereotype image. Still looking for ethnic diversity, I replaced Ebony with an Eskimo boy and later with Sammy, a white boy. The series ended in 1952, and as I continued my career in instructional comics, I never recognized that my rendering of Ebony, when viewed historically, was in conflict with the rage

I felt when I saw anti-Semitism in art and literature.

While I didn't experience any guilt over my creation of Ebony, I became conscious of the problem over the years while teaching sequential art, as my lectures invariably had to confront the issue of stereotype. I concluded that there was "bad" stereotype and "good" stereotype; intention was the key. Since stereotype is an essential tool in the language of graphic storytelling, it is incumbent on cartoonists to recognize its impact on social judgment. In twenty-first-century America, we struggle with "racial profiling." We are in an era that requires graphic portrayers to be sensitive to unfair stereotypes.

So it is with this background and an awareness of the influence of imagery on the popular culture that I began to produce graphic novels with themes of Jewish ethnicity and the prejudice Jews still face. A few years ago, as I was examining folktales and literary classics for possible graphic adaptation, I became aware of the origins of the ethnic stereotypes we accept without question. Upon examining the illustrations of the original editions of *Oliver Twist*, I found an unquestionable example of visual defamation in classic literature. The memory of their awful use by the Nazis in World War II, one hundred years later, added evidence to the persistence of evil stereotyping. Combating it became an obsessive pursuit, and I realized that I had no choice but to undertake a truer portrait of Fagin by telling his life story in the only way I could.

This book, therefore, is not an adaptation of *Oliver Twist*! It is the story of Fagin the Jew.

—WILL EISNER, FLORIDA, 2003

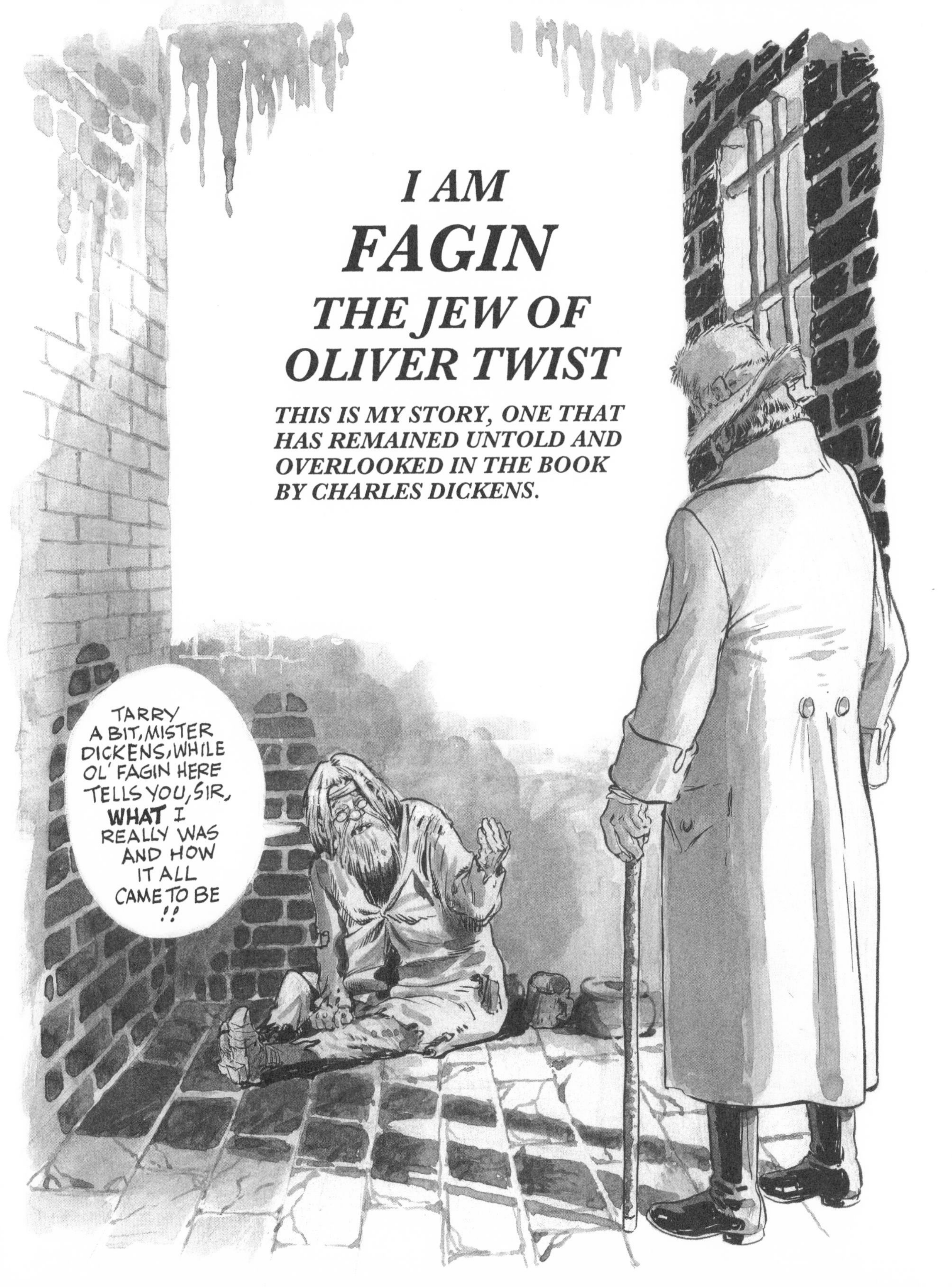
I AM
FAGIN
THE JEW OF
OLIVER TWIST
THIS IS MY STORY, ONE THAT HAS REMAINED UNTOLD AND OVERLOOKED IN THE BOOK BY CHARLES DICKENS.
TARRY A BIT, MISTER DICKENS, WHILE OL' FAGIN HERE TELLS YOU, SIR, WHAT I REALLY WAS AND HOW IT ALL CAME TO BE !!

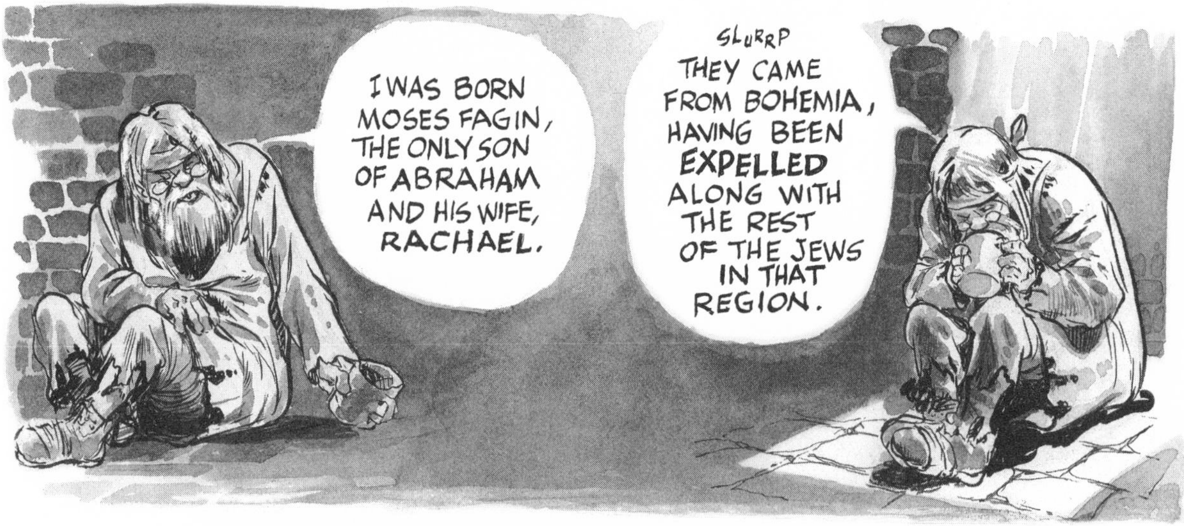
I WAS BORN MOSES FAGIN, THE ONLY SON OF ABRAHAM AND HIS WIFE, RACHAEL.
SLURRP
THEY CAME FROM BOHEMIA, HAVING BEEN EXPELLED ALONG WITH THE REST OF THE JEWS IN THAT REGION.

My parents arrived in London along with other Jews fleeing Middle Europe. How they managed the journey, God only knows.

Here they found a better community, where Jews were not subject to special laws or legal pogroms. England was a country that had long been a refuge for Spanish and Portuguese Jews known as Sephardim. They were the earliest to arrive and had become well established, whereas the newly arriving Middle Europeans were regarded as lower class. Germans, Poles, and the like were called Ashkenazim.

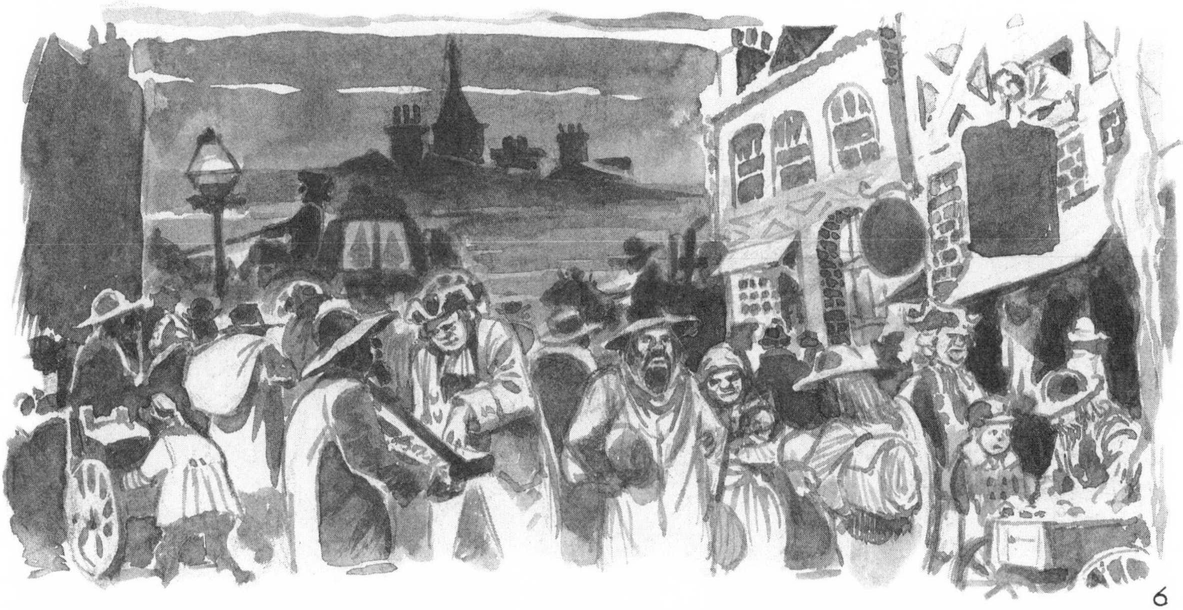

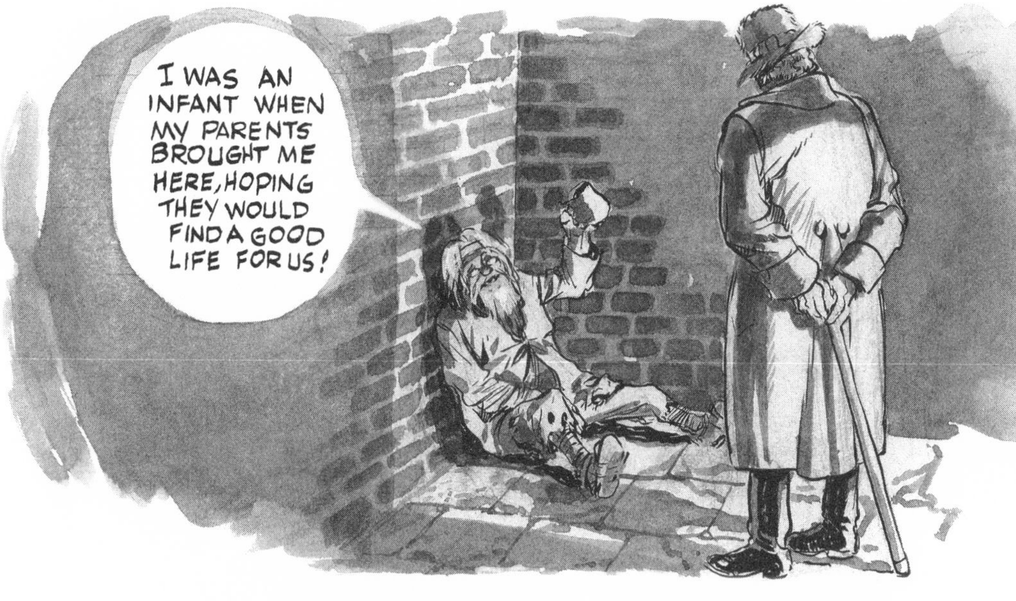
I WAS AN INFANT WHEN MY PARENTS BROUGHT ME HERE, HOPING THEY WOULD FIND A GOOD LIFE FOR US!

But for us, even London life was not so simple. These were grim times, and yet the best of times for us newcomers. We were uneducated and endured a pauperdom perfumed by the promise of opportunity.

Aye, 'twas, not to put too fine a point on it, a time when opportunity bloomed in the dirty streets of London. It was where, when I was still a mere tyke, my parents put me out to peddle needles and buttons.

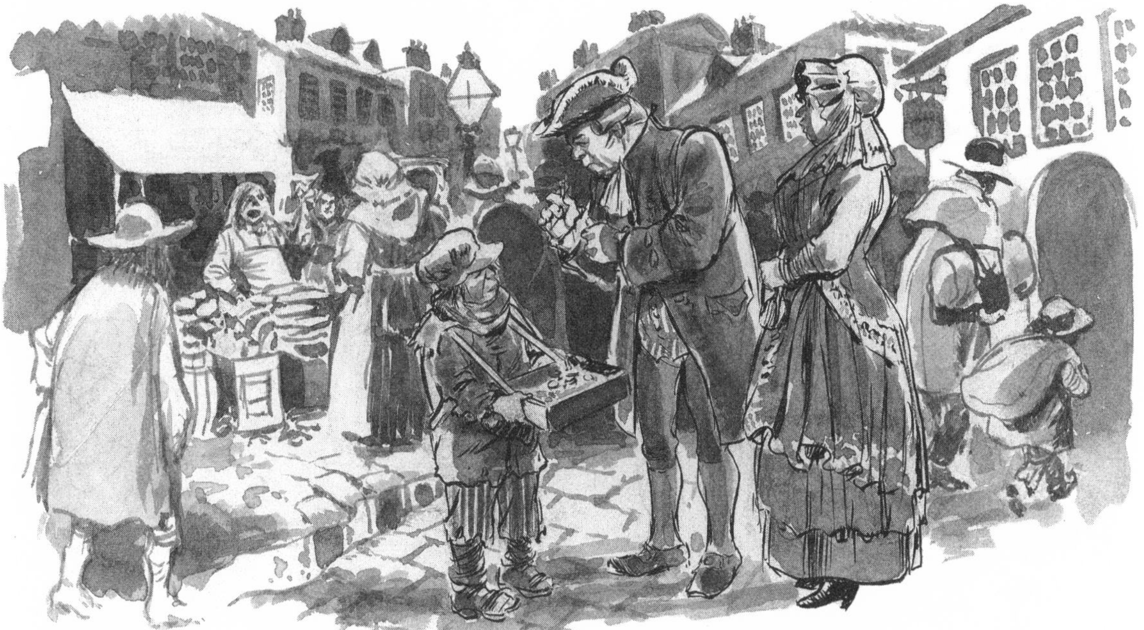

I was "educated" by my father, who, having learned by emulating other Jews, had become skilled in the trades of the street.

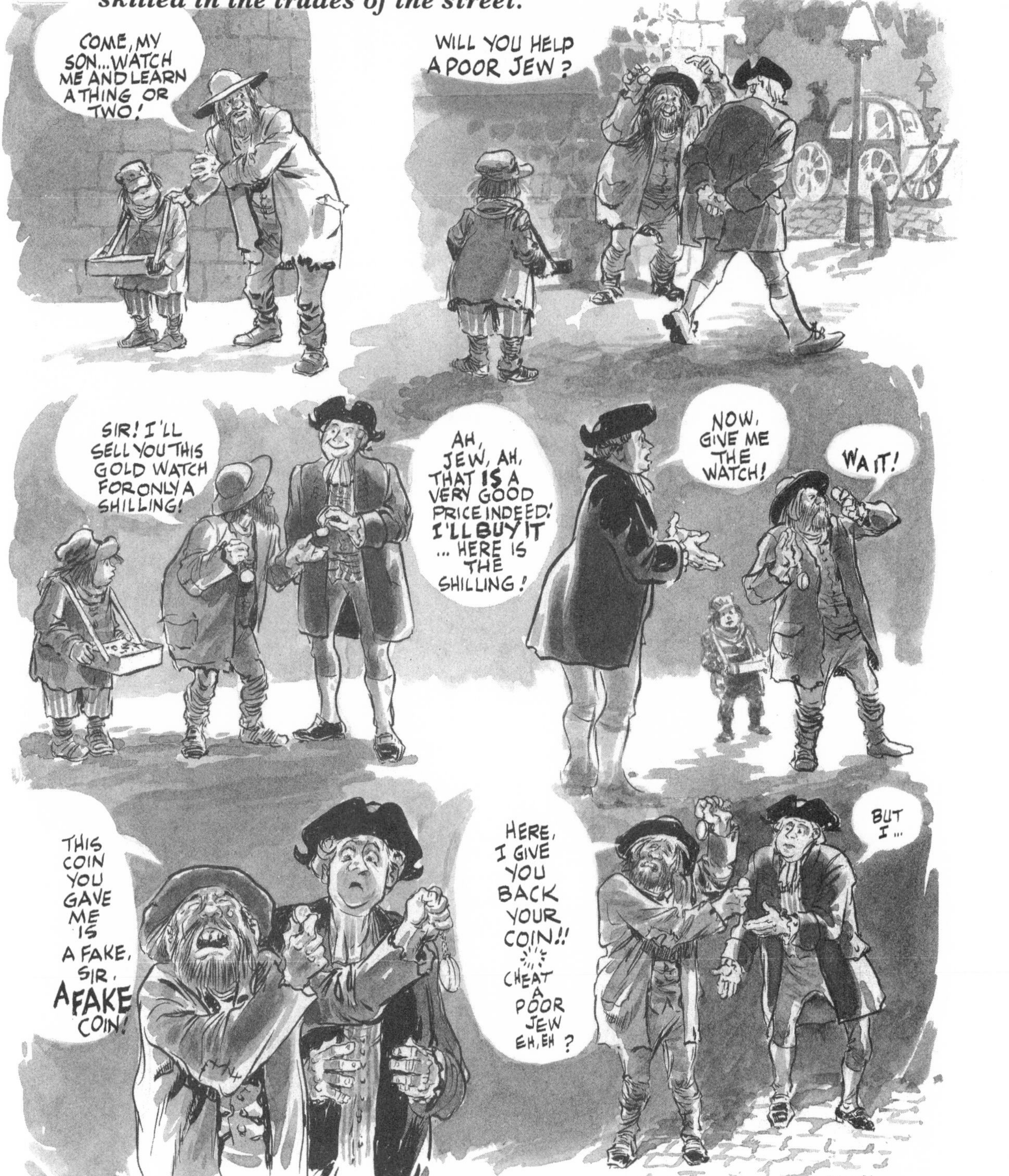
COME, MY SON... WATCH ME AND LEARN A THING OR TWO!
WILL YOU HELP A POOR JEW?
SIR! I'LL SELL YOU THIS GOLD WATCH FOR ONLY A SHILLING!
AH, JEW, AH, THAT IS A VERY GOOD PRICE INDEED! I'LL BUY IT ... HERE IS THE SHILLING!
NOW, GIVE ME THE WATCH!
WAIT!
THIS COIN YOU GAVE ME IS A FAKE, SIR. A FAKE COIN!
HERE, I GIVE YOU BACK YOUR COIN!! CHEAT A POOR JEW EH, EH?
BUT I...

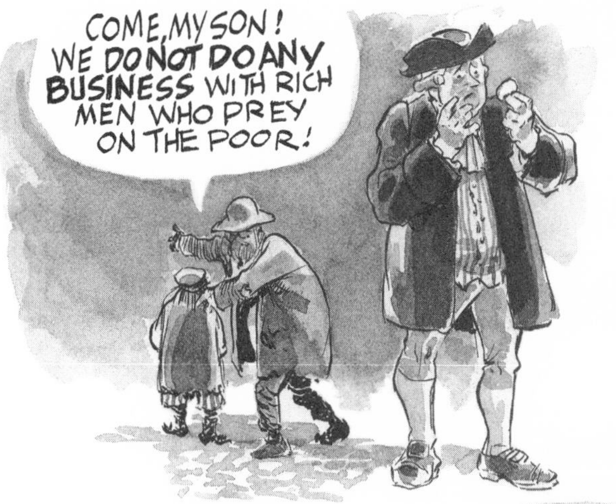
COME, MY SON! WE DO NOT DO ANY BUSINESS WITH RICH MEN WHO PREY ON THE POOR!

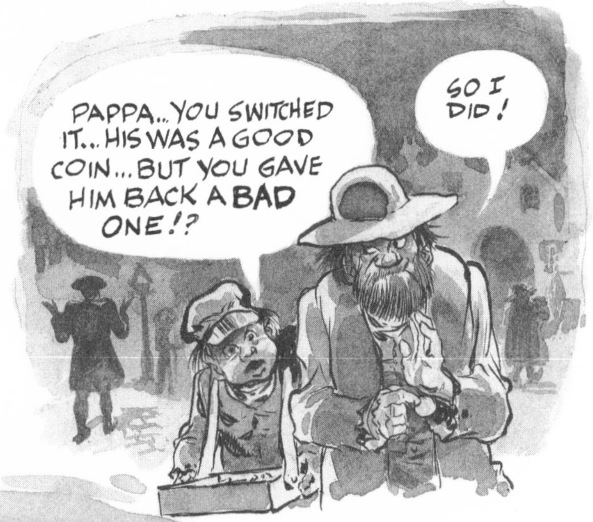
PAPPA... YOU SWITCHED IT... HIS WAS A GOOD COIN... BUT YOU GAVE HIM BACK A BAD ONE!?
SO I DID!

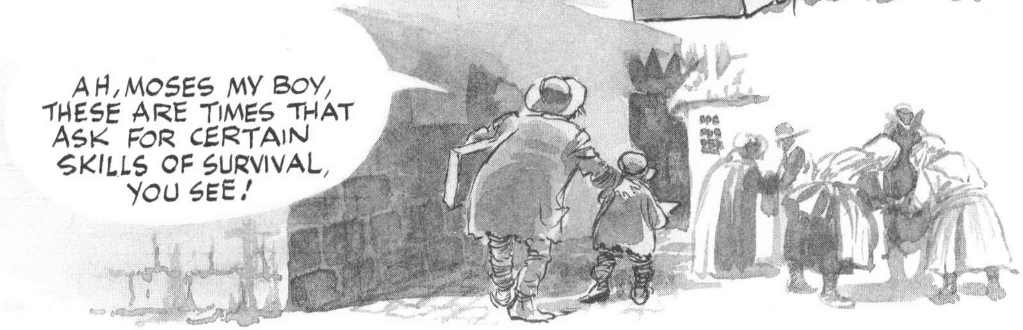
AH, MOSES MY BOY, THESE ARE TIMES THAT ASK FOR CERTAIN SKILLS OF SURVIVAL, YOU SEE!

This was the nature of my formative years... until I neared my thirteenth birthday.

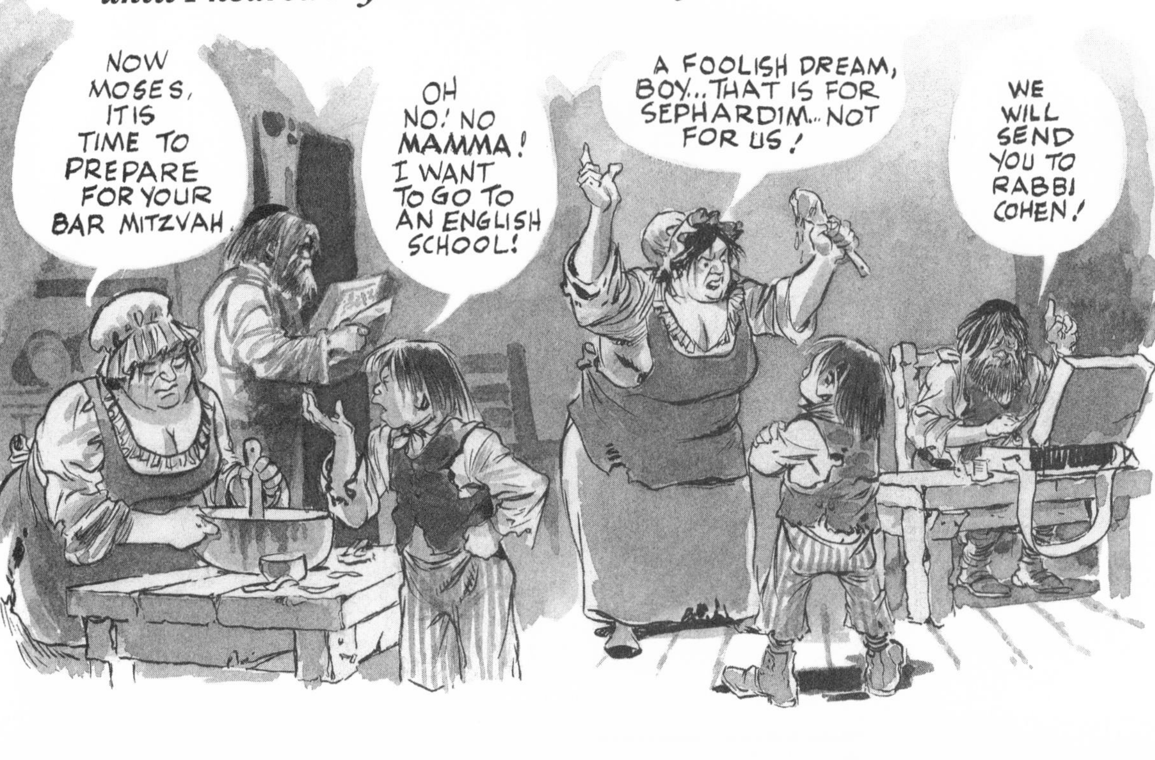
NOW MOSES, IT IS TIME TO PREPARE FOR YOUR BAR MITZVAH.
OH NO! NO MAMMA! I WANT TO GO TO AN ENGLISH SCHOOL!
A FOOLISH DREAM, BOY... THAT IS FOR SEPHARDIM... NOT FOR US!
WE WILL SEND YOU TO RABBI COHEN!

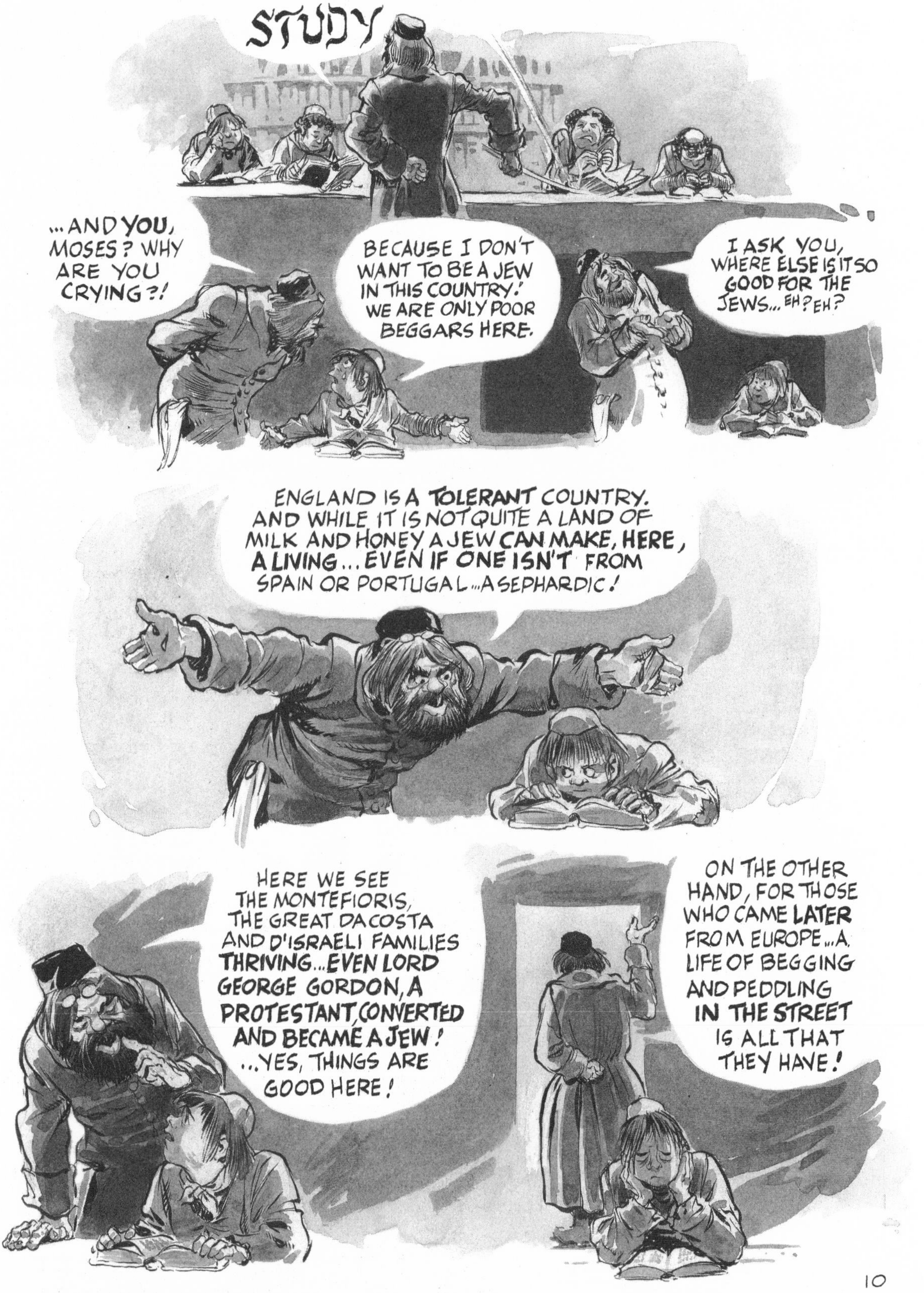

STUDY
...AND YOU, MOSES? WHY ARE YOU CRYING?!
BECAUSE I DON'T WANT TO BE A JEW IN THIS COUNTRY! WE ARE ONLY POOR BEGGARS HERE.
I ASK YOU, WHERE ELSE IS IT SO GOOD FOR THE JEWS... EH? EH?
ENGLAND IS A TOLERANT COUNTRY. AND WHILE IT IS NOT QUITE A LAND OF MILK AND HONEY A JEW CAN MAKE, HERE, A LIVING... EVEN IF ONE ISN'T FROM SPAIN OR PORTUGAL...A SEPHARDIC!
HERE WE SEE THE MONTEFIORIS, THE GREAT DACOSTA AND D'ISRAELI FAMILIES THRIVING...EVEN LORD GEORGE GORDON, A PROTESTANT, CONVERTED AND BECAME A JEW! ...YES, THINGS ARE GOOD HERE!
ON THE OTHER HAND, FOR THOSE WHO CAME LATER FROM EUROPE...A LIFE OF BEGGING AND PEDDLING IN THE STREET IS ALL THAT THEY HAVE!

Meanwhile, even as I began my young manhood, I remained in the streets with my father.

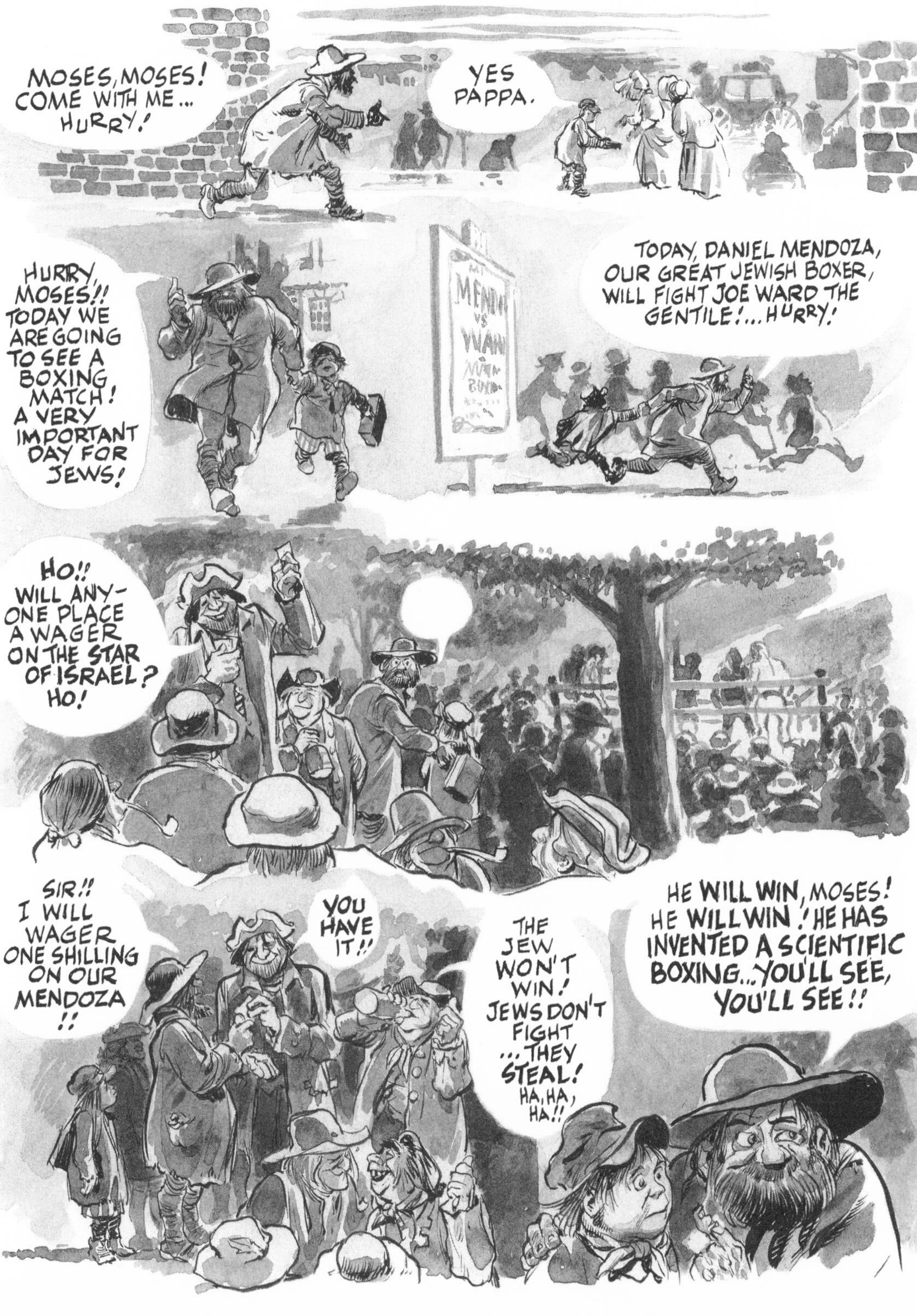

MOSES, MOSES! COME WITH ME... HURRY!
YES PAPPA.
HURRY, MOSES!! TODAY WE ARE GOING TO SEE A BOXING MATCH! A VERY IMPORTANT DAY FOR JEWS!
TODAY, DANIEL MENDOZA, OUR GREAT JEWISH BOXER, WILL FIGHT JOE WARD THE GENTILE!... HURRY!
HO!! WILL ANY-ONE PLACE A WAGER ON THE STAR OF ISRAEL? HO!
SIR!! I WILL WAGER ONE SHILLING ON OUR MENDOZA!!
YOU HAVE IT!!
THE JEW WON'T WIN! JEWS DON'T FIGHT ...THEY STEAL! HA, HA, HA!!
HE WILL WIN, MOSES! HE WILL WIN! HE HAS INVENTED A SCIENTIFIC BOXING... YOU'LL SEE, YOU'LL SEE!!

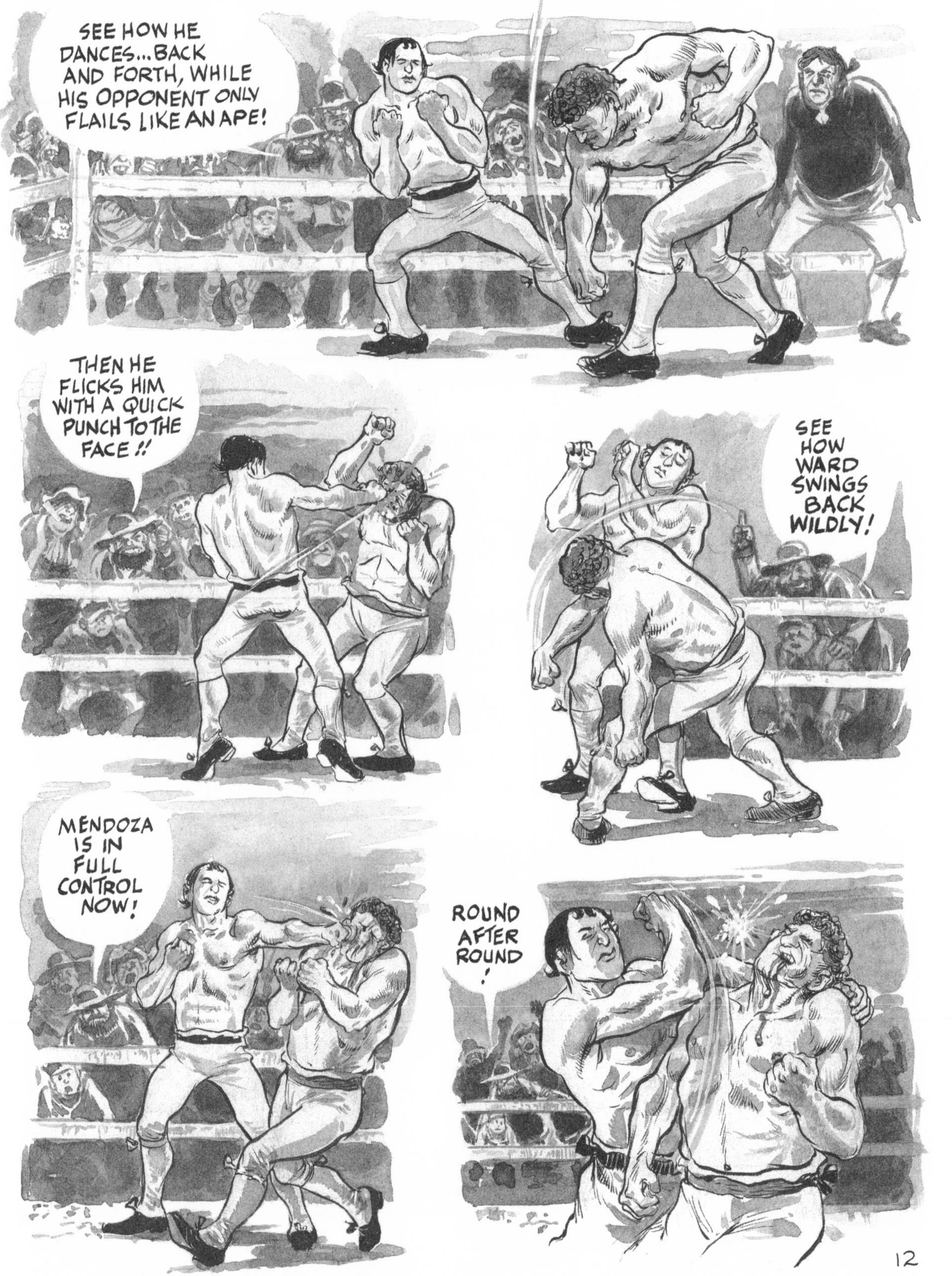
SEE HOW HE DANCES...BACK AND FORTH, WHILE HIS OPPONENT ONLY FLAILS LIKE AN APE!
THEN HE FLICKS HIM WITH A QUICK PUNCH TO THE FACE !!
SEE HOW WARD SWINGS BACK WILDLY!
MENDOZA IS IN FULL CONTROL NOW!
ROUND AFTER ROUND !

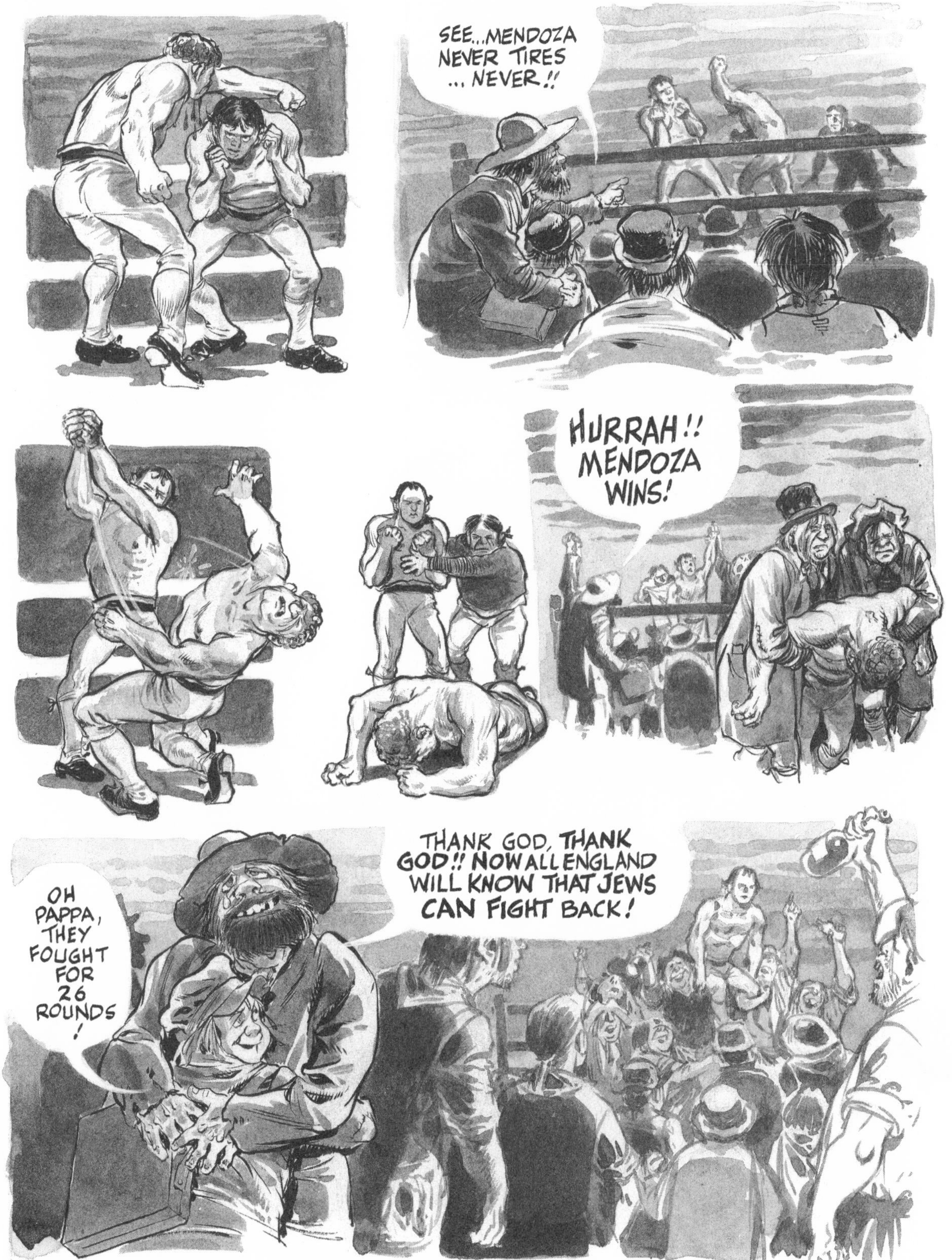
SEE... MENDOZA NEVER TIRES ... NEVER!!
HURRAH!! MENDOZA WINS!
OH PAPPA, THEY FOUGHT FOR 26 ROUNDS!
THANK GOD, THANK GOD!! NOW ALL ENGLAND WILL KNOW THAT JEWS CAN FIGHT BACK!

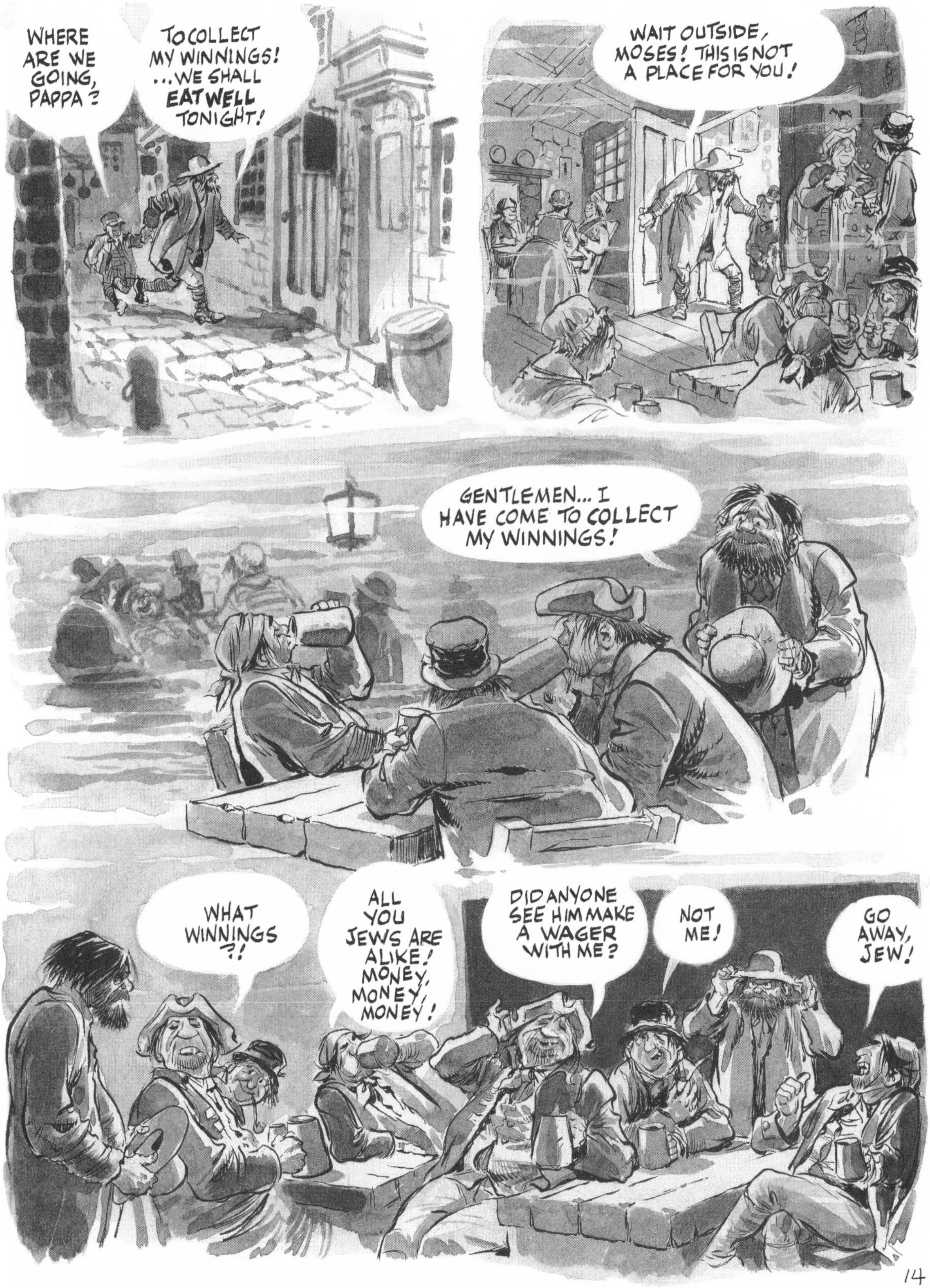
WHERE ARE WE GOING, PAPPA?
TO COLLECT MY WINNINGS! ...WE SHALL **EAT WELL** TONIGHT!
WAIT OUTSIDE, MOSES! THIS IS NOT A PLACE FOR YOU!
GENTLEMEN... I HAVE COME TO COLLECT MY WINNINGS!
WHAT WINNINGS ?!
ALL YOU JEWS ARE ALIKE! MONEY, MONEY, MONEY!
DID ANYONE SEE HIM MAKE A WAGER WITH ME?
NOT ME!
GO AWAY, JEW!

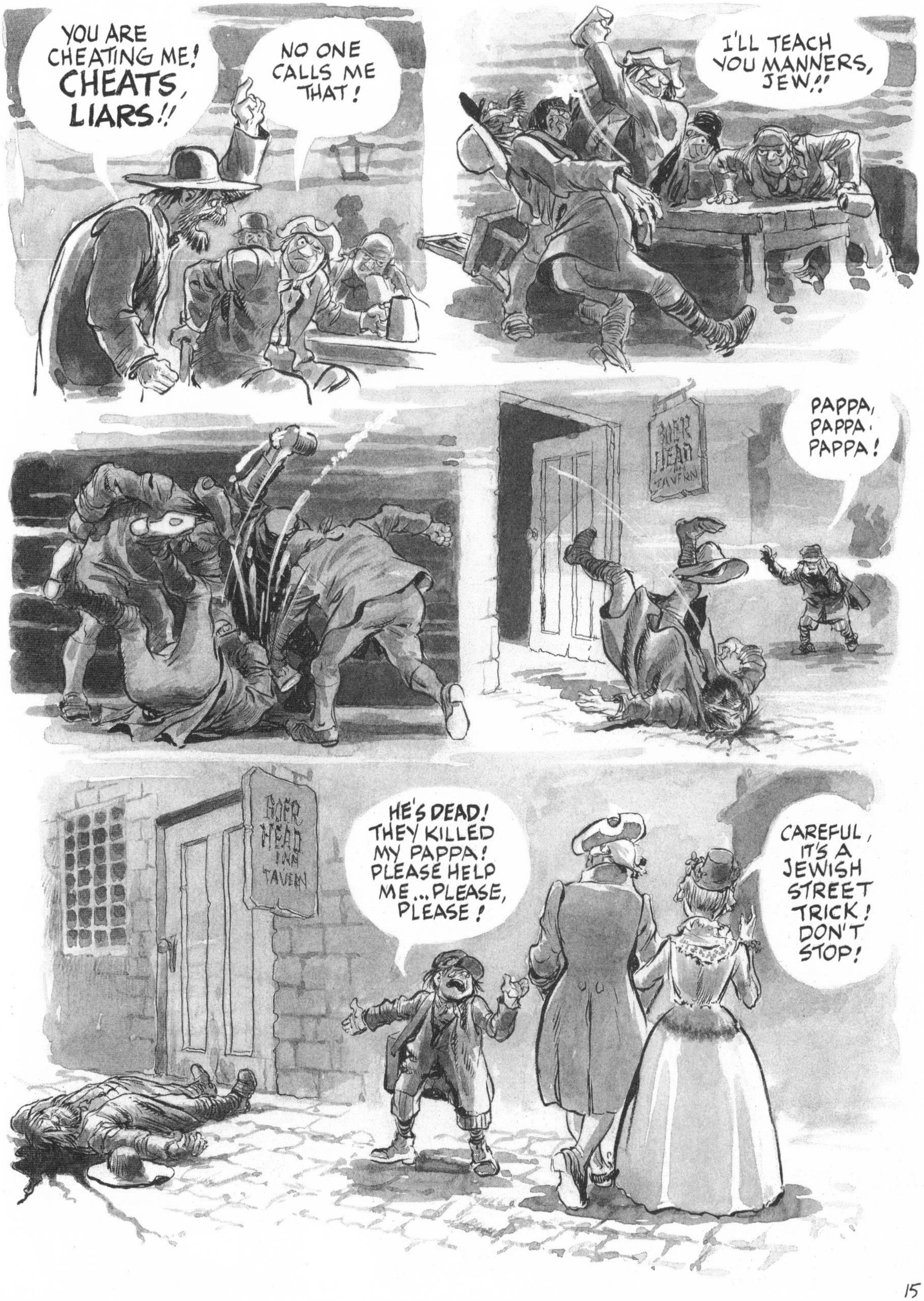
YOU ARE CHEATING ME! CHEATS, LIARS!!
NO ONE CALLS ME THAT!
I'LL TEACH YOU MANNERS, JEW!!
BOER HEAD TAVERN
PAPPA, PAPPA. PAPPA!
BOER HEAD INN TAVERN
HE'S DEAD! THEY KILLED MY PAPPA! PLEASE HELP ME... PLEASE, PLEASE!
CAREFUL, IT'S A JEWISH STREET TRICK! DON'T STOP!

My father's death left me the sole support of my mother. One day...

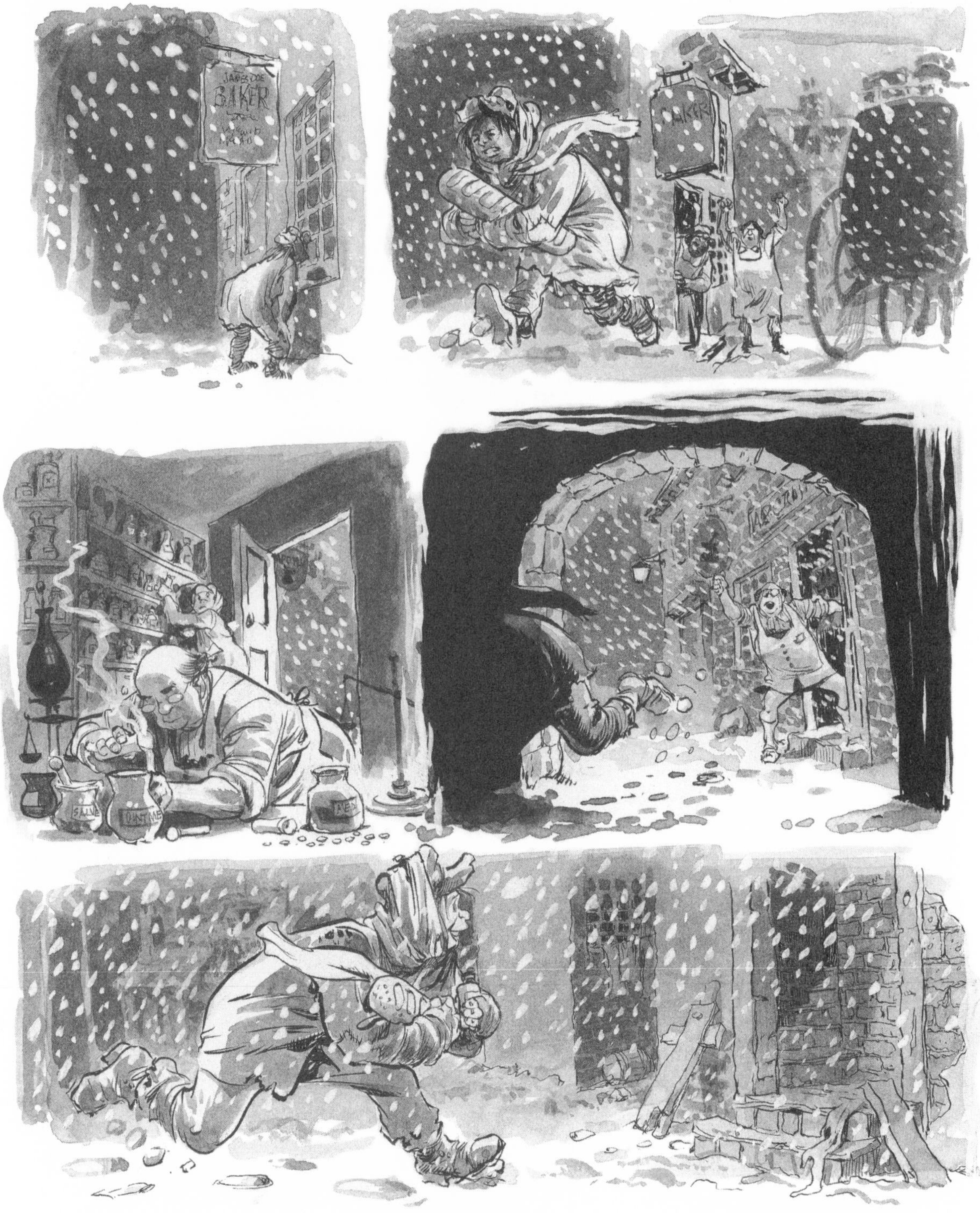
BAKER

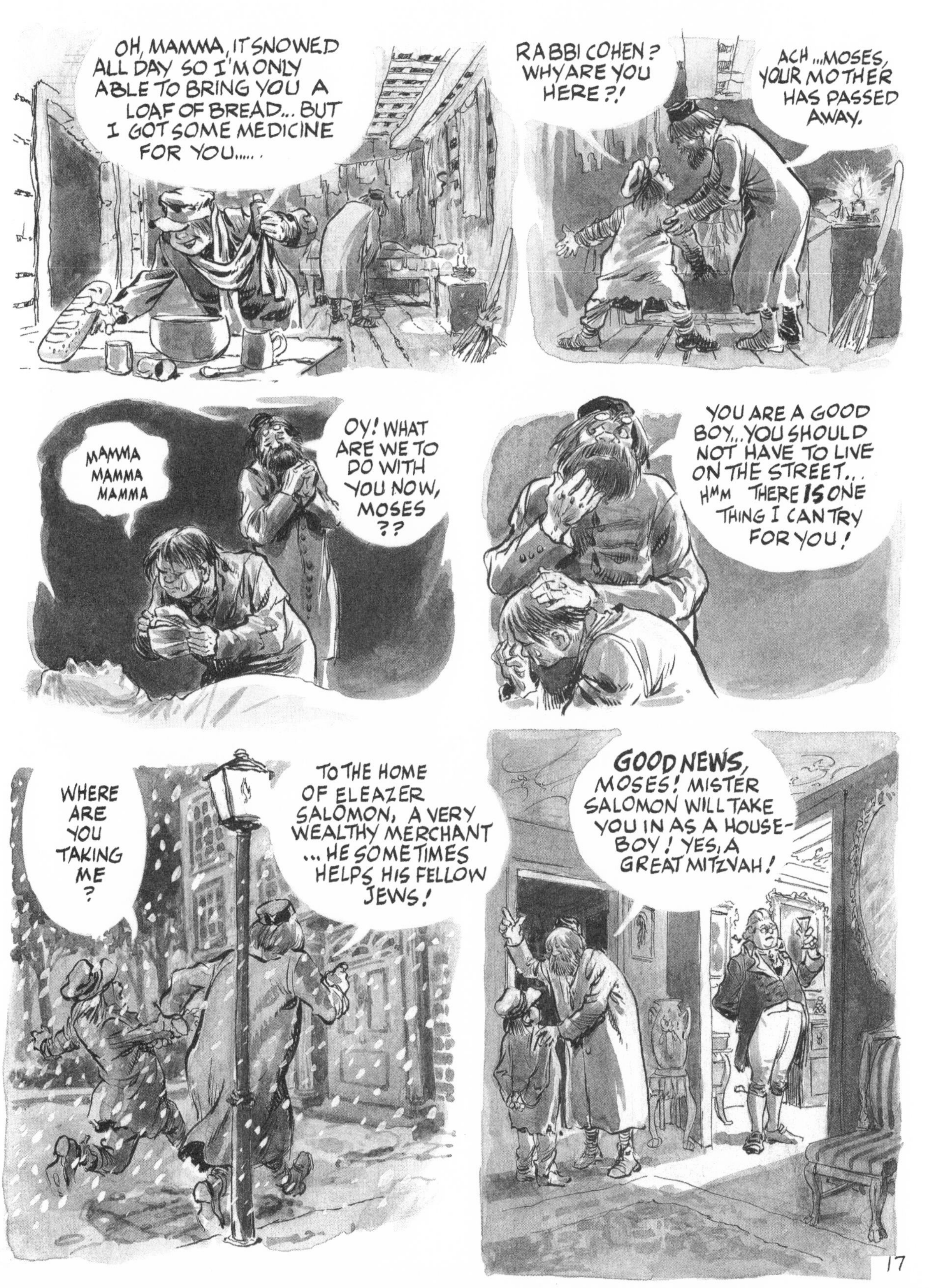
OH, MAMMA, IT SNOWED ALL DAY SO I'M ONLY ABLE TO BRING YOU A LOAF OF BREAD... BUT I GOT SOME MEDICINE FOR YOU.....
RABBI COHEN? WHY ARE YOU HERE?!
ACH ...MOSES, YOUR MOTHER HAS PASSED AWAY.
MAMMA MAMMA MAMMA
OY! WHAT ARE WE TO DO WITH YOU NOW, MOSES ??
YOU ARE A GOOD BOY... YOU SHOULD NOT HAVE TO LIVE ON THE STREET... HMM THERE IS ONE THING I CAN TRY FOR YOU!
WHERE ARE YOU TAKING ME ?
TO THE HOME OF ELEAZER SALOMON, A VERY WEALTHY MERCHANT ... HE SOMETIMES HELPS HIS FELLOW JEWS!
GOOD NEWS, MOSES! MISTER SALOMON WILL TAKE YOU IN AS A HOUSE-BOY! YES, A GREAT MITZVAH!

As a houseboy in the Salomon household I could accompany the master and see a very different side of Jewish life.

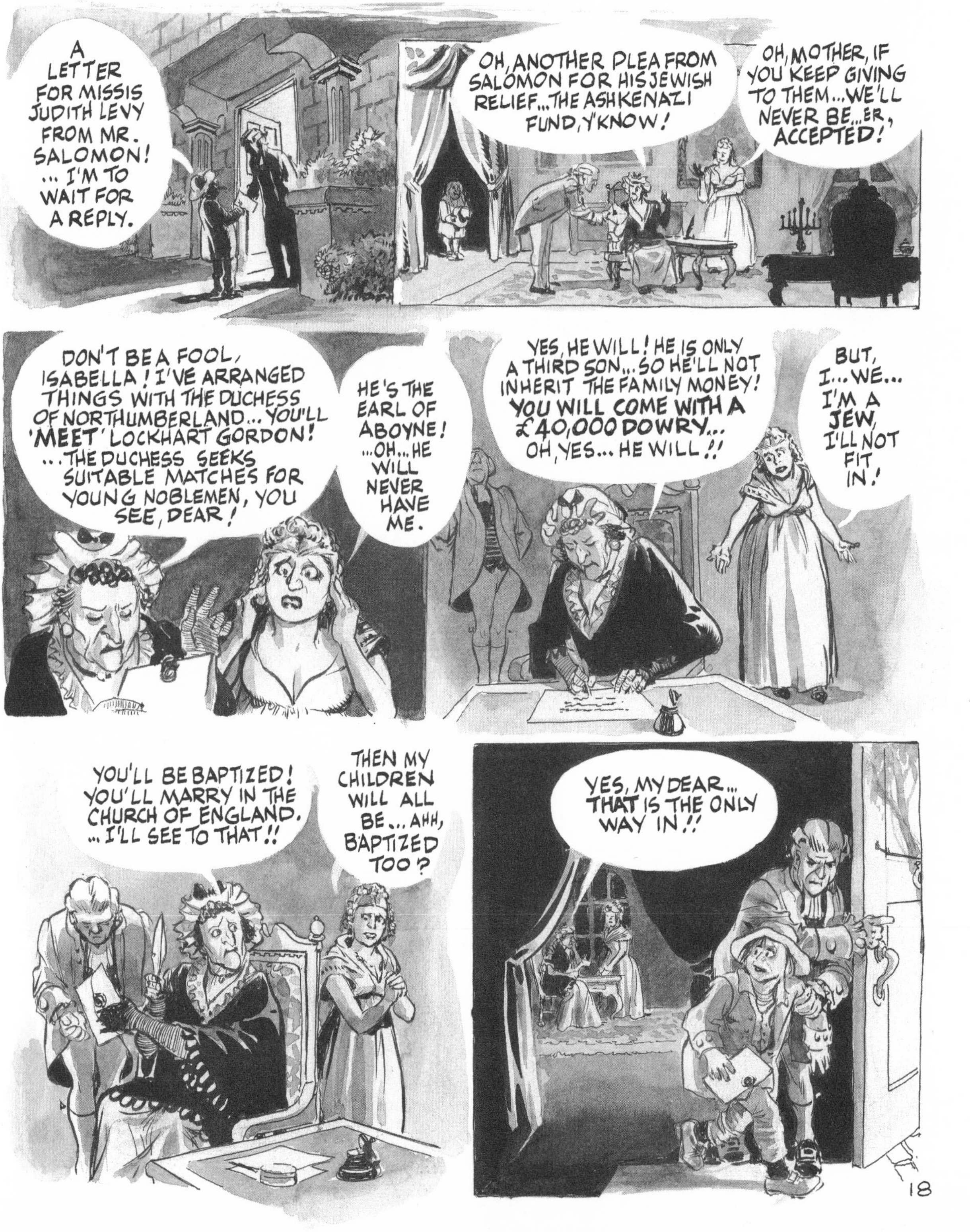
A LETTER FOR MISSIS JUDITH LEVY FROM MR. SALOMON! ... I'M TO WAIT FOR A REPLY.
OH, ANOTHER PLEA FROM SALOMON FOR HIS JEWISH RELIEF... THE ASHKENAZI FUND, Y'KNOW!
OH, MOTHER, IF YOU KEEP GIVING TO THEM... WE'LL NEVER BE... ER, ACCEPTED!
DON'T BE A FOOL, ISABELLA! I'VE ARRANGED THINGS WITH THE DUCHESS OF NORTHUMBERLAND... YOU'LL 'MEET' LOCKHART GORDON! ... THE DUCHESS SEEKS SUITABLE MATCHES FOR YOUNG NOBLEMEN, YOU SEE, DEAR!
HE'S THE EARL OF ABOYNE! ...OH... HE WILL NEVER HAVE ME.
YES, HE WILL! HE IS ONLY A THIRD SON... SO HE'LL NOT INHERIT THE FAMILY MONEY! YOU WILL COME WITH A £40,000 DOWRY... OH, YES... HE WILL!!
BUT, I... WE... I'M A JEW, I'LL NOT FIT IN!
YOU'LL BE BAPTIZED! YOU'LL MARRY IN THE CHURCH OF ENGLAND. ... I'LL SEE TO THAT!!
THEN MY CHILDREN WILL ALL BE... AHH, BAPTIZED TOO?
YES, MY DEAR... THAT IS THE ONLY WAY IN!!

The reputation of the Jews in the London slums continued to soil the status of their betters. This only prodded Mr. Salomon and his colleagues into stronger efforts to build a fund for the school. Mr. Salomon, at last undeterred by Jewish class prejudices, called on Mr. Isaac D'Israeli, a leader in the Sephardic community.

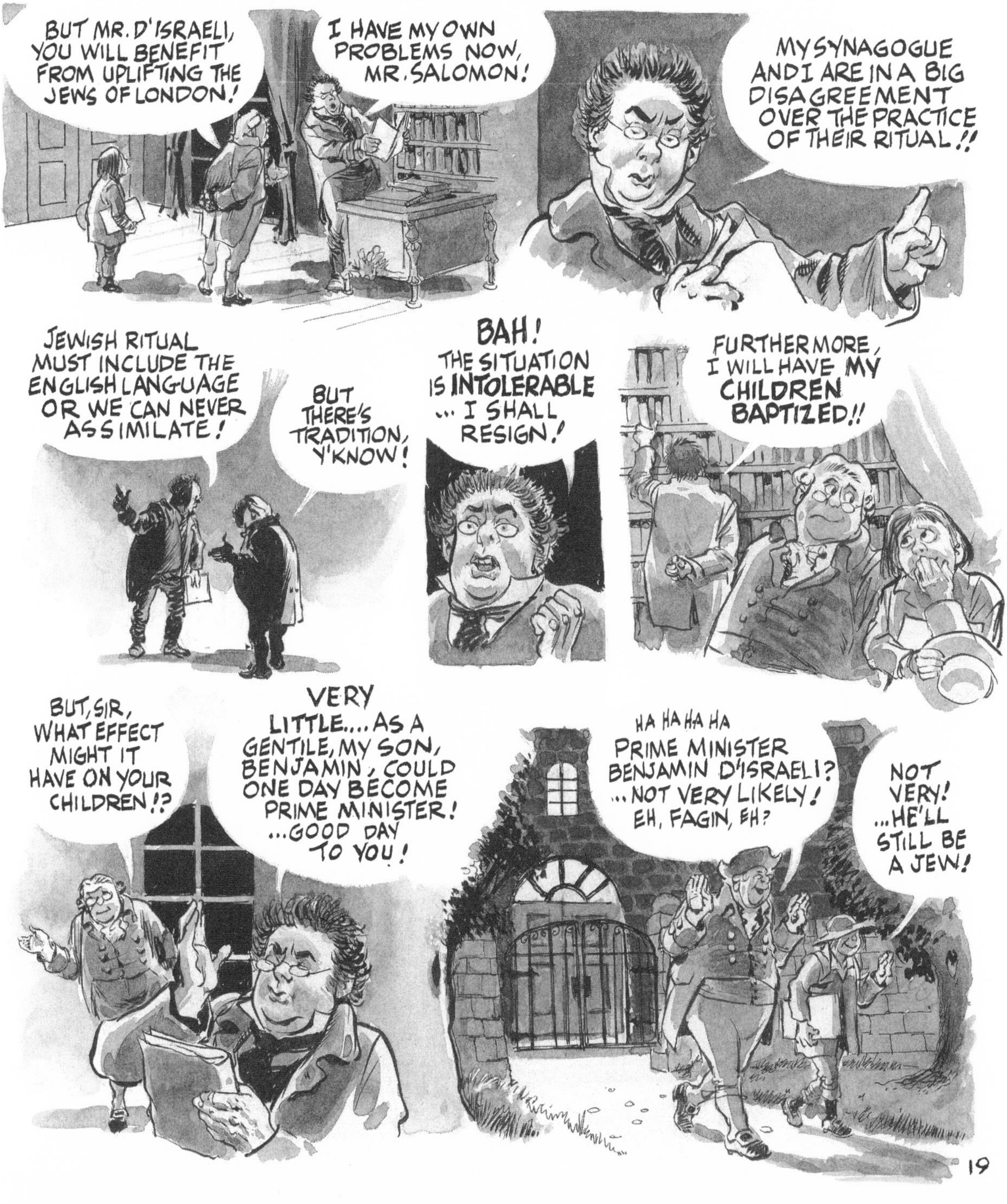

BUT MR. D'ISRAELI, YOU WILL BENEFIT FROM UPLIFTING THE JEWS OF LONDON!
I HAVE MY OWN PROBLEMS NOW, MR. SALOMON!
MY SYNAGOGUE AND I ARE IN A BIG DISAGREEMENT OVER THE PRACTICE OF THEIR RITUAL!!
JEWISH RITUAL MUST INCLUDE THE ENGLISH LANGUAGE OR WE CAN NEVER ASSIMILATE!
BUT THERE'S TRADITION, Y'KNOW!
BAH! THE SITUATION IS INTOLERABLE ... I SHALL RESIGN!
FURTHERMORE, I WILL HAVE MY CHILDREN BAPTIZED!!
BUT, SIR, WHAT EFFECT MIGHT IT HAVE ON YOUR CHILDREN!?
VERY LITTLE.... AS A GENTILE, MY SON, BENJAMIN, COULD ONE DAY BECOME PRIME MINISTER! ...GOOD DAY TO YOU!
HA HA HA HA
PRIME MINISTER BENJAMIN D'ISRAELI? ...NOT VERY LIKELY! EH, FAGIN, EH?
NOT VERY! ...HE'LL STILL BE A JEW!

During the time I spent observing life in the Salomon household, I learned how Jews succeeded in rising in this world.

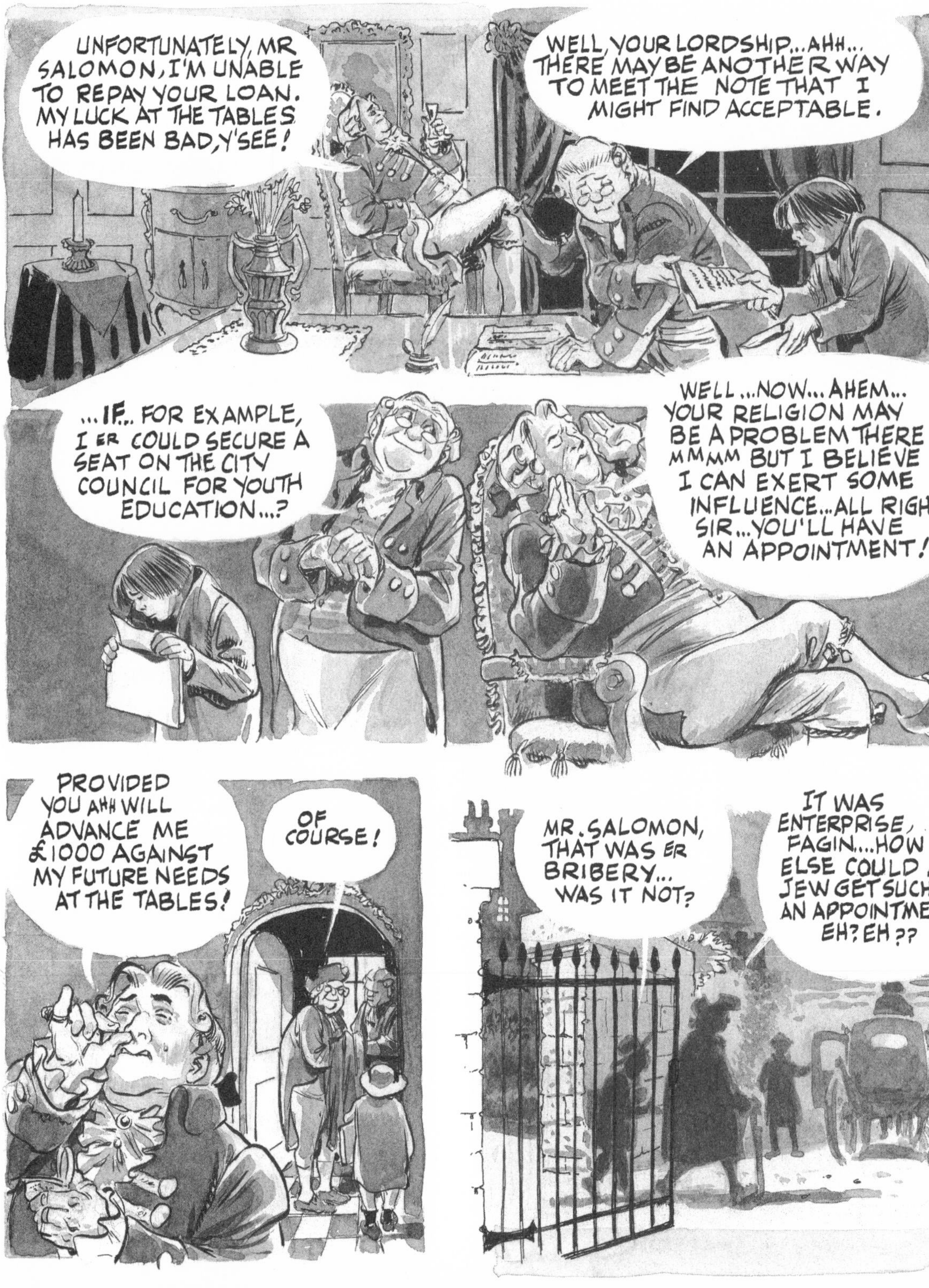

UNFORTUNATELY, MR SALOMON, I'M UNABLE TO REPAY YOUR LOAN. MY LUCK AT THE TABLES HAS BEEN BAD, Y'SEE!
WELL, YOUR LORDSHIP... AHH... THERE MAY BE ANOTHER WAY TO MEET THE NOTE THAT I MIGHT FIND ACCEPTABLE.
...IF... FOR EXAMPLE, I ER COULD SECURE A SEAT ON THE CITY COUNCIL FOR YOUTH EDUCATION...?
WELL...NOW...AHEM... YOUR RELIGION MAY BE A PROBLEM THERE MMMM BUT I BELIEVE I CAN EXERT SOME INFLUENCE...ALL RIGHT SIR...YOU'LL HAVE AN APPOINTMENT!
PROVIDED YOU AHH WILL ADVANCE ME £1000 AGAINST MY FUTURE NEEDS AT THE TABLES!
OF COURSE!
MR. SALOMON, THAT WAS ER BRIBERY... WAS IT NOT?
IT WAS ENTERPRISE, FAGIN...HOW ELSE COULD A JEW GET SUCH AN APPOINTMENT EH? EH??

Mr. Salomon still pursued his search for funds to uplift the lower-class Jews of London by establishing a school to educate young Ashkenazim and help them advance by ways other than crime.

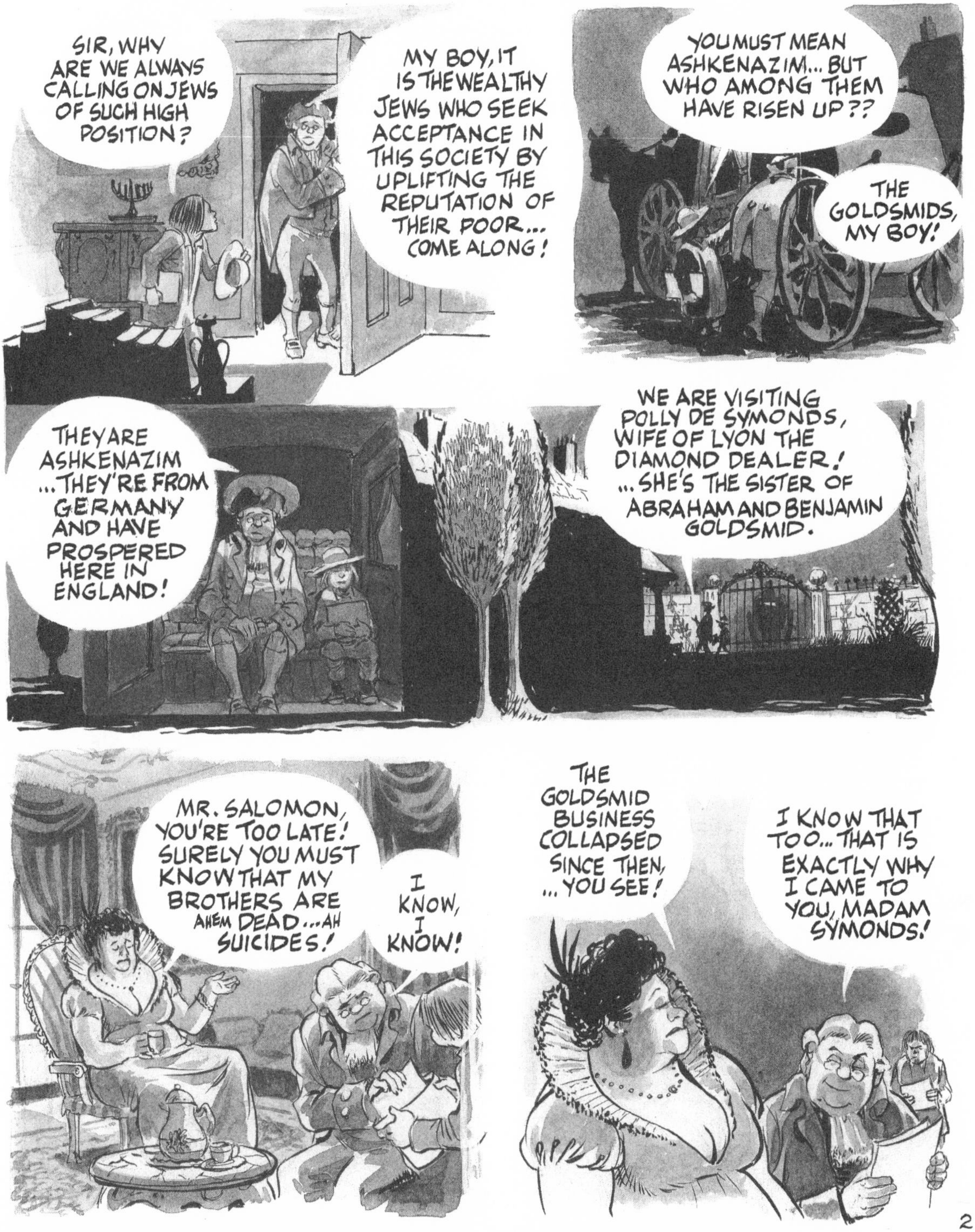
SIR, WHY ARE WE ALWAYS CALLING ON JEWS OF SUCH HIGH POSITION?
MY BOY, IT IS THE WEALTHY JEWS WHO SEEK ACCEPTANCE IN THIS SOCIETY BY UPLIFTING THE REPUTATION OF THEIR POOR... COME ALONG!
YOU MUST MEAN ASHKENAZIM... BUT WHO AMONG THEM HAVE RISEN UP??
THE GOLDSMIDS, MY BOY!
THEY ARE ASHKENAZIM ...THEY'RE FROM GERMANY AND HAVE PROSPERED HERE IN ENGLAND!
WE ARE VISITING POLLY DE SYMONDS, WIFE OF LYON THE DIAMOND DEALER! ...SHE'S THE SISTER OF ABRAHAM AND BENJAMIN GOLDSMID.
MR. SALOMON, YOU'RE TOO LATE! SURELY YOU MUST KNOW THAT MY BROTHERS ARE AHEM DEAD... AH SUICIDES!
I KNOW, I KNOW!
THE GOLDSMID BUSINESS COLLAPSED SINCE THEN, ...YOU SEE!
I KNOW THAT TOO... THAT IS EXACTLY WHY I CAME TO YOU, MADAM SYMONDS!

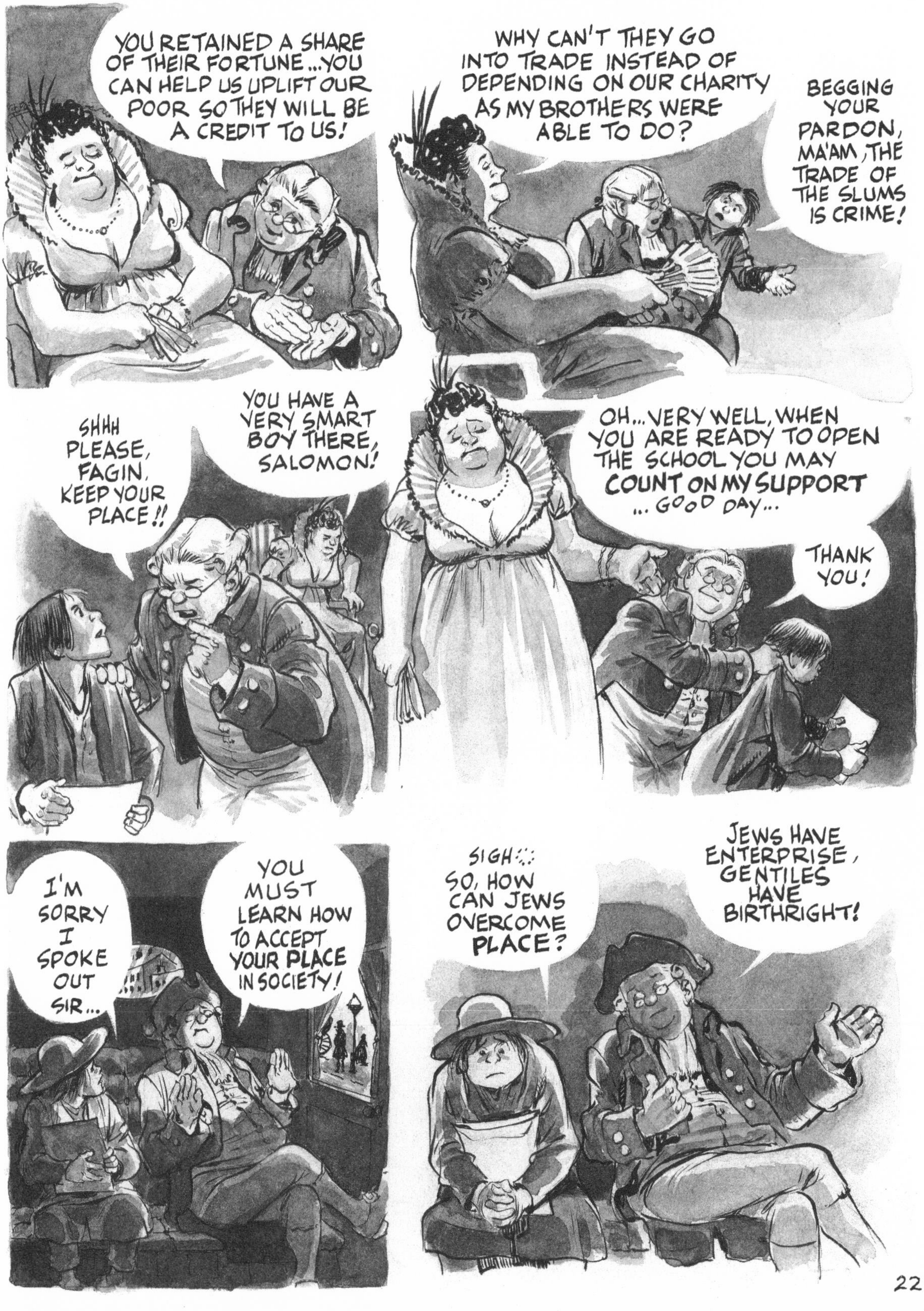
YOU RETAINED A SHARE OF THEIR FORTUNE...YOU CAN HELP US UPLIFT OUR POOR SO THEY WILL BE A CREDIT TO US!
WHY CAN'T THEY GO INTO TRADE INSTEAD OF DEPENDING ON OUR CHARITY AS MY BROTHERS WERE ABLE TO DO?
BEGGING YOUR PARDON, MA'AM, THE TRADE OF THE SLUMS IS CRIME!
YOU HAVE A VERY SMART BOY THERE, SALOMON!
SHHH PLEASE, FAGIN, KEEP YOUR PLACE!!
OH...VERY WELL, WHEN YOU ARE READY TO OPEN THE SCHOOL YOU MAY COUNT ON MY SUPPORT ...GOOD DAY...
THANK YOU!
I'M SORRY I SPOKE OUT SIR...
YOU MUST LEARN HOW TO ACCEPT YOUR PLACE IN SOCIETY!
SIGH...
SO, HOW CAN JEWS OVERCOME PLACE?
JEWS HAVE ENTERPRISE, GENTILES HAVE BIRTHRIGHT!

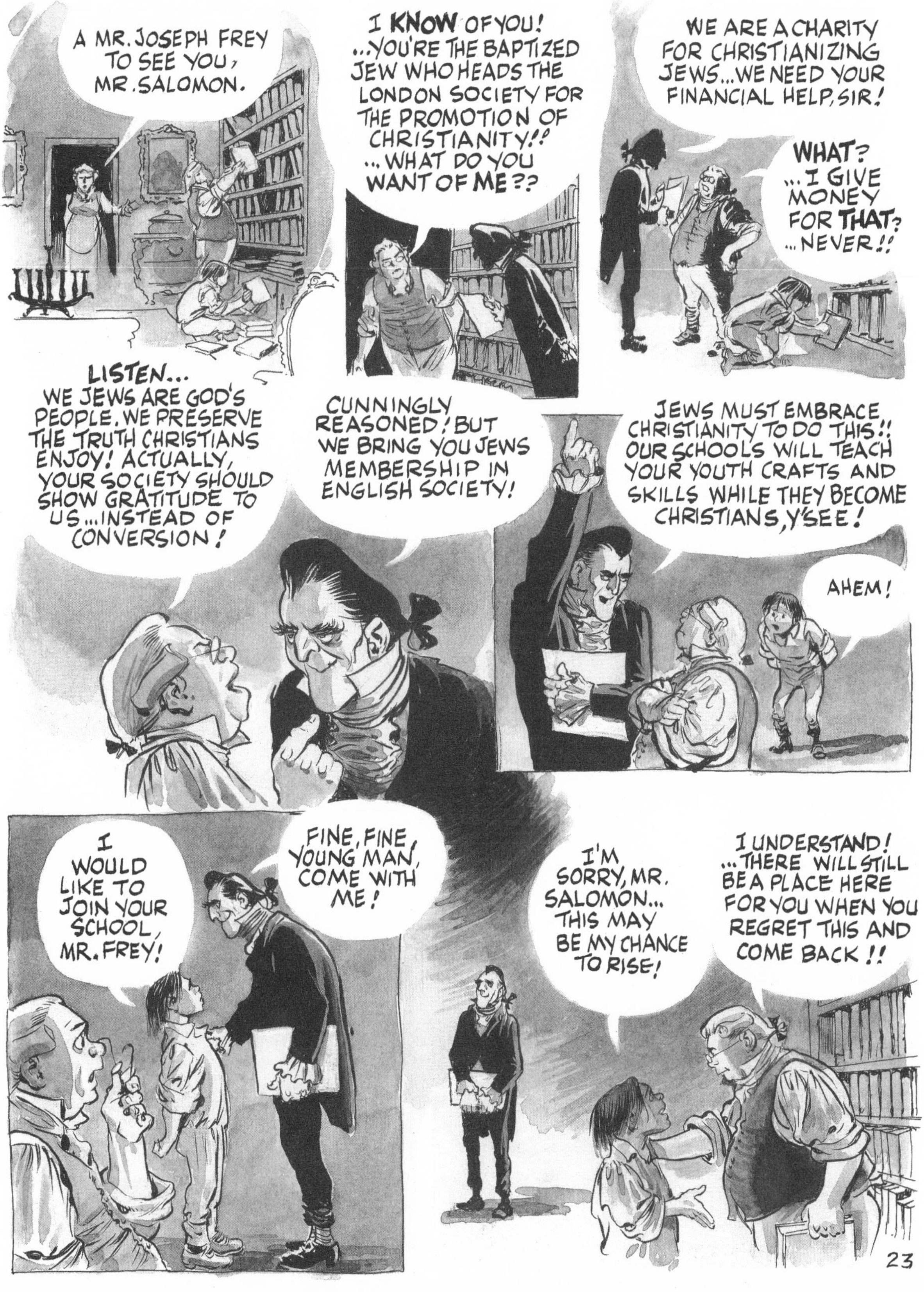

A MR. JOSEPH FREY TO SEE YOU, MR. SALOMON.
I KNOW OF YOU! ...YOU'RE THE BAPTIZED JEW WHO HEADS THE LONDON SOCIETY FOR THE PROMOTION OF CHRISTIANITY!! ...WHAT DO YOU WANT OF ME??
WE ARE A CHARITY FOR CHRISTIANIZING JEWS...WE NEED YOUR FINANCIAL HELP, SIR!
WHAT? ...I GIVE MONEY FOR THAT? ...NEVER!!
LISTEN... WE JEWS ARE GOD'S PEOPLE. WE PRESERVE THE TRUTH CHRISTIANS ENJOY! ACTUALLY, YOUR SOCIETY SHOULD SHOW GRATITUDE TO US...INSTEAD OF CONVERSION!
CUNNINGLY REASONED! BUT WE BRING YOU JEWS MEMBERSHIP IN ENGLISH SOCIETY!
JEWS MUST EMBRACE CHRISTIANITY TO DO THIS!! OUR SCHOOLS WILL TEACH YOUR YOUTH CRAFTS AND SKILLS WHILE THEY BECOME CHRISTIANS, Y'SEE!
AHEM!
I WOULD LIKE TO JOIN YOUR SCHOOL, MR. FREY!
FINE, FINE, YOUNG MAN, COME WITH ME!
I'M SORRY, MR. SALOMON... THIS MAY BE MY CHANCE TO RISE!
I UNDERSTAND! ...THERE WILL STILL BE A PLACE HERE FOR YOU WHEN YOU REGRET THIS AND COME BACK!!

One year later, Joseph Frey's school for the Christianizing of young Jews lay in failure. Mr. Frey was reprimanded and reassigned by his backers for an indiscreet affair with a Mrs. Josephson. All I had accumulated in my time there was some skill at sewing, basket weaving, and repair, which would be of use to me later in life. But Christianizing me had failed.

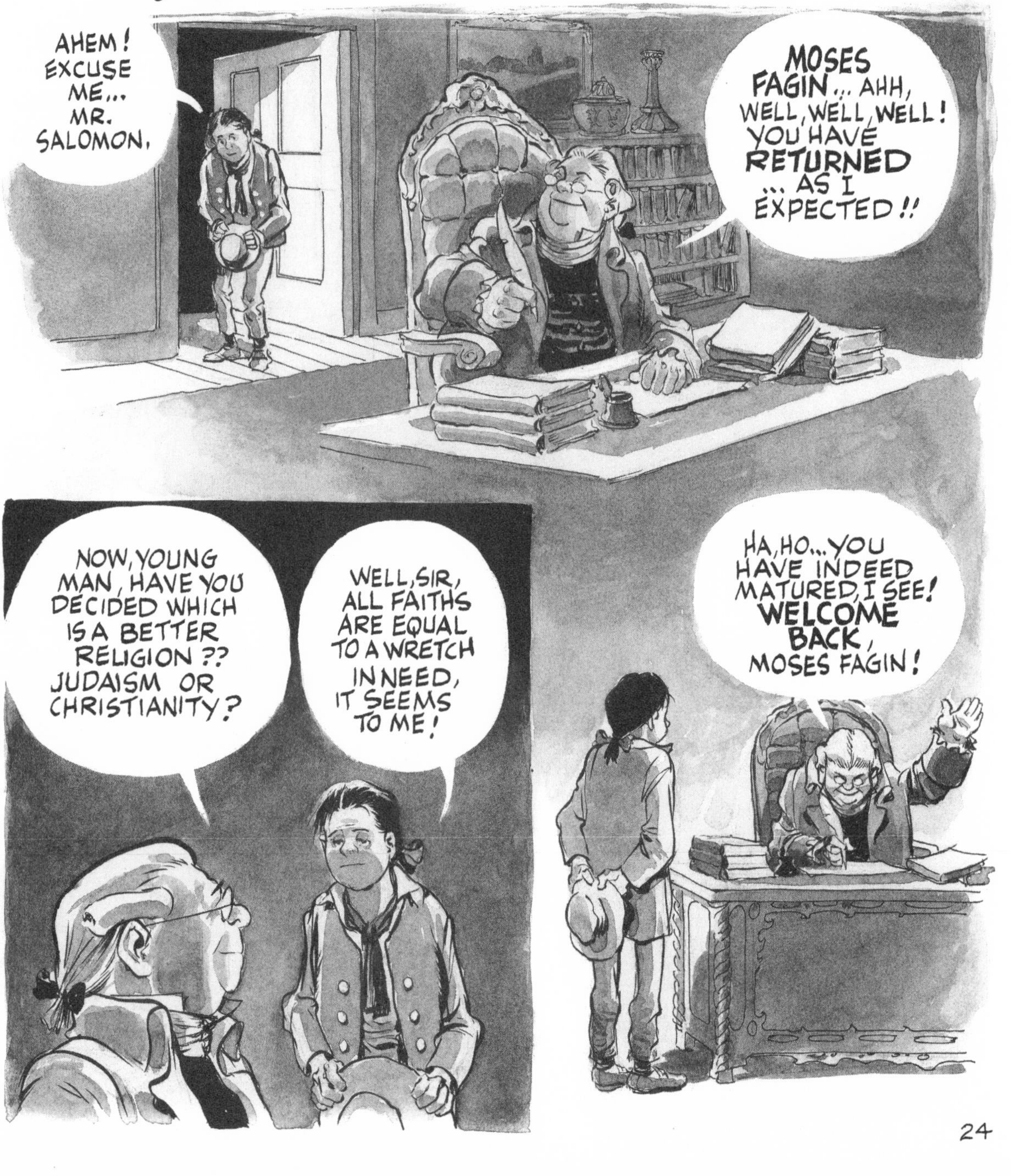
AHEM! EXCUSE ME... MR. SALOMON.
MOSES FAGIN... AHH, WELL, WELL, WELL! YOU HAVE RETURNED ... AS I EXPECTED!!
NOW, YOUNG MAN, HAVE YOU DECIDED WHICH IS A BETTER RELIGION?? JUDAISM OR CHRISTIANITY?
WELL, SIR, ALL FAITHS ARE EQUAL TO A WRETCH IN NEED, IT SEEMS TO ME!
HA, HO... YOU HAVE INDEED MATURED, I SEE! WELCOME BACK, MOSES FAGIN!

Well … a few years passed and I was in my seventeenth year, still a servant in the Salomon house. Then one day …

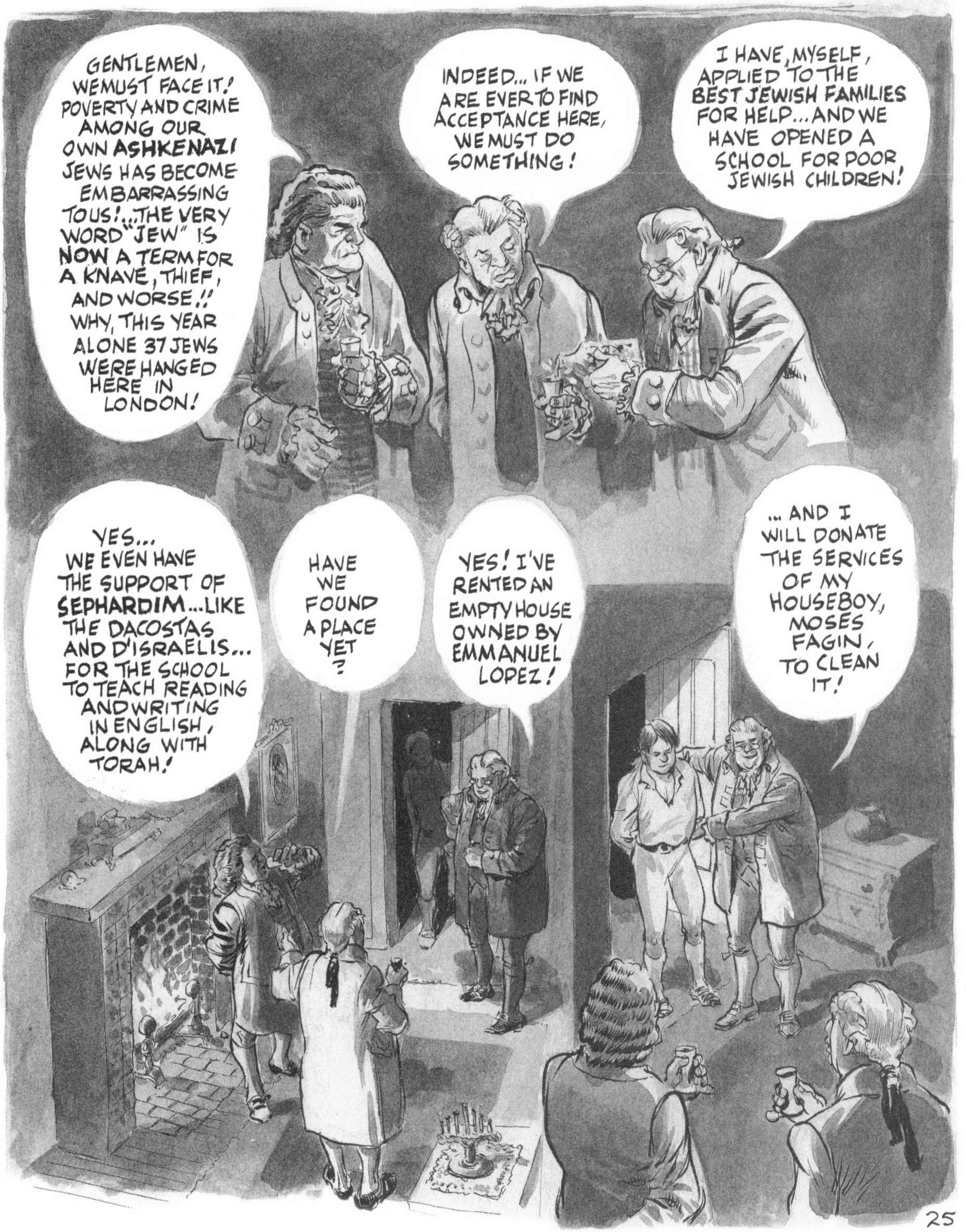
GENTLEMEN, WE MUST FACE IT! POVERTY AND CRIME AMONG OUR OWN ASHKENAZI JEWS HAS BECOME EMBARRASSING TO US!... THE VERY WORD "JEW" IS NOW A TERM FOR A KNAVE, THIEF, AND WORSE!! WHY, THIS YEAR ALONE 37 JEWS WERE HANGED HERE IN LONDON!
INDEED... IF WE ARE EVER TO FIND ACCEPTANCE HERE, WE MUST DO SOMETHING!
I HAVE, MYSELF, APPLIED TO THE BEST JEWISH FAMILIES FOR HELP... AND WE HAVE OPENED A SCHOOL FOR POOR JEWISH CHILDREN!
YES... WE EVEN HAVE THE SUPPORT OF SEPHARDIM... LIKE THE DACOSTAS AND D'ISRAELIS... FOR THE SCHOOL TO TEACH READING AND WRITING IN ENGLISH, ALONG WITH TORAH!
HAVE WE FOUND A PLACE YET?
YES! I'VE RENTED AN EMPTY HOUSE OWNED BY EMMANUEL LOPEZ!
... AND I WILL DONATE THE SERVICES OF MY HOUSEBOY, MOSES FAGIN, TO CLEAN IT!

And so I went to work at the school...

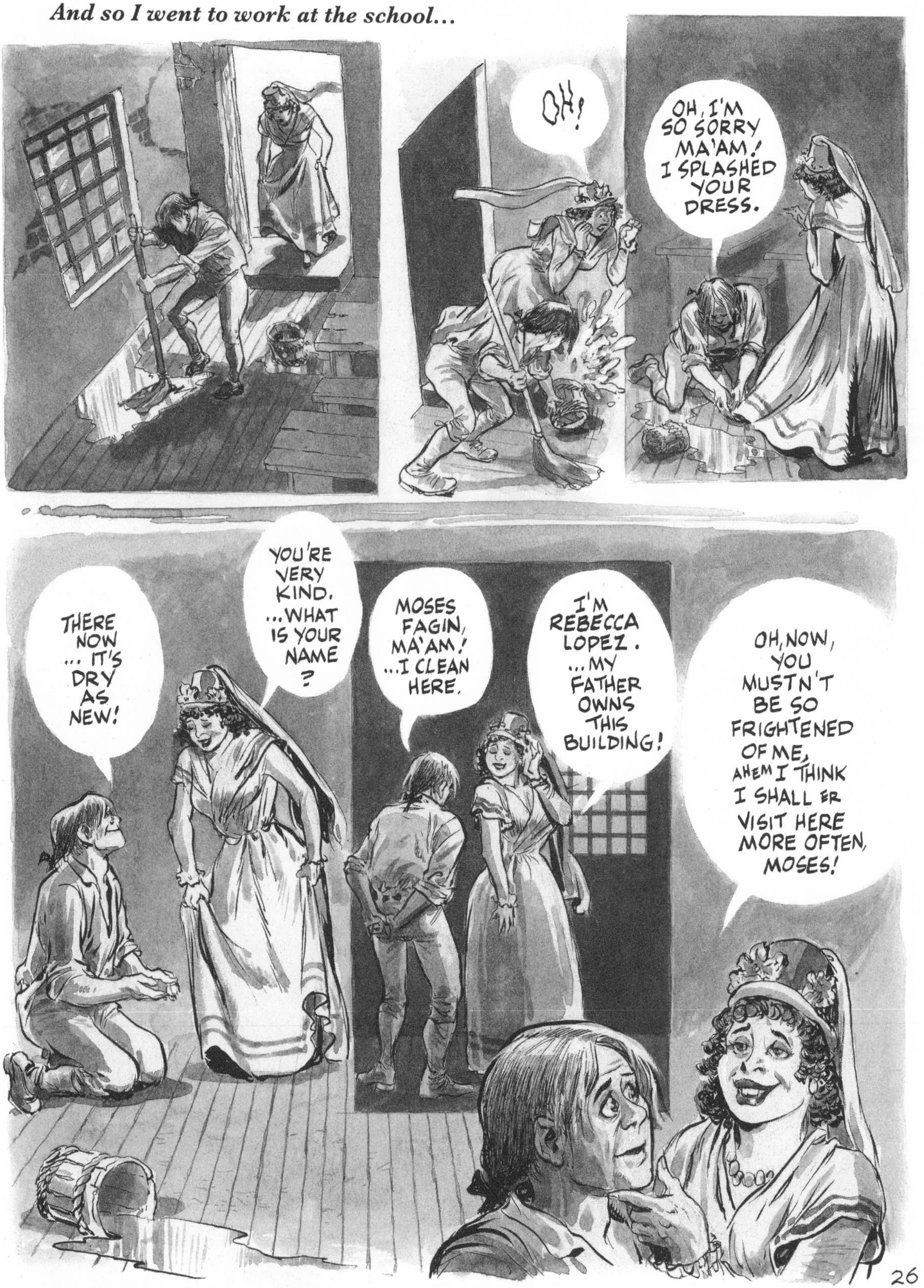
OH!
OH, I'M SO SORRY MA'AM! I SPLASHED YOUR DRESS.
THERE NOW ... IT'S DRY AS NEW!
YOU'RE VERY KIND. ...WHAT IS YOUR NAME?
MOSES FAGIN, MA'AM! ...I CLEAN HERE.
I'M REBECCA LOPEZ. ...MY FATHER OWNS THIS BUILDING!
OH, NOW, YOU MUSTN'T BE SO FRIGHTENED OF ME, AHEM I THINK I SHALL ER VISIT HERE MORE OFTEN, MOSES!

So began my short romance with Rebecca Lopez.

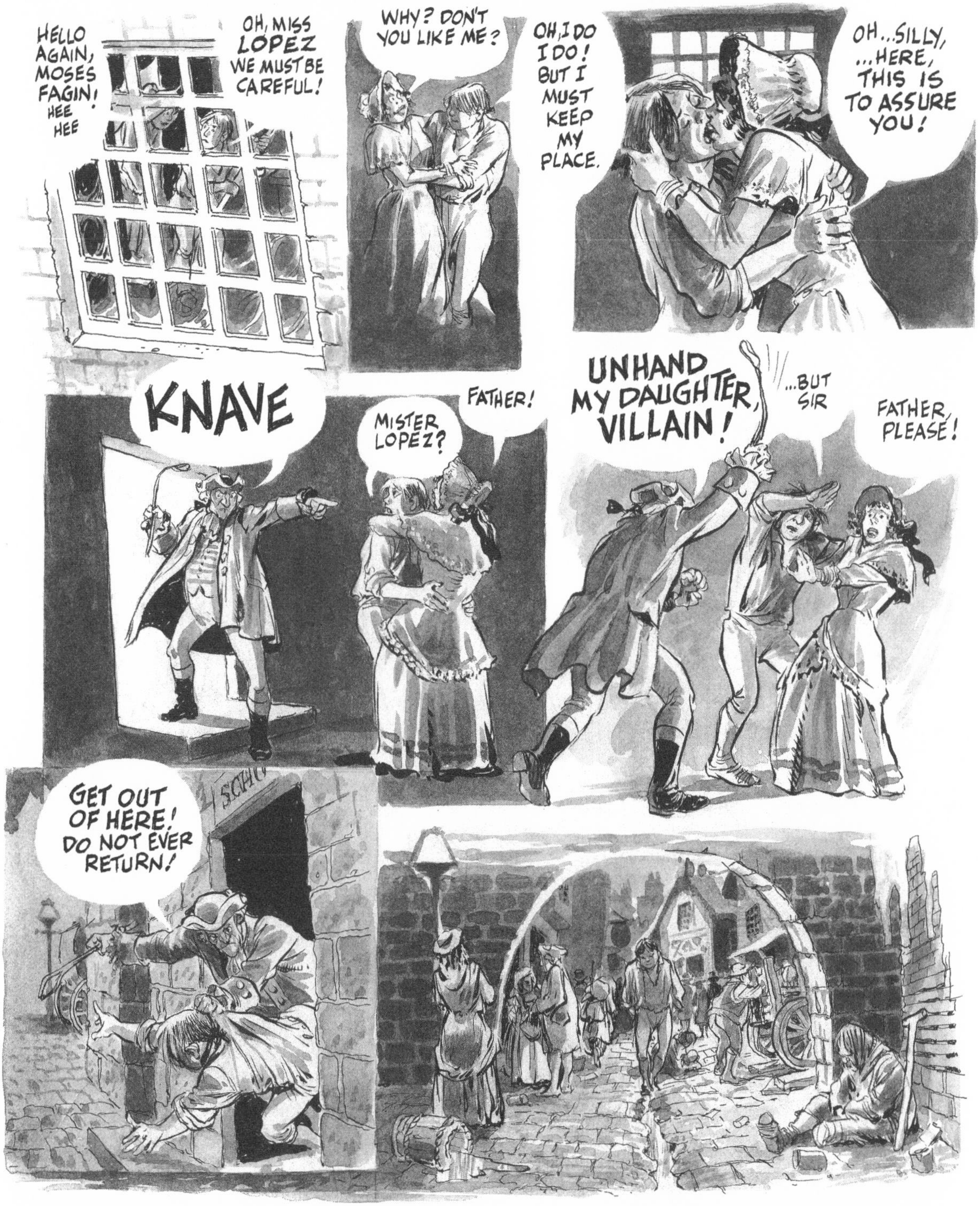

HELLO AGAIN, MOSES FAGIN! HEE HEE
OH, MISS LOPEZ WE MUST BE CAREFUL!
WHY? DON'T YOU LIKE ME?
OH, I DO I DO! BUT I MUST KEEP MY PLACE.
OH...SILLY, ...HERE, THIS IS TO ASSURE YOU!
KNAVE
MISTER LOPEZ?
FATHER!
UNHAND MY DAUGHTER, VILLAIN!
...BUT SIR
FATHER, PLEASE!
GET OUT OF HERE! DO NOT EVER RETURN!

So it ended ... as did my place in the school, and with it all hope for improvement in my station. With this turn of events began my return to the dregs of the streets of London.

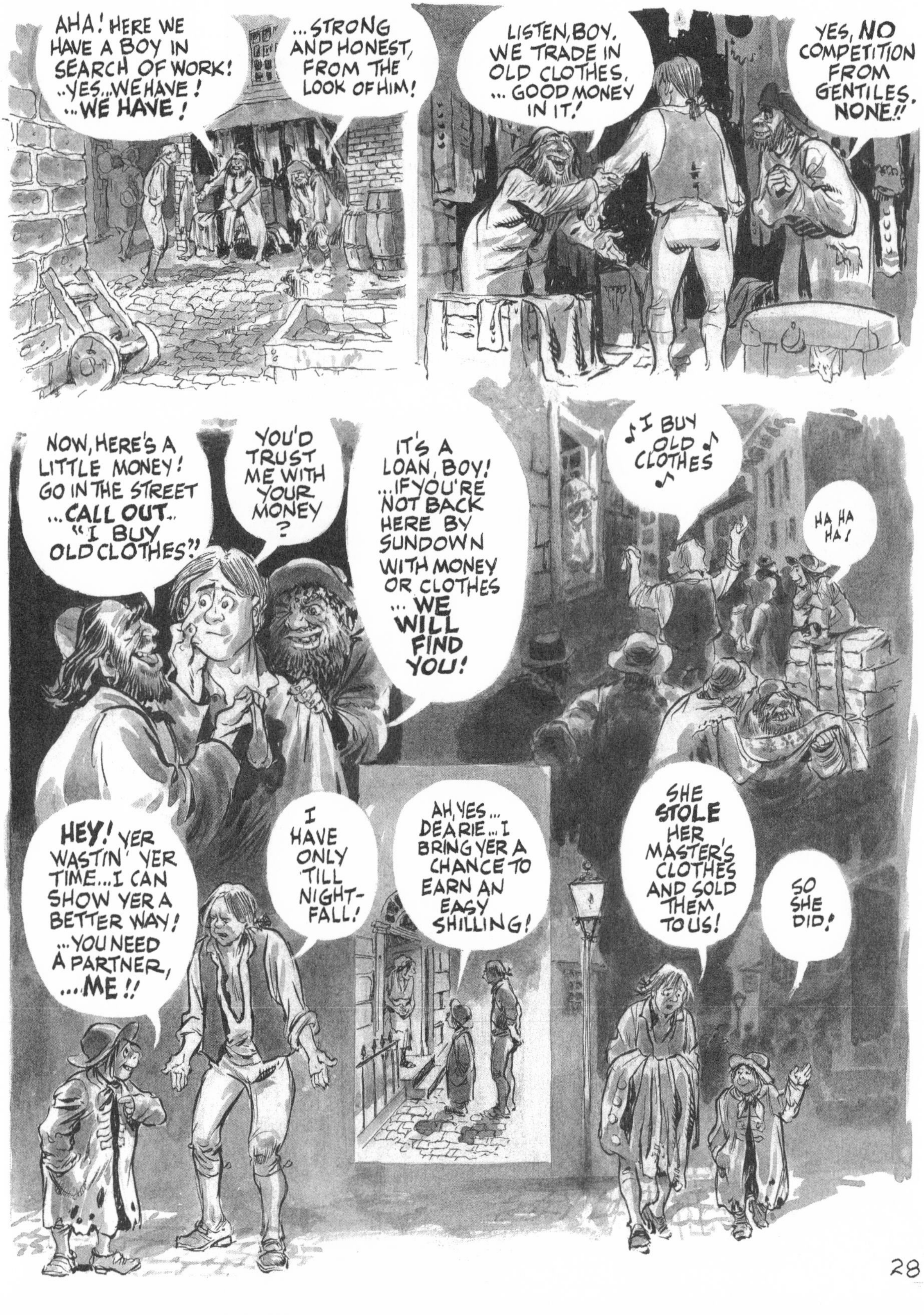

AHA! HERE WE HAVE A BOY IN SEARCH OF WORK! ..YES...WE HAVE! ...WE HAVE!
...STRONG AND HONEST, FROM THE LOOK OF HIM!
LISTEN, BOY. WE TRADE IN OLD CLOTHES. ... GOOD MONEY IN IT!
YES, NO COMPETITION FROM GENTILES. NONE!!
NOW, HERE'S A LITTLE MONEY! GO IN THE STREET ...CALL OUT.. "I BUY OLD CLOTHES"!
YOU'D TRUST ME WITH YOUR MONEY?
IT'S A LOAN, BOY! ...IF YOU'RE NOT BACK HERE BY SUNDOWN WITH MONEY OR CLOTHES ...WE WILL FIND YOU!
♪ I BUY OLD CLOTHES ♪
HA HA HA!
HEY! YER WASTIN' YER TIME...I CAN SHOW YER A BETTER WAY! ...YOU NEED A PARTNER, ...ME!!
I HAVE ONLY TILL NIGHT-FALL!
AH, YES... DEARIE... I BRING YER A CHANCE TO EARN AN EASY SHILLING!
SHE STOLE HER MASTER'S CLOTHES AND SOLD THEM TO US!
SO SHE DID!

Ah, how the business of survival does take perilous turns. Before long, I was more deeply involved in the trade of the streets than ever.

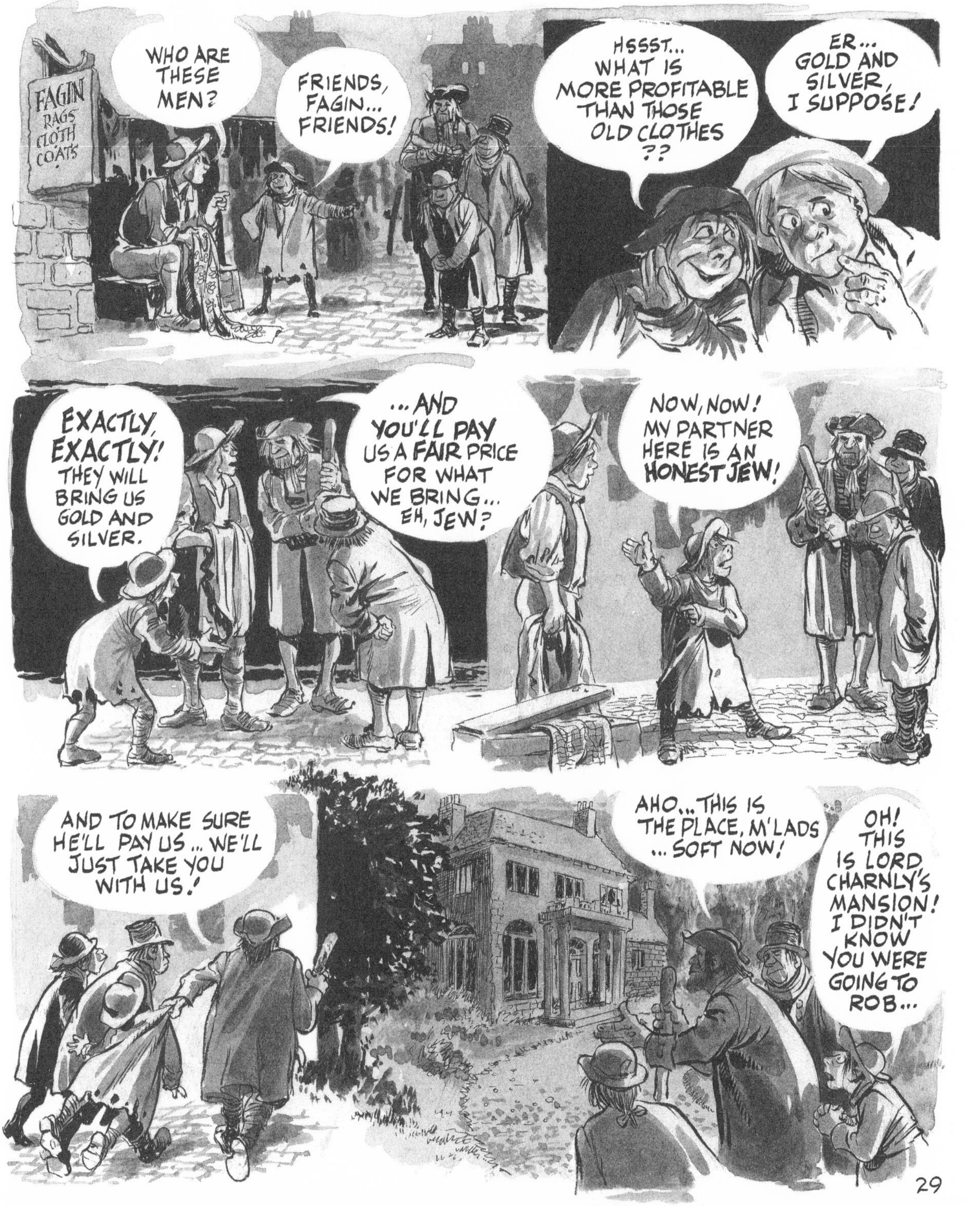
FAGIN RAGS CLOTH COATS
WHO ARE THESE MEN?
FRIENDS, FAGIN... FRIENDS!
HSSST... WHAT IS MORE PROFITABLE THAN THOSE OLD CLOTHES ??
ER... GOLD AND SILVER, I SUPPOSE!
EXACTLY, EXACTLY! THEY WILL BRING US GOLD AND SILVER.
...AND YOU'LL PAY US A FAIR PRICE FOR WHAT WE BRING... EH, JEW?
NOW, NOW! MY PARTNER HERE IS AN HONEST JEW!
AND TO MAKE SURE HE'LL PAY US... WE'LL JUST TAKE YOU WITH US!
AHO... THIS IS THE PLACE, M'LADS ... SOFT NOW!
OH! THIS IS LORD CHARNLY'S MANSION! I DIDN'T KNOW YOU WERE GOING TO ROB...

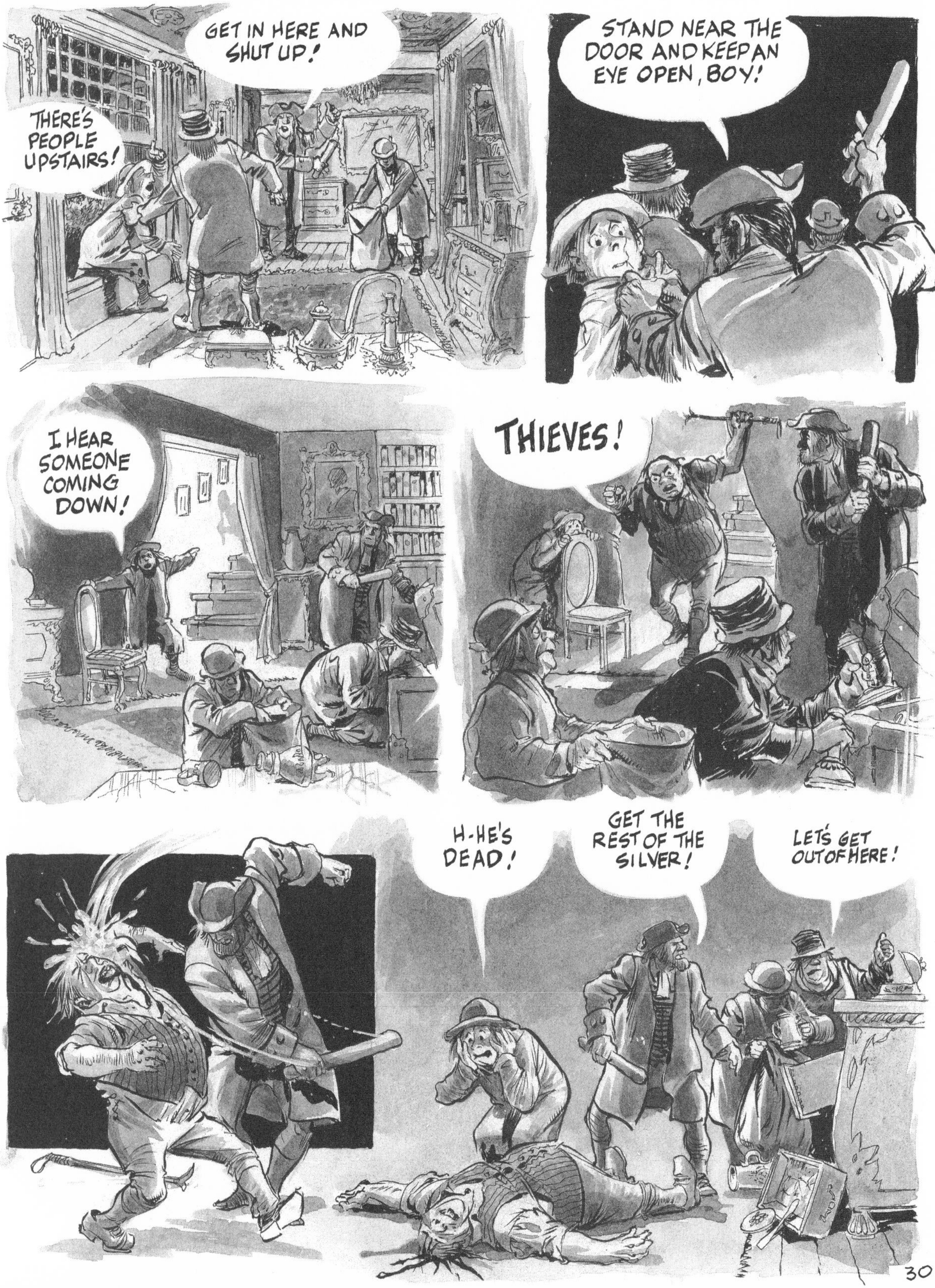
THERE'S PEOPLE UPSTAIRS!
GET IN HERE AND SHUT UP!
STAND NEAR THE DOOR AND KEEP AN EYE OPEN, BOY!
I HEAR SOMEONE COMING DOWN!
THIEVES!
H-HE'S DEAD!
GET THE REST OF THE SILVER!
LET'S GET OUT OF HERE!

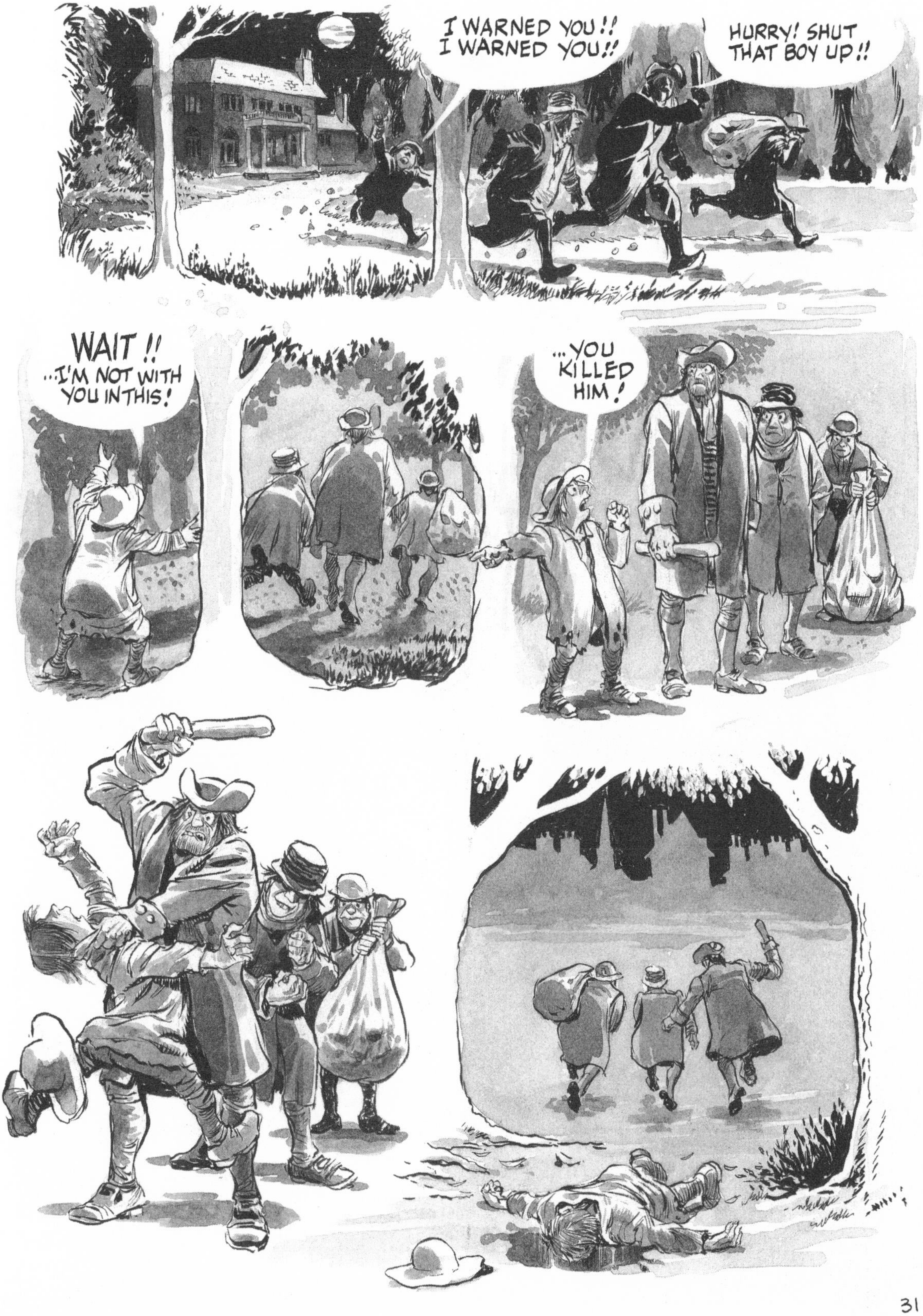

I WARNED YOU!! I WARNED YOU!!
HURRY! SHUT THAT BOY UP!!
WAIT!! ..I'M NOT WITH YOU IN THIS!
...YOU KILLED HIM!

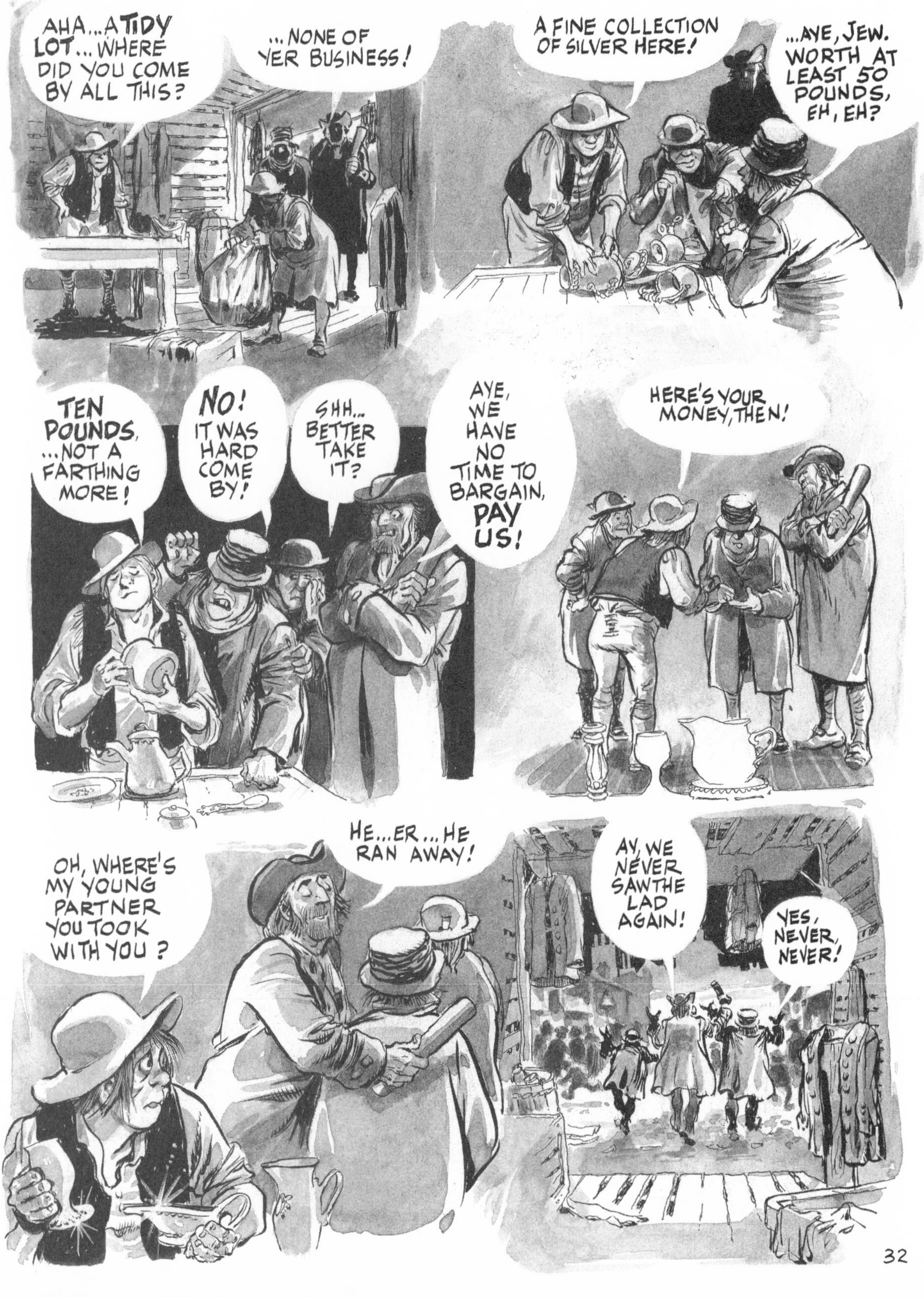
AHA...A TIDY LOT...WHERE DID YOU COME BY ALL THIS?
...NONE OF YER BUSINESS!
A FINE COLLECTION OF SILVER HERE!
...AYE, JEW. WORTH AT LEAST 50 POUNDS, EH, EH?
TEN POUNDS, ...NOT A FARTHING MORE!
NO! IT WAS HARD COME BY!
SHH... BETTER TAKE IT?
AYE, WE HAVE NO TIME TO BARGAIN, PAY US!
HERE'S YOUR MONEY, THEN!
OH, WHERE'S MY YOUNG PARTNER YOU TOOK WITH YOU?
HE...ER...HE RAN AWAY!
AY, WE NEVER SAW THE LAD AGAIN!
YES, NEVER, NEVER!

By now I had learned that in this trade, it was best not to ask questions. So I stored my newly purchased treasures in a safe place. They would bring me a tidy profit. I could sleep well ...

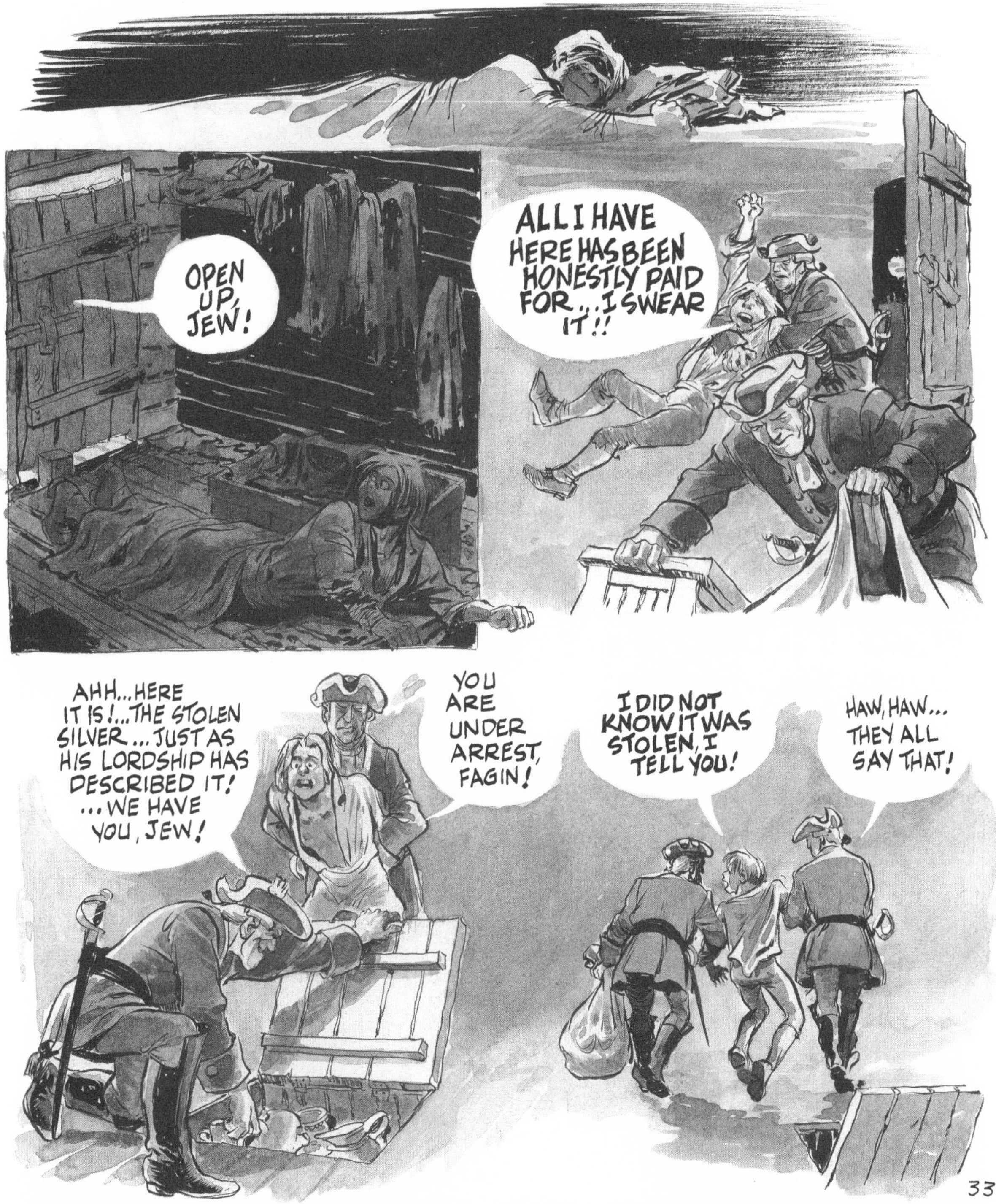

OPEN UP, JEW!
ALL I HAVE HERE HAS BEEN HONESTLY PAID FOR... I SWEAR IT!!
AHH... HERE IT IS!... THE STOLEN SILVER... JUST AS HIS LORDSHIP HAS DESCRIBED IT! ... WE HAVE YOU, JEW!
YOU ARE UNDER ARREST, FAGIN!
I DID NOT KNOW IT WAS STOLEN, I TELL YOU!
HAW, HAW... THEY ALL SAY THAT!

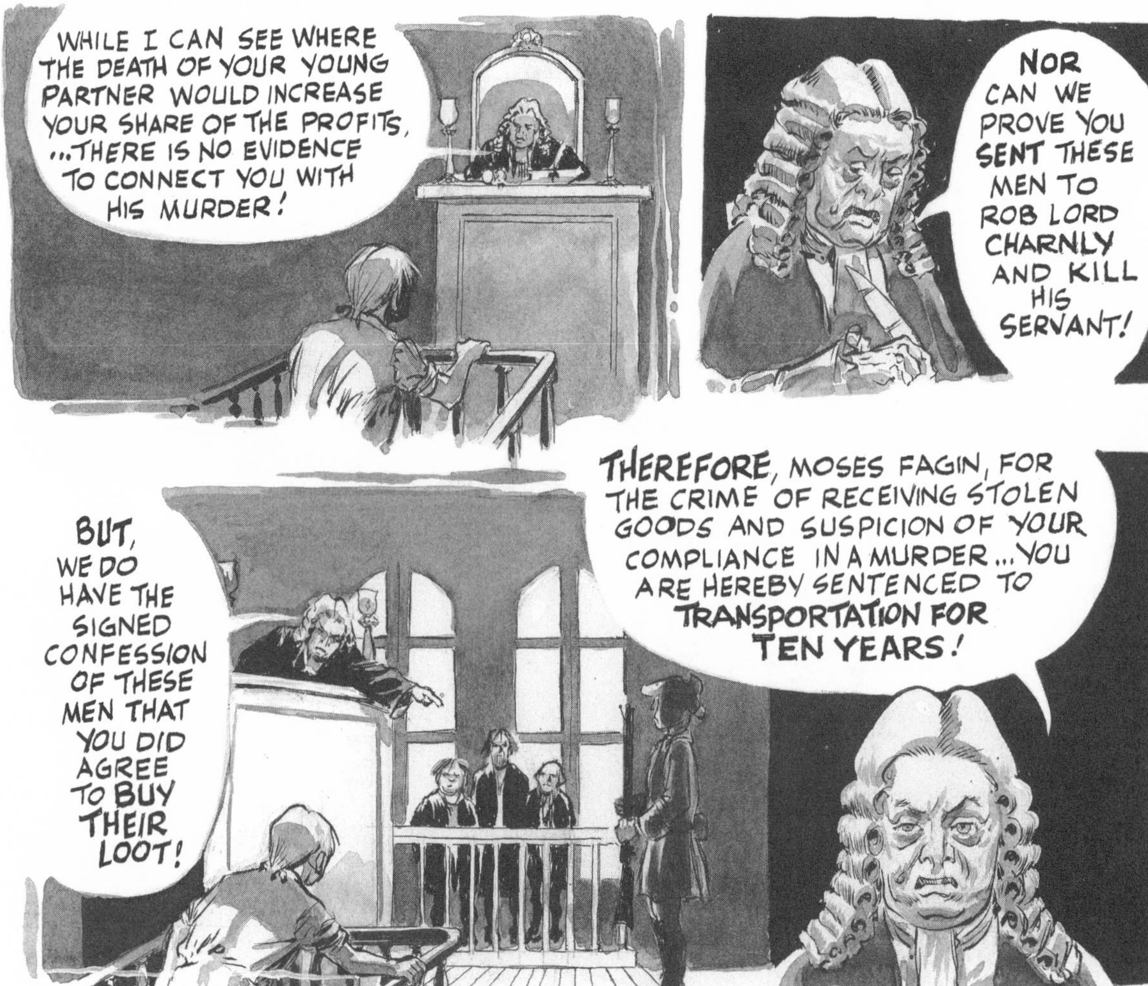
WHILE I CAN SEE WHERE THE DEATH OF YOUR YOUNG PARTNER WOULD INCREASE YOUR SHARE OF THE PROFITS, ...THERE IS NO EVIDENCE TO CONNECT YOU WITH HIS MURDER!
NOR CAN WE PROVE YOU SENT THESE MEN TO ROB LORD CHARNLY AND KILL HIS SERVANT!
BUT, WE DO HAVE THE SIGNED CONFESSION OF THESE MEN THAT YOU DID AGREE TO BUY THEIR LOOT!
THEREFORE, MOSES FAGIN, FOR THE CRIME OF RECEIVING STOLEN GOODS AND SUSPICION OF YOUR COMPLIANCE IN A MURDER... YOU ARE HEREBY SENTENCED TO TRANSPORTATION FOR TEN YEARS!

It was the very next week that I was herded with other convicts on a ship bound for one of England's western colonies, where convicts sentenced to transportation were to fulfill their sentences. There they were enslaved to colonists who bought their services from the Crown.

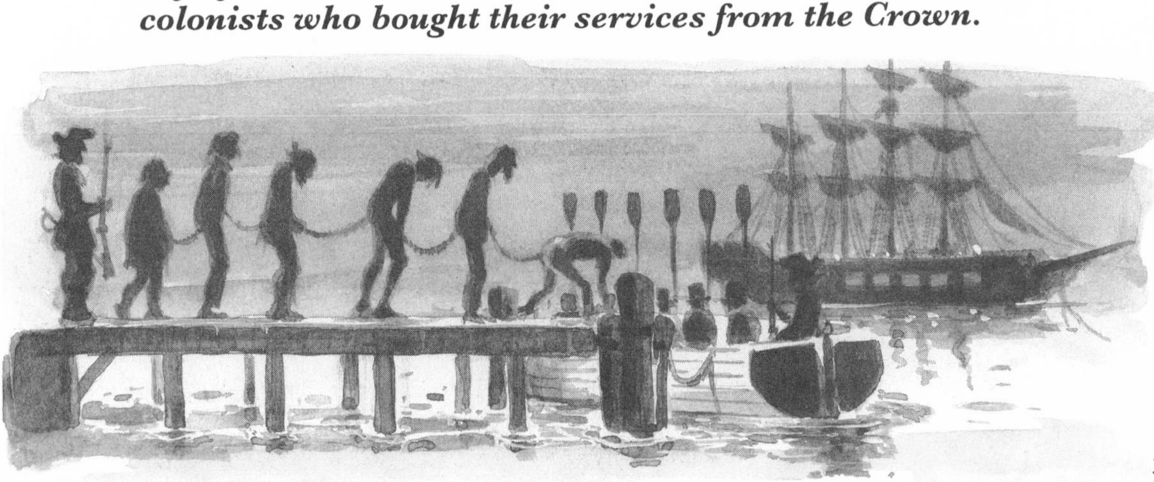

In the penal colony I was "bought" by a plantation owner, and for a year I was part of a gang clearing a swamp. There was little to eat and hard work from dawn to dusk ... but I knew how to find food.

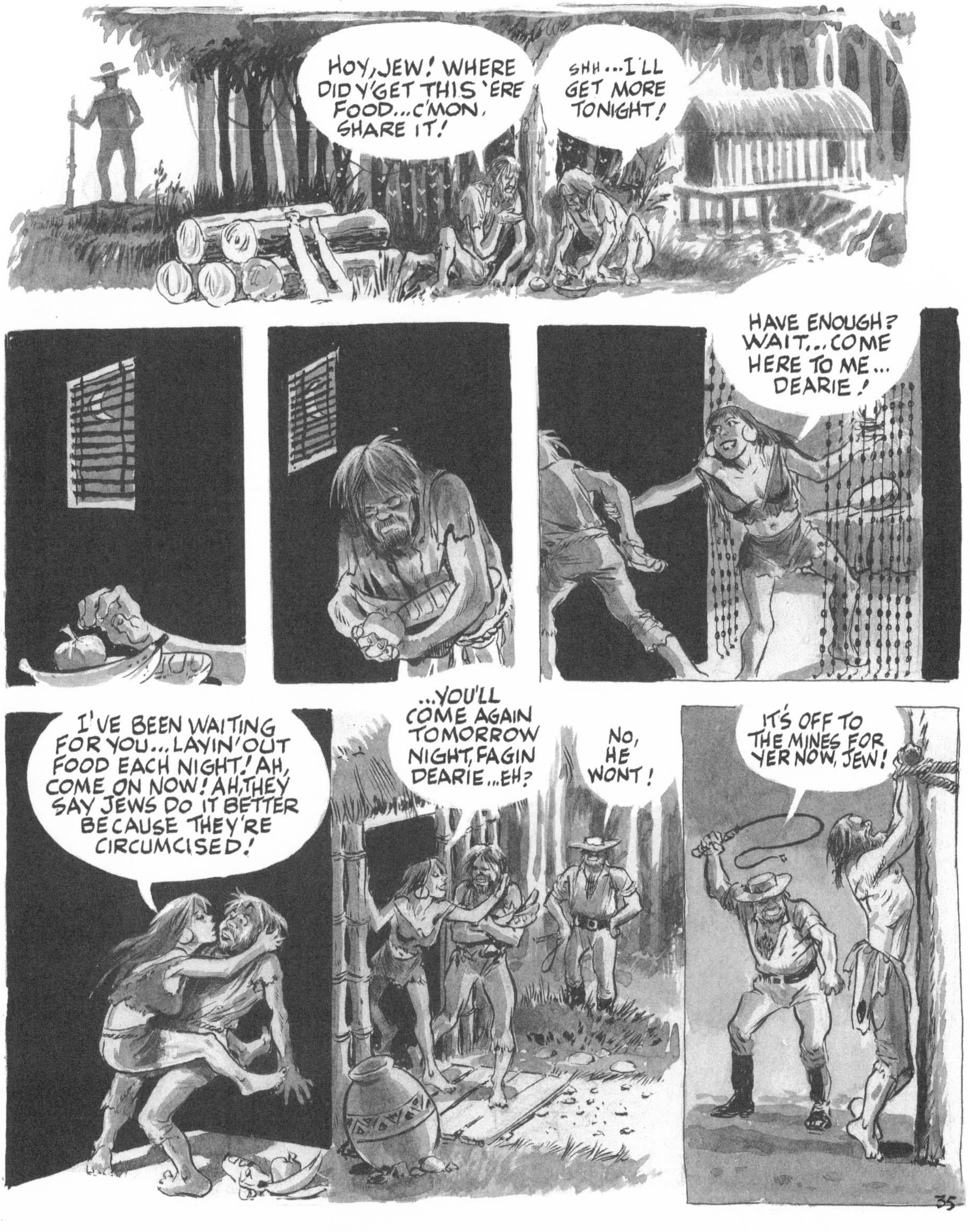
HOY, JEW! WHERE DID Y'GET THIS 'ERE FOOD...C'MON, SHARE IT!
SHH...I'LL GET MORE TONIGHT!
HAVE ENOUGH? WAIT...COME HERE TO ME... DEARIE!
I'VE BEEN WAITING FOR YOU...LAYIN' OUT FOOD EACH NIGHT! AH, COME ON NOW! AH, THEY SAY JEWS DO IT BETTER BECAUSE THEY'RE CIRCUMCISED!
...YOU'LL COME AGAIN TOMORROW NIGHT, FAGIN DEARIE...EH?
NO, HE WONT!
IT'S OFF TO THE MINES FOR YER NOW, JEW!

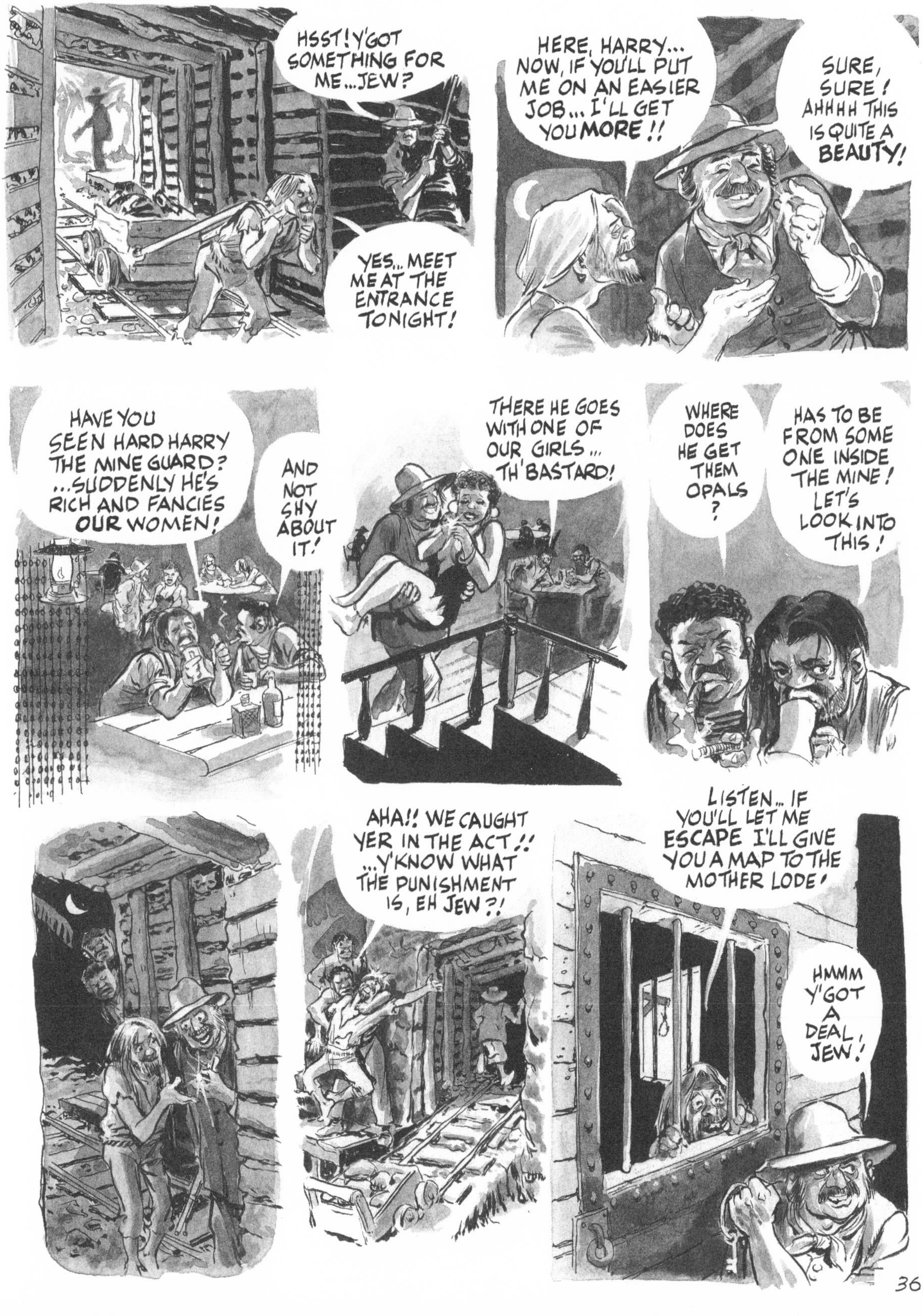
HSST! Y'GOT SOMETHING FOR ME...JEW?
YES... MEET ME AT THE ENTRANCE TONIGHT!
HERE, HARRY... NOW, IF YOU'LL PUT ME ON AN EASIER JOB... I'LL GET YOU MORE!!
SURE, SURE! AHHHH THIS IS QUITE A BEAUTY!
HAVE YOU SEEN HARD HARRY THE MINE GUARD? ...SUDDENLY HE'S RICH AND FANCIES OUR WOMEN!
AND NOT SHY ABOUT IT!
THERE HE GOES WITH ONE OF OUR GIRLS... TH'BASTARD!
WHERE DOES HE GET THEM OPALS?
HAS TO BE FROM SOME ONE INSIDE THE MINE! LET'S LOOK INTO THIS!
AHA!! WE CAUGHT YER IN THE ACT!! ...Y'KNOW WHAT THE PUNISHMENT IS, EH JEW?!
LISTEN... IF YOU'LL LET ME ESCAPE I'LL GIVE YOU A MAP TO THE MOTHER LODE!
HMMM Y'GOT A DEAL, JEW!

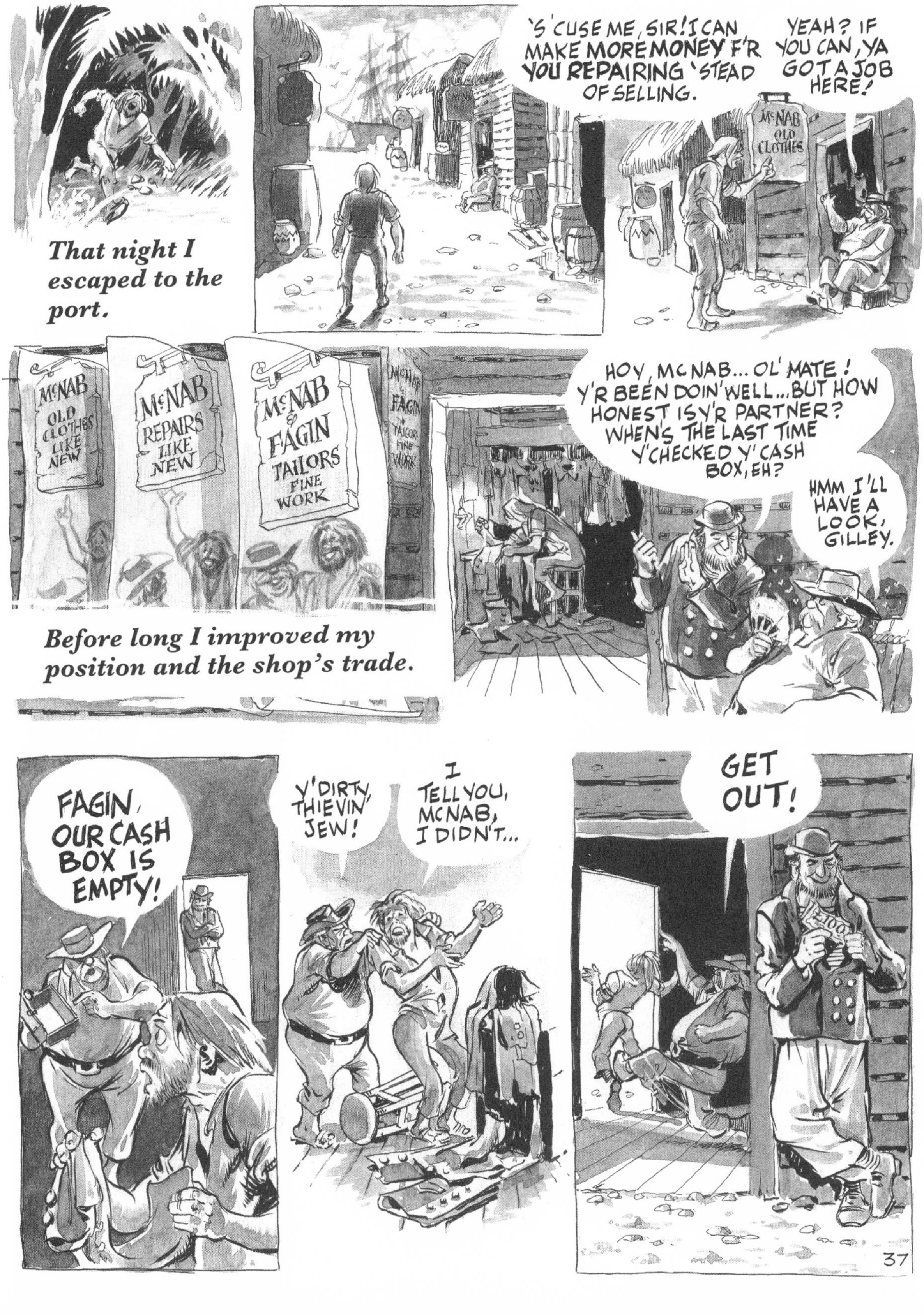

That night I escaped to the port.
'S'CUSE ME, SIR! I CAN MAKE MORE MONEY F'R YOU REPAIRING 'STEAD OF SELLING.
YEAH? IF YOU CAN, YA GOT A JOB HERE!
McNAB OLD CLOTHES
McNAB OLD CLOTHES LIKE NEW
McNAB REPAIRS LIKE NEW
McNAB & FAGIN TAILORS FINE WORK
McNAB & FAGIN TAILORS FINE WORK
Before long I improved my position and the shop's trade.
HOY, McNAB... OL' MATE! Y'R BEEN DOIN' WELL... BUT HOW HONEST IS Y'R PARTNER? WHEN'S THE LAST TIME Y'CHECKED Y' CASH BOX, EH?
HMM I'LL HAVE A LOOK, GILLEY.
FAGIN, OUR CASH BOX IS EMPTY!
Y'DIRTY, THIEVIN' JEW!
I TELL YOU, McNAB, I DIDN'T...
GET OUT!

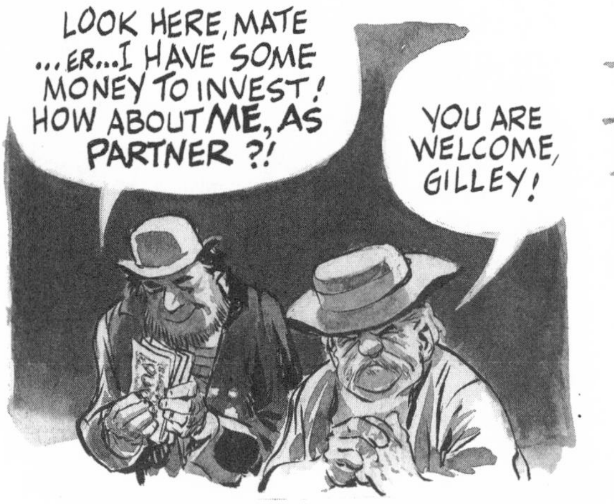
LOOK HERE, MATE ...ER...I HAVE SOME MONEY TO INVEST! HOW ABOUT ME, AS PARTNER ?!
YOU ARE WELCOME, GILLEY!

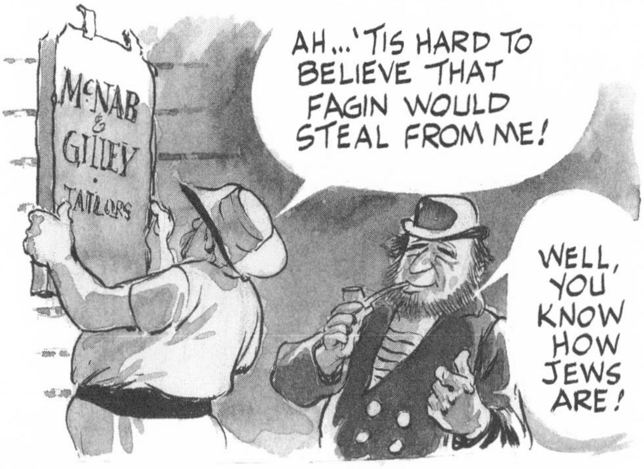
McNAB & GILLEY TAILORS
AH...'TIS HARD TO BELIEVE THAT FAGIN WOULD STEAL FROM ME!
WELL, YOU KNOW HOW JEWS ARE!

Once again I was at liberty, actually a prisoner-at-large. To avoid arrest I kept to the docks hoping for any opportunity that would give me shelter.

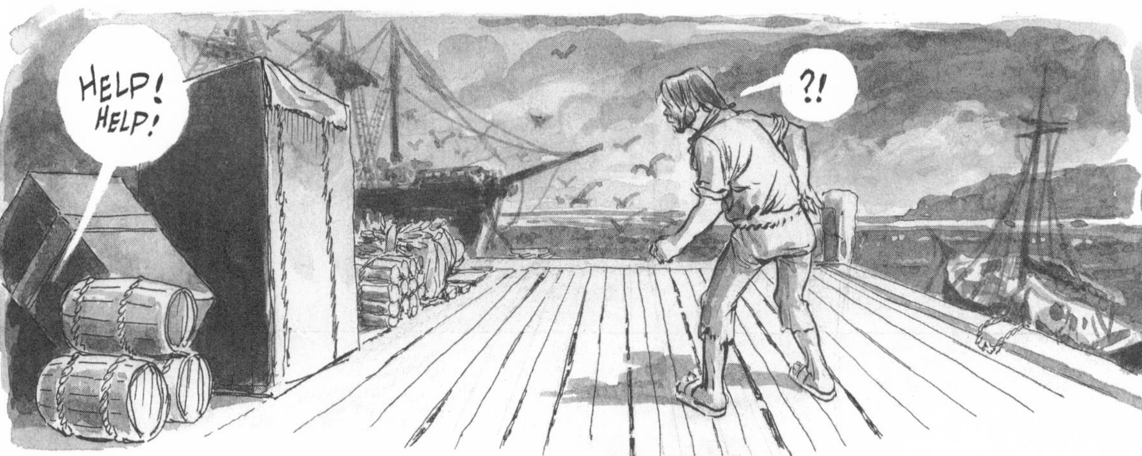
HELP! HELP!
?!

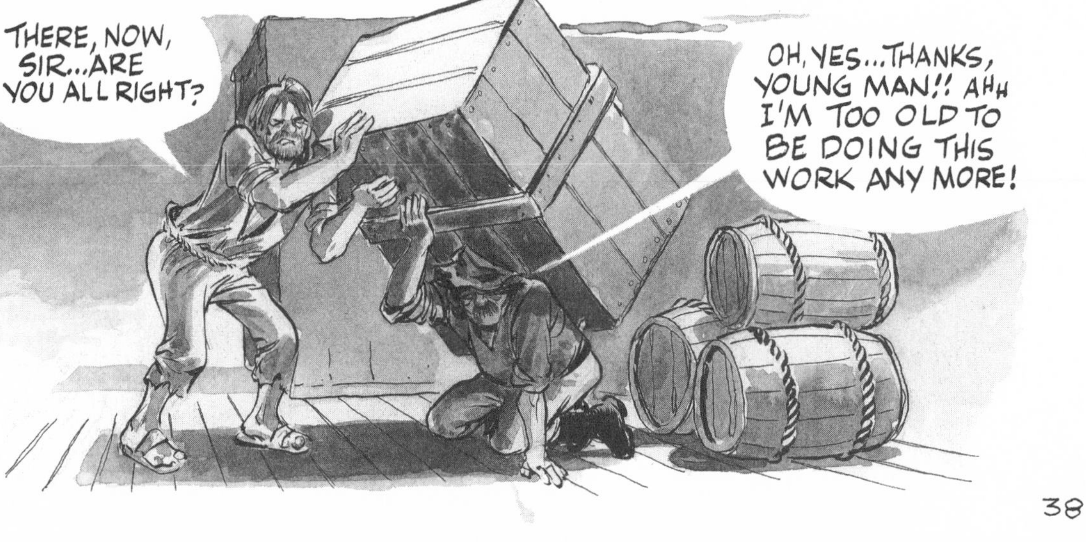
THERE, NOW, SIR...ARE YOU ALL RIGHT?
OH, YES...THANKS, YOUNG MAN!! AHH I'M TOO OLD TO BE DOING THIS WORK ANY MORE!

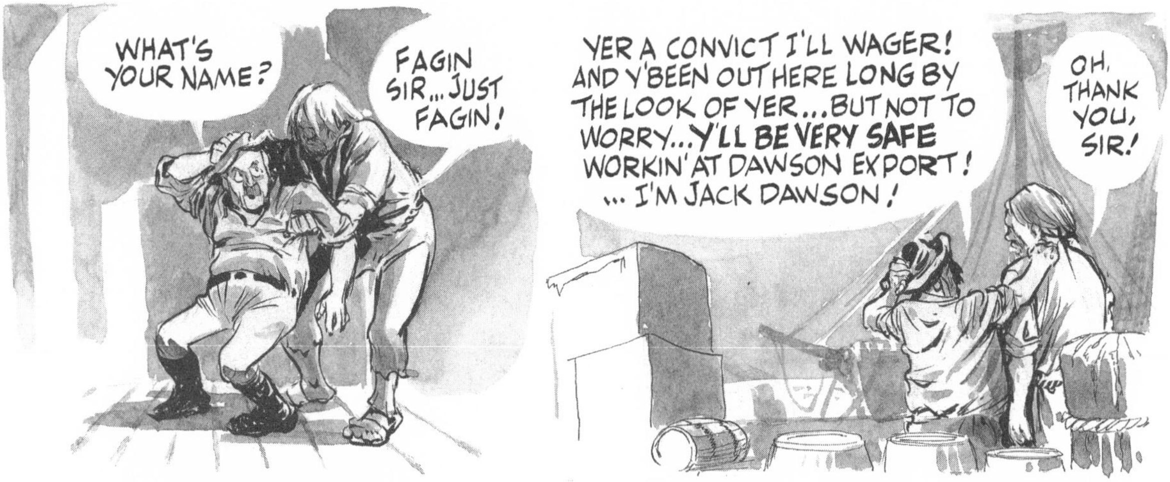
WHAT'S YOUR NAME?
FAGIN SIR... JUST FAGIN!
YER A CONVICT I'LL WAGER! AND Y'BEEN OUT HERE LONG BY THE LOOK OF YER... BUT NOT TO WORRY... Y'LL BE VERY SAFE WORKIN' AT DAWSON EXPORT! ... I'M JACK DAWSON!
OH, THANK YOU, SIR!

Mr. Dawson was a good man, fair and kind, and he provided me with a safe haven. Meanwhile, my anger over the betrayal at McNab kept boiling inside me, and before long I devised a plan to avenge myself.

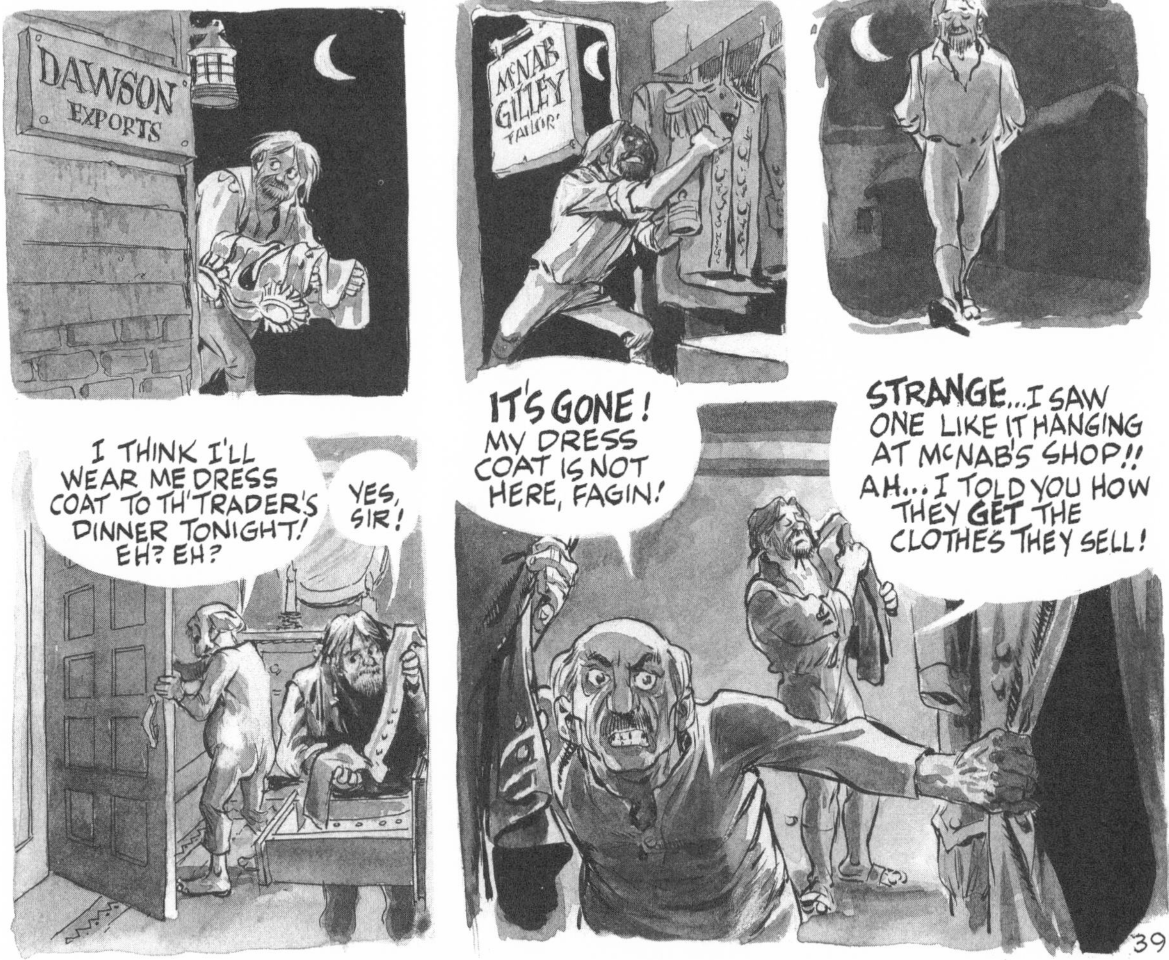
DAWSON EXPORTS
McNAB GILLEY
I THINK I'LL WEAR ME DRESS COAT TO TH' TRADER'S DINNER TONIGHT! EH? EH?
YES, SIR!
IT'S GONE! MY DRESS COAT IS NOT HERE, FAGIN!
STRANGE... I SAW ONE LIKE IT HANGING AT McNAB'S SHOP!! AH... I TOLD YOU HOW THEY GET THE CLOTHES THEY SELL!

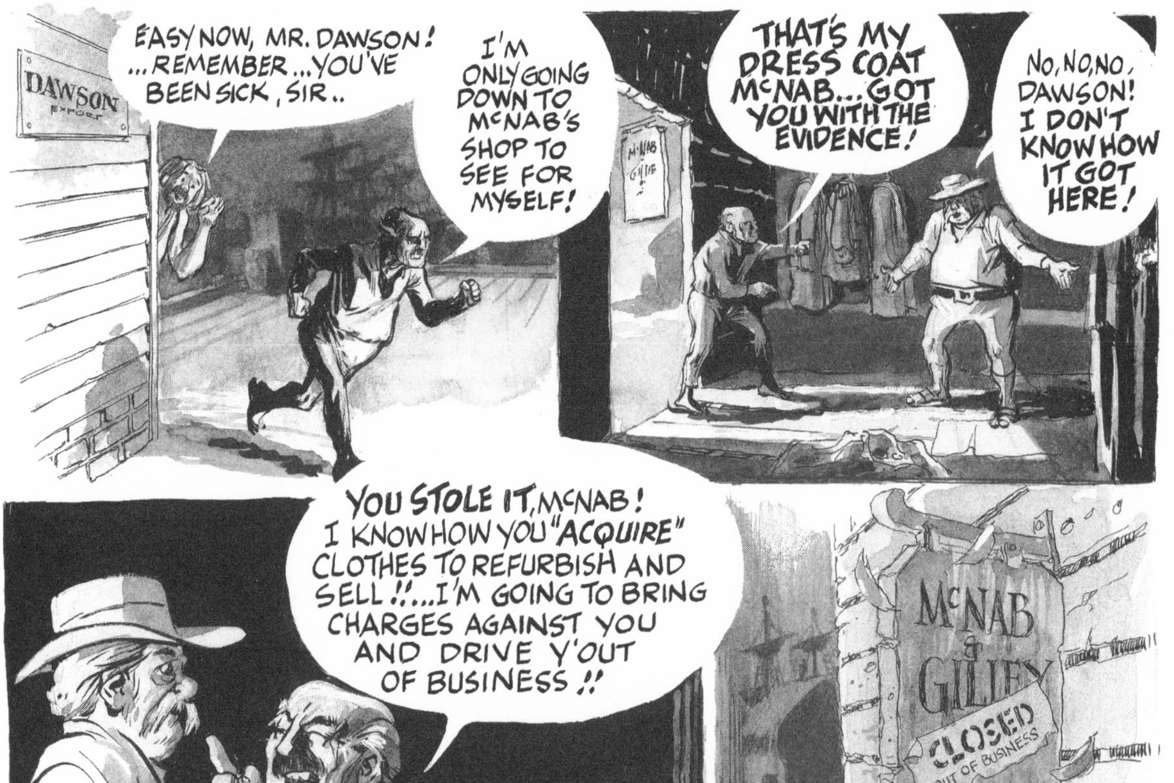
DAWSON EXPORT
EASY NOW, MR. DAWSON! ...REMEMBER...YOU'VE BEEN SICK, SIR..
I'M ONLY GOING DOWN TO McNAB'S SHOP TO SEE FOR MYSELF!
THAT'S MY DRESS COAT McNAB...GOT YOU WITH THE EVIDENCE!
NO, NO, NO, DAWSON! I DON'T KNOW HOW IT GOT HERE!
YOU STOLE IT, McNAB! I KNOW HOW YOU "ACQUIRE" CLOTHES TO REFURBISH AND SELL!!...I'M GOING TO BRING CHARGES AGAINST YOU AND DRIVE Y'OUT OF BUSINESS!!
McNAB & GILLEY
CLOSED
OUT OF BUSINESS

My plan worked perfectly … now at last I had a chance to establish myself. It was possible for convicts to do this if they had someone to "stake" them.

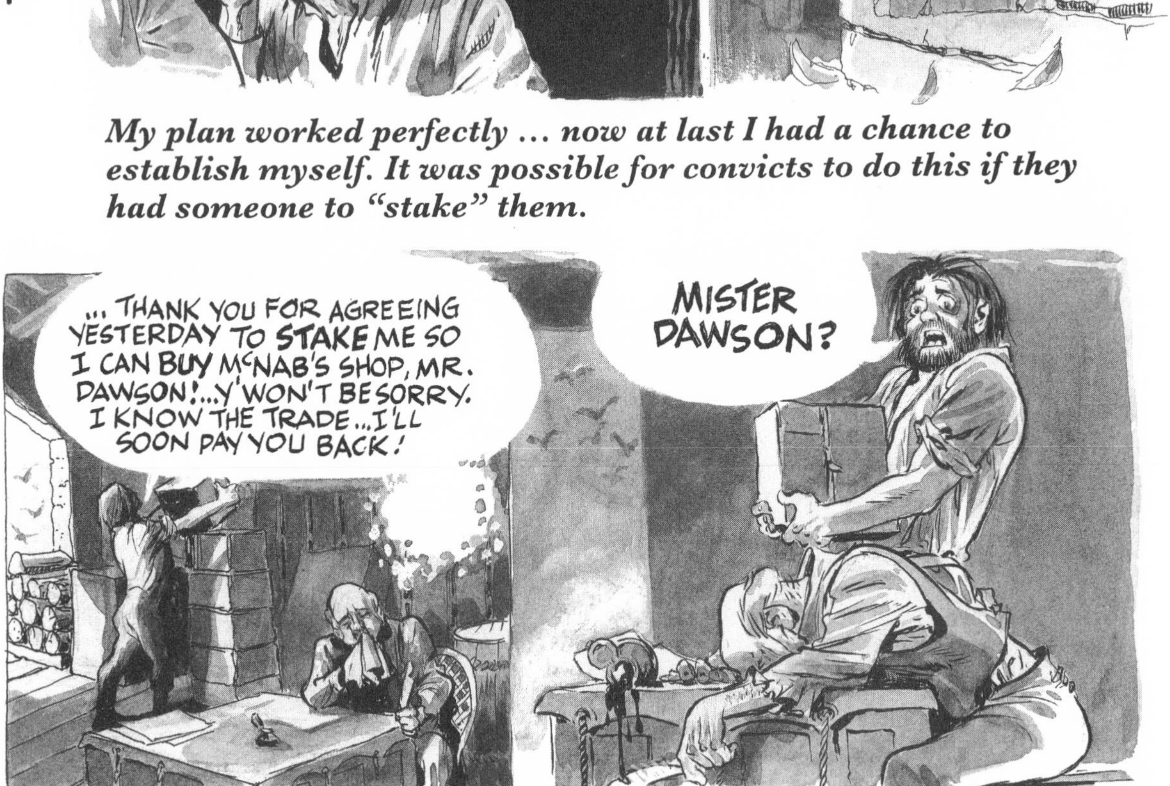
... THANK YOU FOR AGREEING YESTERDAY TO STAKE ME SO I CAN BUY McNAB'S SHOP, MR. DAWSON!...Y'WON'T BE SORRY. I KNOW THE TRADE...I'LL SOON PAY YOU BACK!
MISTER DAWSON?

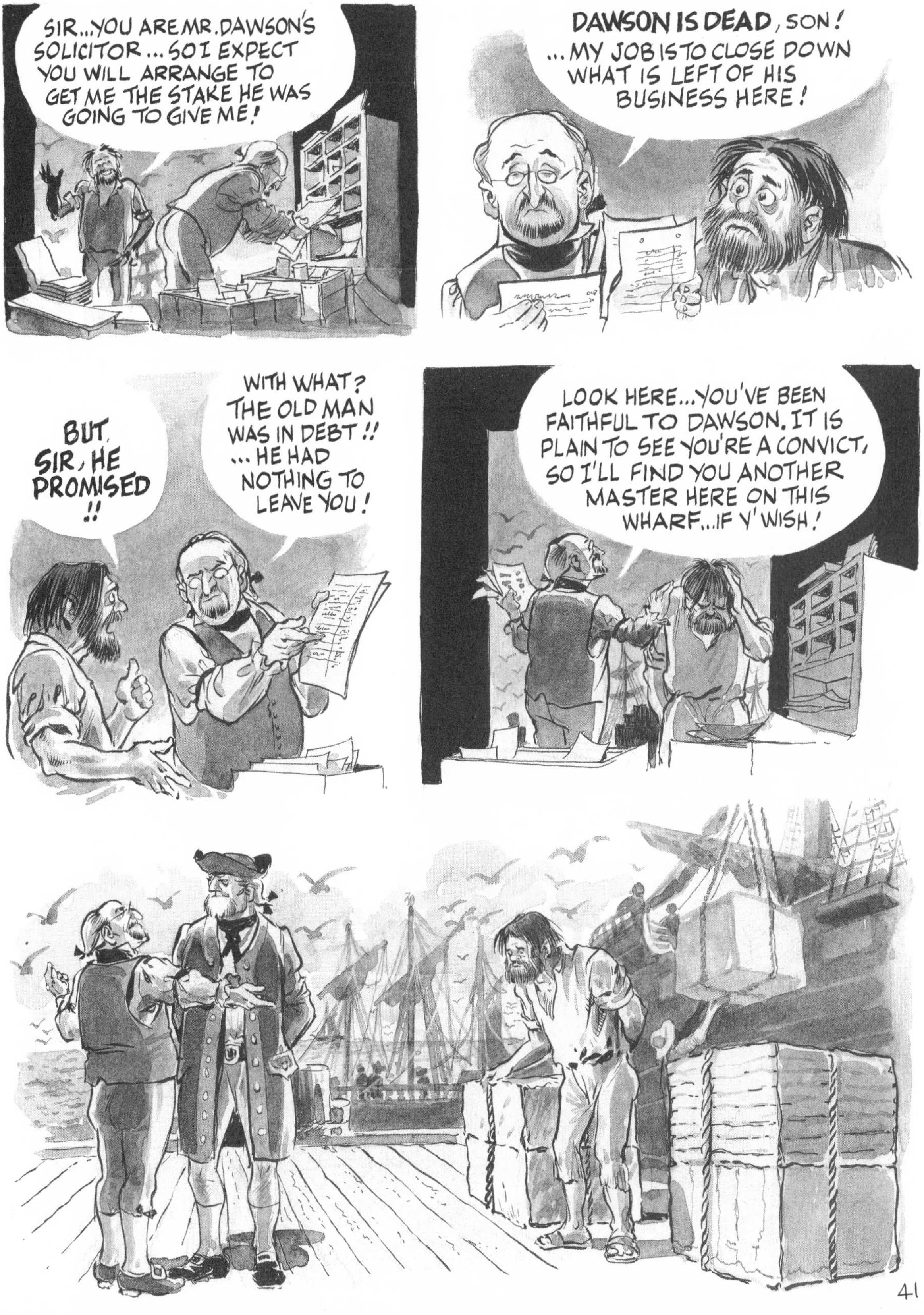
SIR...YOU ARE MR. DAWSON'S SOLICITOR ... SO I EXPECT YOU WILL ARRANGE TO GET ME THE STAKE HE WAS GOING TO GIVE ME!
DAWSON IS DEAD, SON! ... MY JOB IS TO CLOSE DOWN WHAT IS LEFT OF HIS BUSINESS HERE!
BUT, SIR, HE PROMISED !!
WITH WHAT? THE OLD MAN WAS IN DEBT !! ... HE HAD NOTHING TO LEAVE YOU!
LOOK HERE...YOU'VE BEEN FAITHFUL TO DAWSON. IT IS PLAIN TO SEE YOU'RE A CONVICT, SO I'LL FIND YOU ANOTHER MASTER HERE ON THIS WHARF...IF Y' WISH!

So I remained there, working out the rest of my sentence, a slave indentured to an honest harbor master, until one day ...

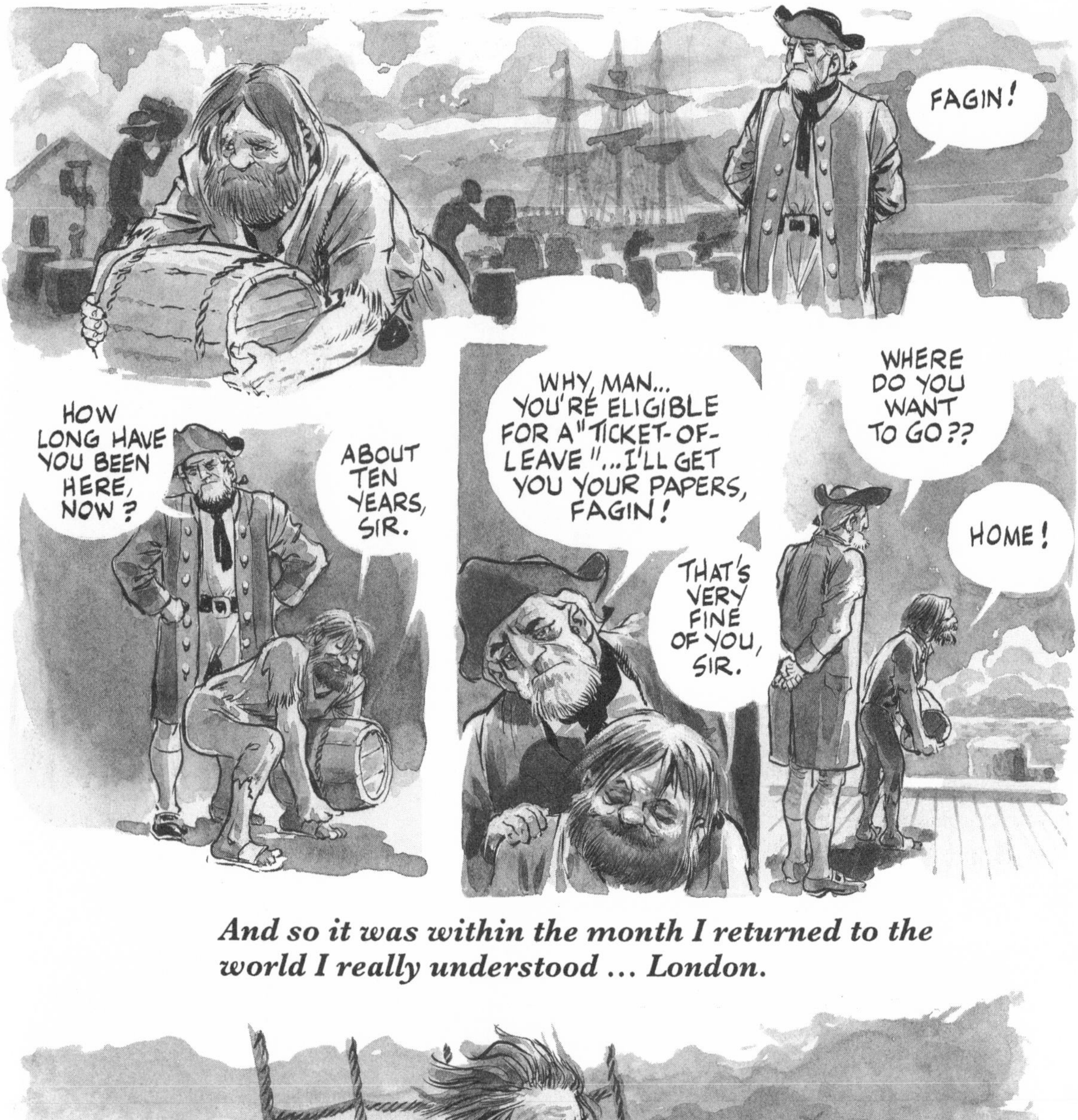
FAGIN!
HOW LONG HAVE YOU BEEN HERE, NOW?
ABOUT TEN YEARS, SIR.
WHY, MAN... YOU'RE ELIGIBLE FOR A "TICKET-OF-LEAVE"... I'LL GET YOU YOUR PAPERS, FAGIN!
THAT'S VERY FINE OF YOU, SIR.
WHERE DO YOU WANT TO GO??
HOME!

And so it was within the month I returned to the world I really understood ... London.

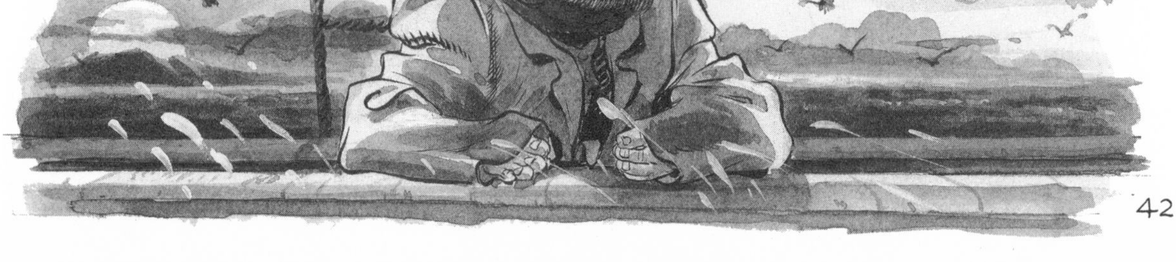

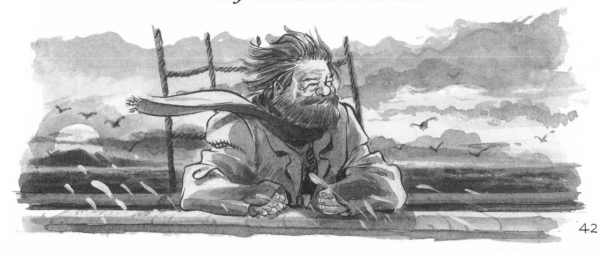

When at last I returned to London, I was aged beyond my years. Broken in body, in fragile health, I was in appearance a shuffling greybeard, the result of the horrors of penal life and imprisonment.

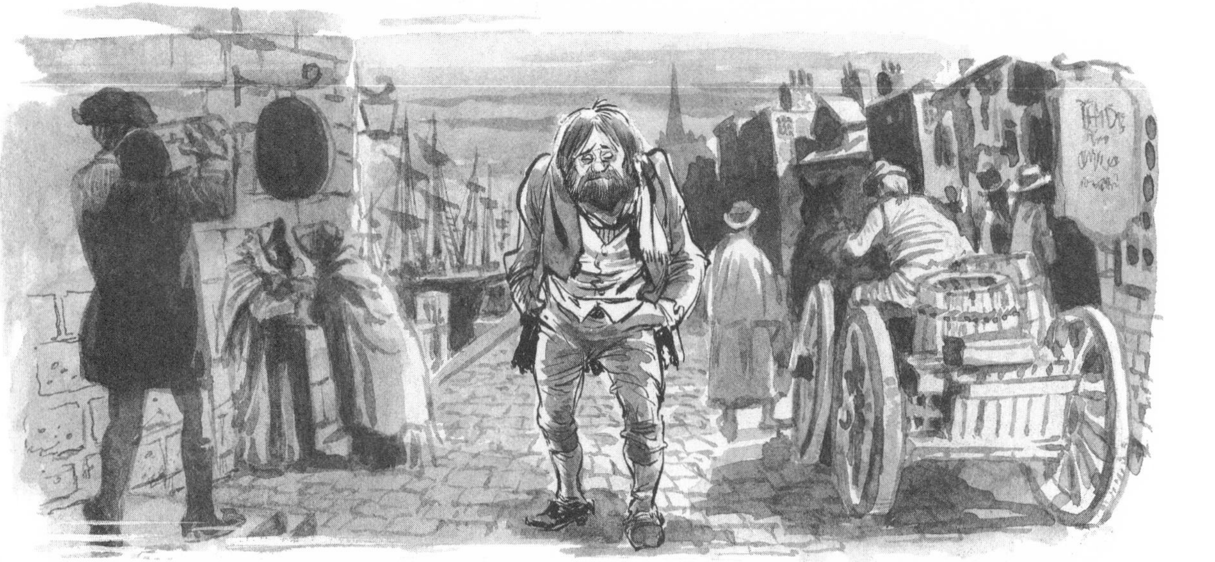

However, I still had my wits about me. Sharper than ever were my skills, which were honed in the penal colonies.

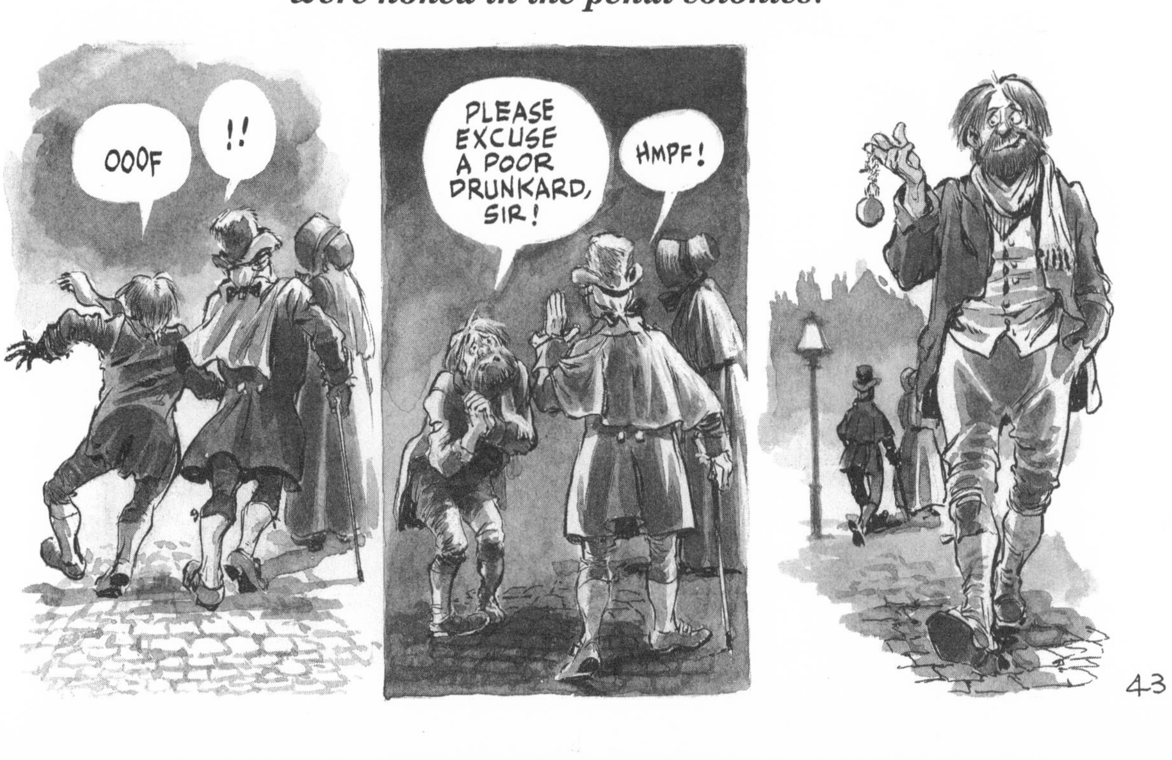
OOOF
!!
PLEASE EXCUSE A POOR DRUNKARD, SIR!
HMPF!

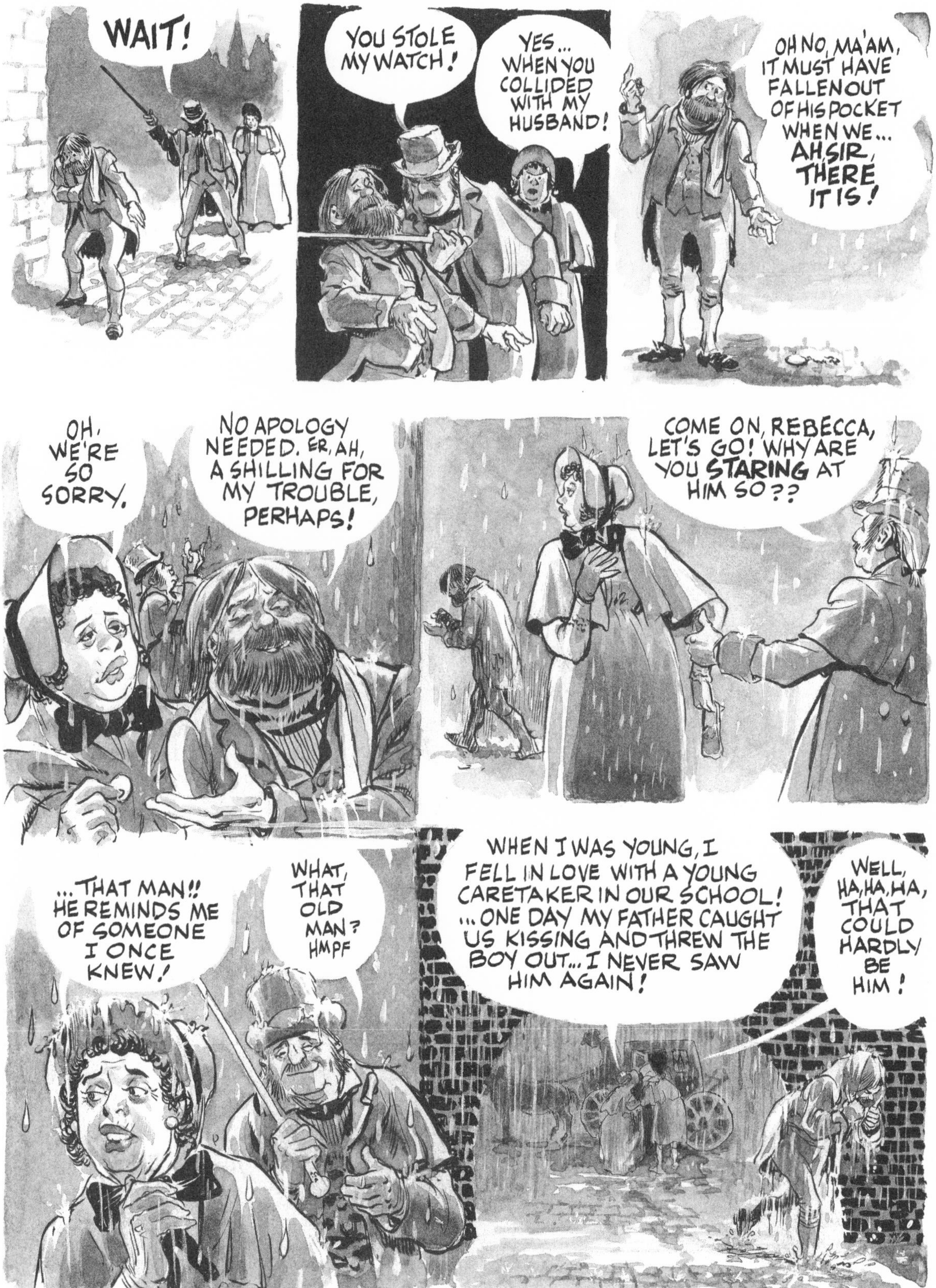
WAIT!
YOU STOLE MY WATCH!
YES... WHEN YOU COLLIDED WITH MY HUSBAND!
OH NO, MA'AM, IT MUST HAVE FALLEN OUT OF HIS POCKET WHEN WE... AH SIR, THERE IT IS!
OH, WE'RE SO SORRY.
NO APOLOGY NEEDED. ER, AH, A SHILLING FOR MY TROUBLE, PERHAPS!
COME ON, REBECCA, LET'S GO! WHY ARE YOU STARING AT HIM SO??
...THAT MAN!! HE REMINDS ME OF SOMEONE I ONCE KNEW!
WHAT, THAT OLD MAN? HMPF
WHEN I WAS YOUNG, I FELL IN LOVE WITH A YOUNG CARETAKER IN OUR SCHOOL! ...ONE DAY MY FATHER CAUGHT US KISSING AND THREW THE BOY OUT... I NEVER SAW HIM AGAIN!
WELL, HA, HA, HA, THAT COULD HARDLY BE HIM!

In London, I had finally established myself. I was no longer naive; gone was the promise that fueled my hope of a grand future. I was what the urchins who worked for me would one day become.

Who knows, were I not a Jew ... had I not lost opportunities or suffered the misfortune of imprisonment or had I been able to stay in Mr. Salomon's employ, I might not be standing in a knot of people in a London street operating a street game with a new partner, a ruffian named Sikes.

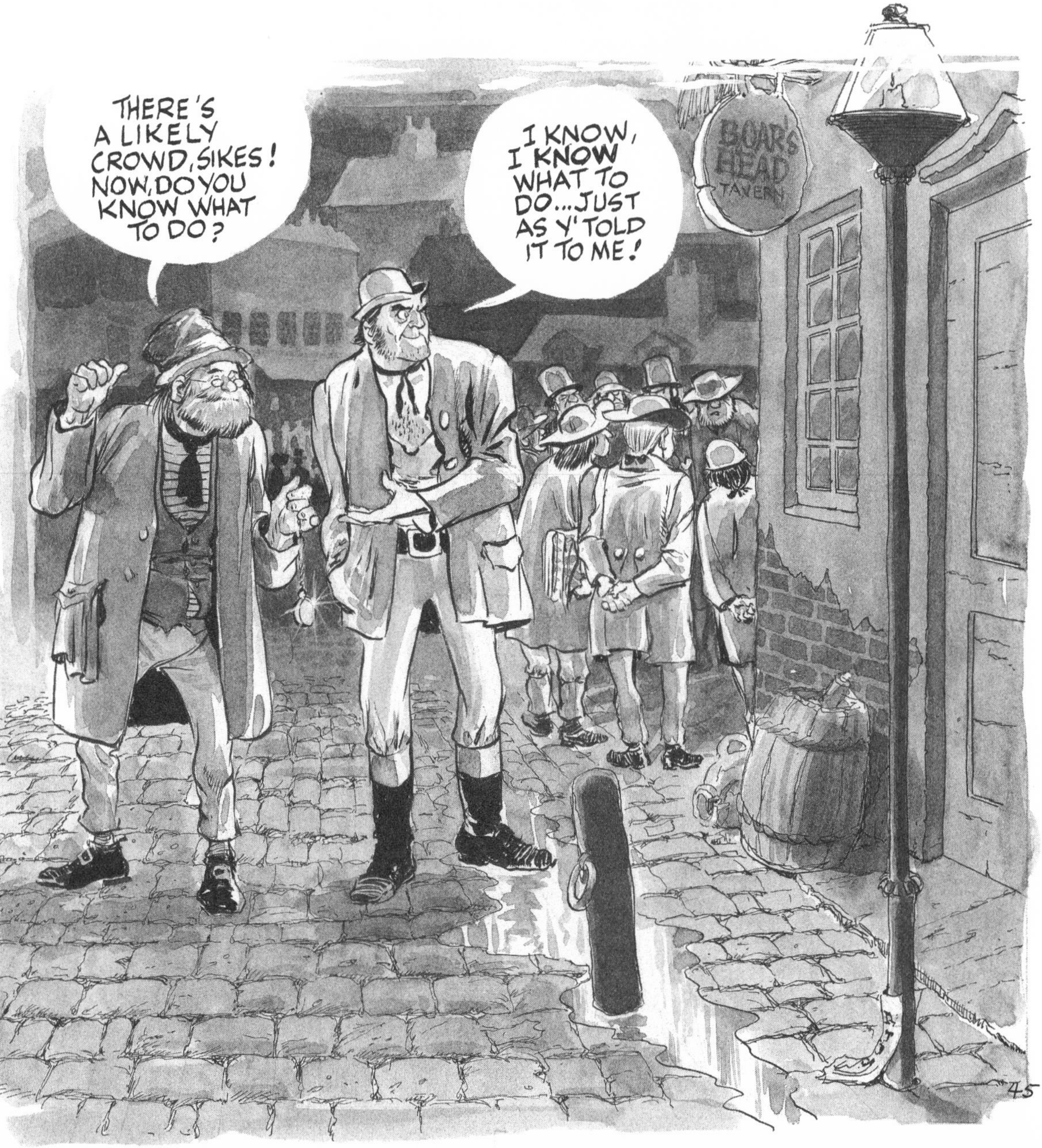
THERE'S A LIKELY CROWD, SIKES! NOW, DO YOU KNOW WHAT TO DO?
I KNOW, I KNOW WHAT TO DO... JUST AS Y'TOLD IT TO ME!
BOAR'S HEAD TAVERN

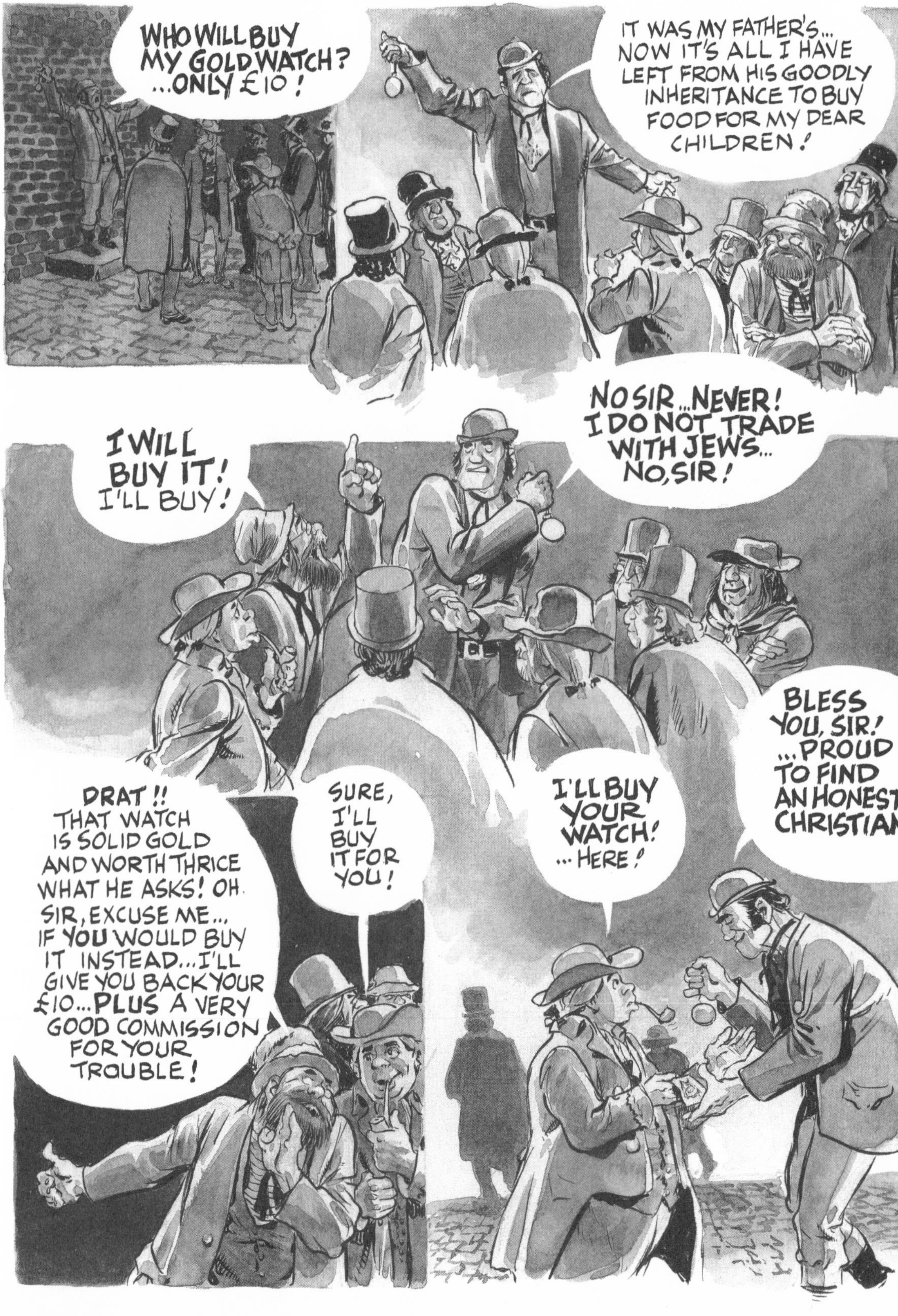
WHO WILL BUY MY GOLD WATCH? ...ONLY £10!
IT WAS MY FATHER'S... NOW IT'S ALL I HAVE LEFT FROM HIS GOODLY INHERITANCE TO BUY FOOD FOR MY DEAR CHILDREN!
I WILL BUY IT! I'LL BUY!
NO SIR...NEVER! I DO NOT TRADE WITH JEWS... NO, SIR!
DRAT!! THAT WATCH IS SOLID GOLD AND WORTH THRICE WHAT HE ASKS! OH SIR, EXCUSE ME... IF YOU WOULD BUY IT INSTEAD... I'LL GIVE YOU BACK YOUR £10... PLUS A VERY GOOD COMMISSION FOR YOUR TROUBLE!
SURE, I'LL BUY IT FOR YOU!
I'LL BUY YOUR WATCH! ... HERE!
BLESS YOU, SIR! ...PROUD TO FIND AN HONEST CHRISTIAN!

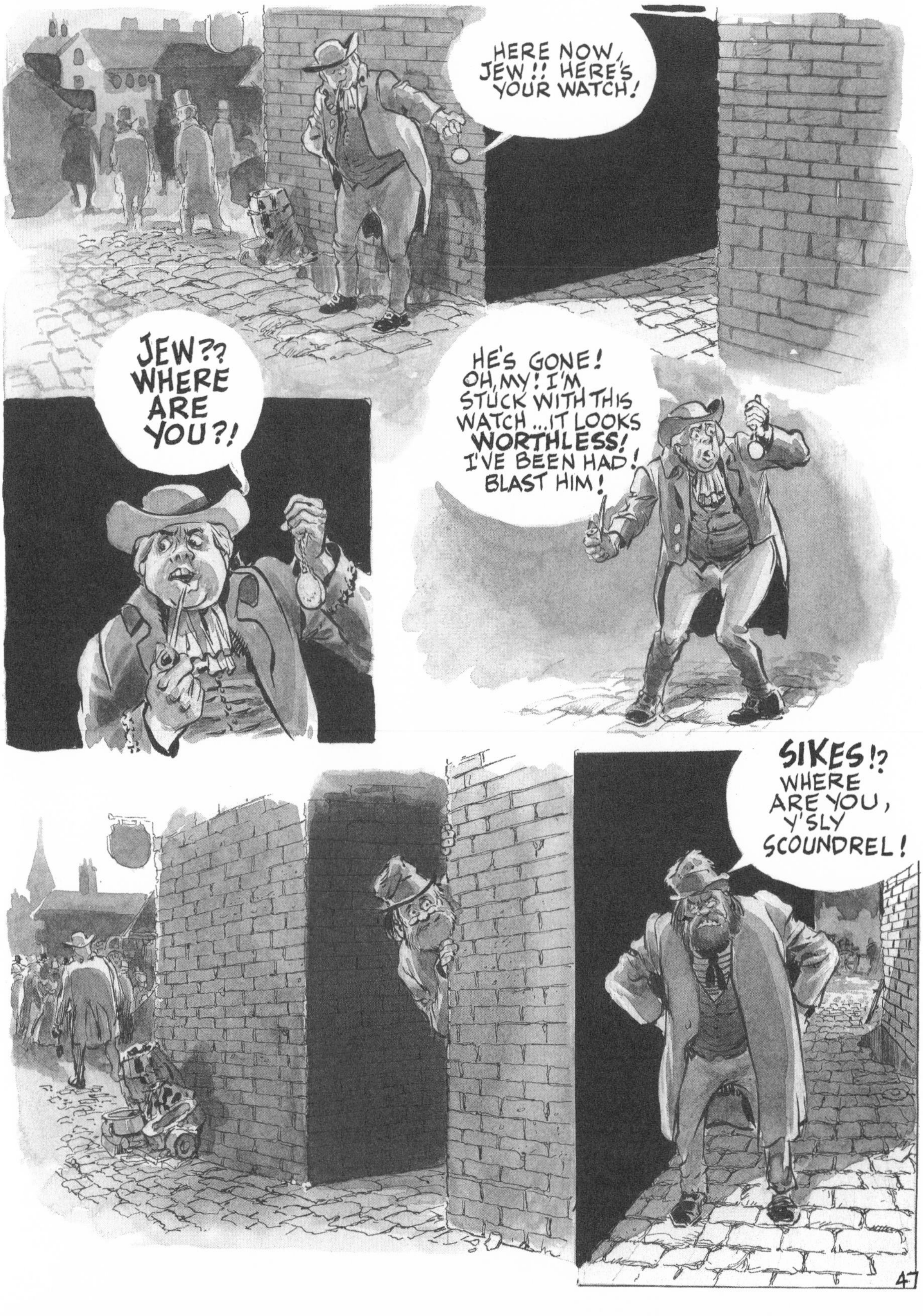

HERE NOW, JEW!! HERE'S YOUR WATCH!
JEW?? WHERE ARE YOU?!
HE'S GONE! OH, MY! I'M STUCK WITH THIS WATCH ...IT LOOKS **WORTHLESS!** I'VE BEEN HAD! BLAST HIM!
SIKES!? WHERE ARE YOU, Y'SLY SCOUNDREL!

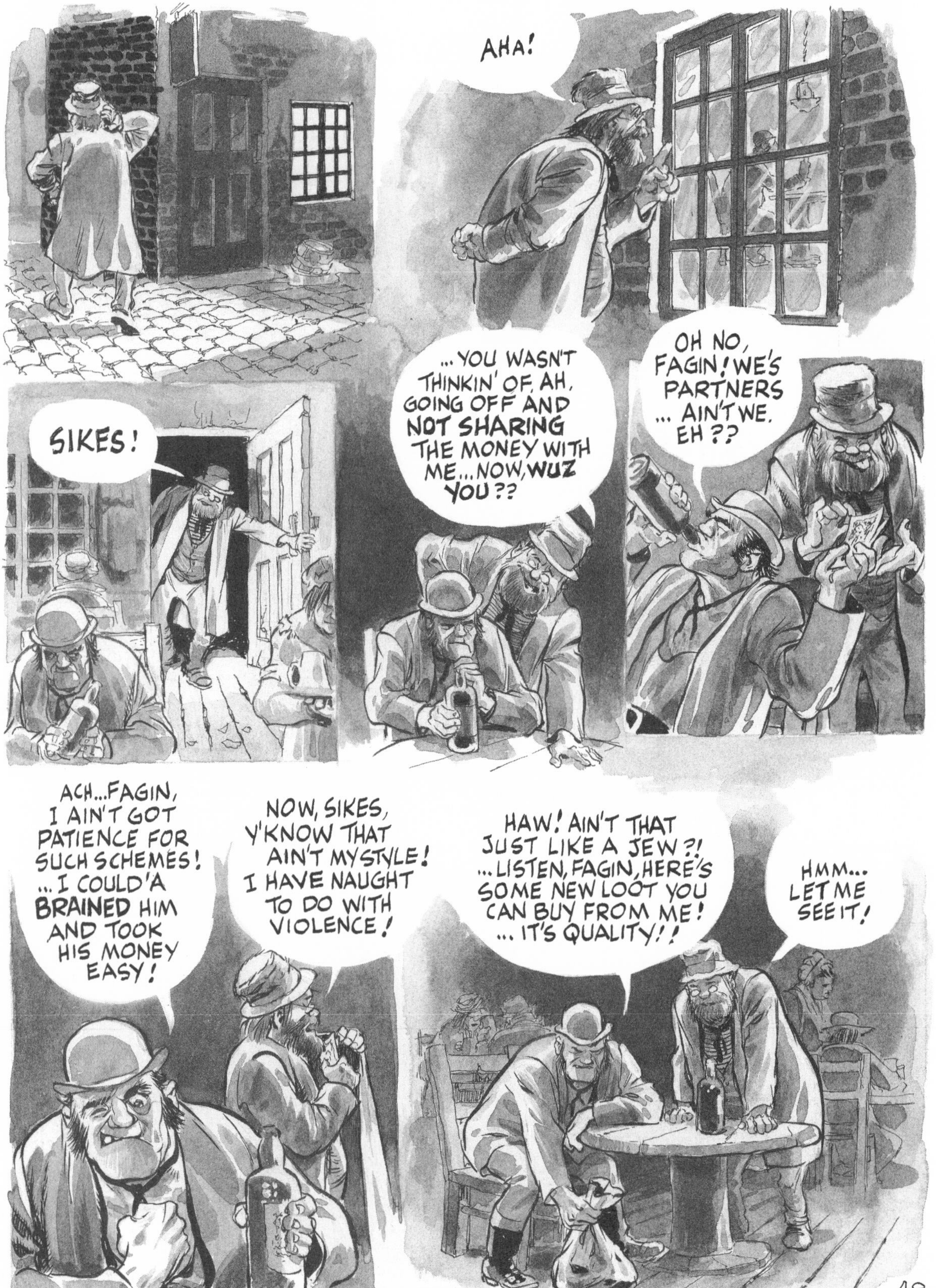
AHA!
SIKES!
... YOU WASN'T THINKIN' OF, AH, GOING OFF AND NOT SHARING THE MONEY WITH ME... NOW, WUZ YOU??
OH NO, FAGIN! WE'S PARTNERS ... AIN'T WE, EH??
ACH... FAGIN, I AIN'T GOT PATIENCE FOR SUCH SCHEMES! ... I COULD'A BRAINED HIM AND TOOK HIS MONEY EASY!
NOW, SIKES, Y'KNOW THAT AIN'T MY STYLE! I HAVE NAUGHT TO DO WITH VIOLENCE!
HAW! AIN'T THAT JUST LIKE A JEW?! ... LISTEN, FAGIN, HERE'S SOME NEW LOOT YOU CAN BUY FROM ME! ... IT'S QUALITY!!
HMM... LET ME SEE IT!

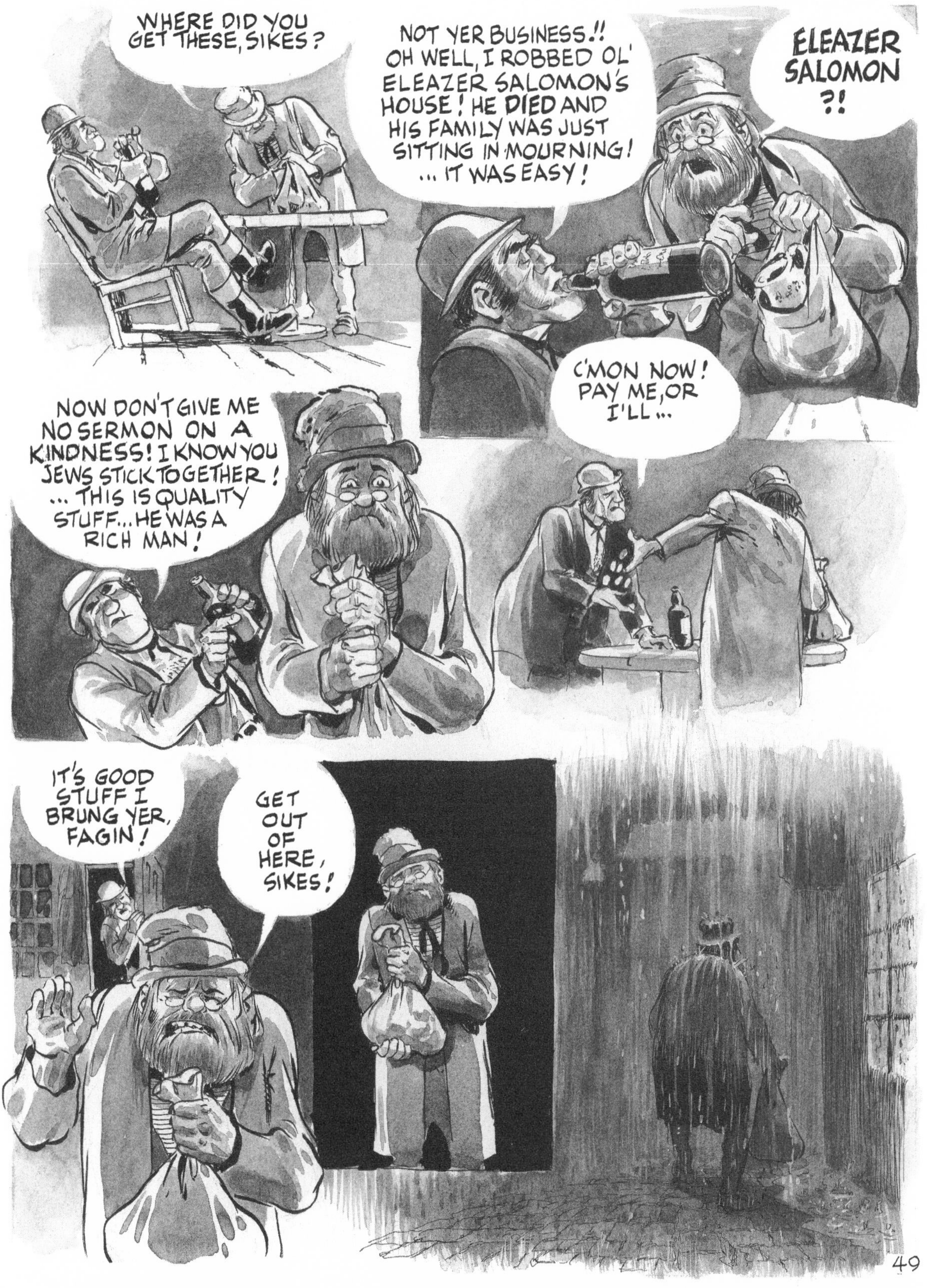
WHERE DID YOU GET THESE, SIKES?
NOT YER BUSINESS.!! OH WELL, I ROBBED OL' ELEAZER SALOMON'S HOUSE! HE **DIED** AND HIS FAMILY WAS JUST SITTING IN MOURNING! ... IT WAS EASY!
ELEAZER SALOMON ?!
C'MON NOW! PAY ME, OR I'LL...
NOW DON'T GIVE ME NO SERMON ON A KINDNESS! I KNOW YOU JEWS STICK TOGETHER! ... THIS IS QUALITY STUFF... HE WAS A RICH MAN!
IT'S GOOD STUFF I BRUNG YER, FAGIN!
GET OUT OF HERE, SIKES!

I returned the loot to Mr. Salomon's home, where for a few moments I mourned over what my life ... what I might have been, had Mr. Lopez not thrown me out of that school so many years ago.

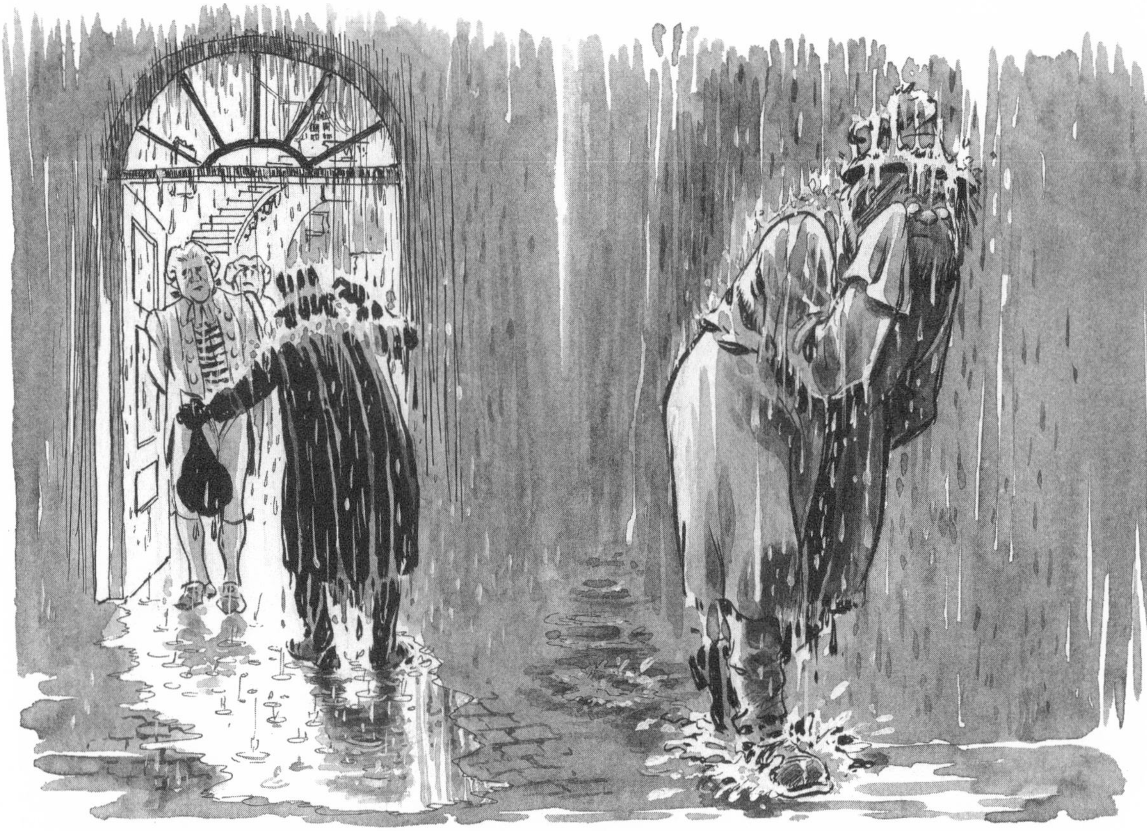

The following years were spent at the only trade I knew ... buying and selling whatever came to hand. I became a haven for the ragged urchins of the street.

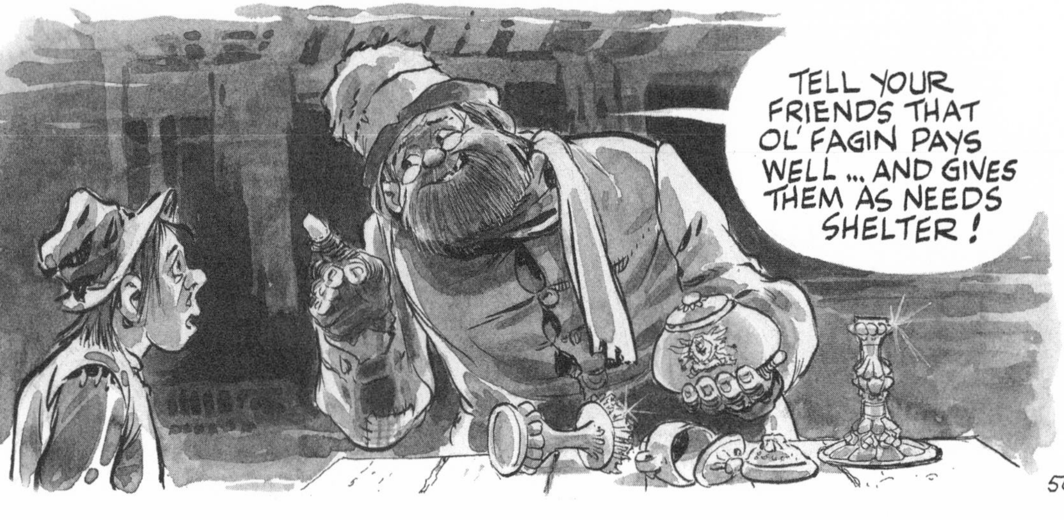
TELL YOUR FRIENDS THAT OL' FAGIN PAYS WELL ... AND GIVES THEM AS NEEDS SHELTER!

And my reputation among the little derelicts soon spread. I became known as a teacher of street arts …

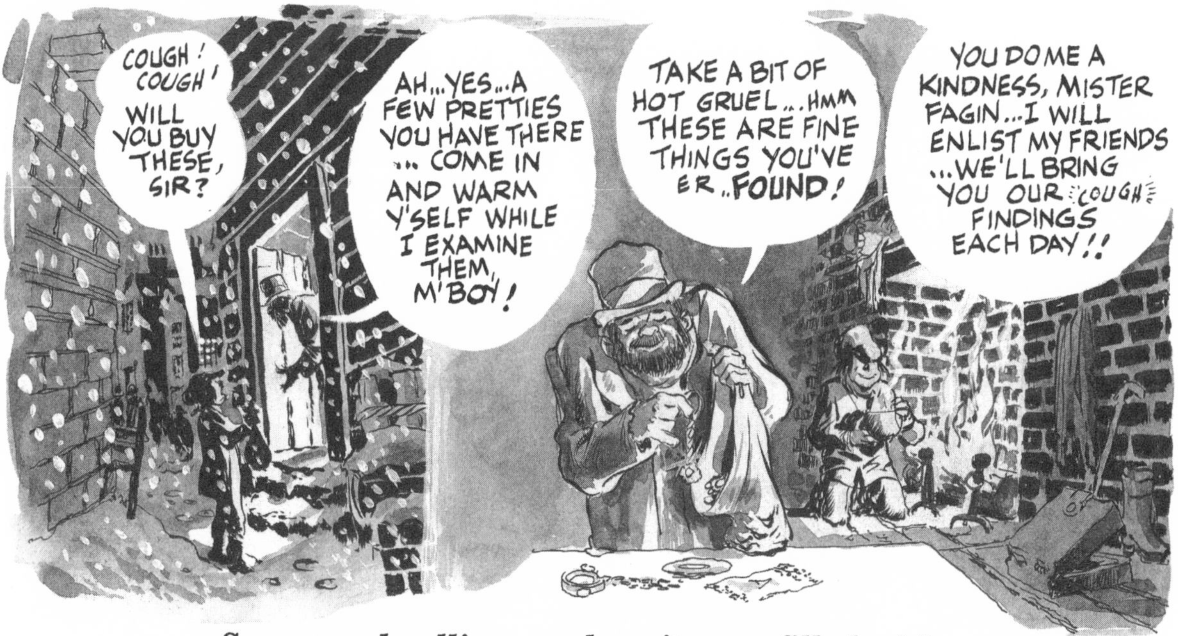
COUGH! COUGH! WILL YOU BUY THESE, SIR?
AH... YES... A FEW PRETTIES YOU HAVE THERE ... COME IN AND WARM Y'SELF WHILE I EXAMINE THEM, M'BOY!
TAKE A BIT OF HOT GRUEL... HMM THESE ARE FINE THINGS YOU'VE ER.. FOUND!
YOU DO ME A KINDNESS, MISTER FAGIN... I WILL ENLIST MY FRIENDS ...WE'LL BRING YOU OUR COUGH FINDINGS EACH DAY!!

Soon my dwelling, such as it was, filled with adept ragamuffins who provided me with an ample source of merchandise I could resell.

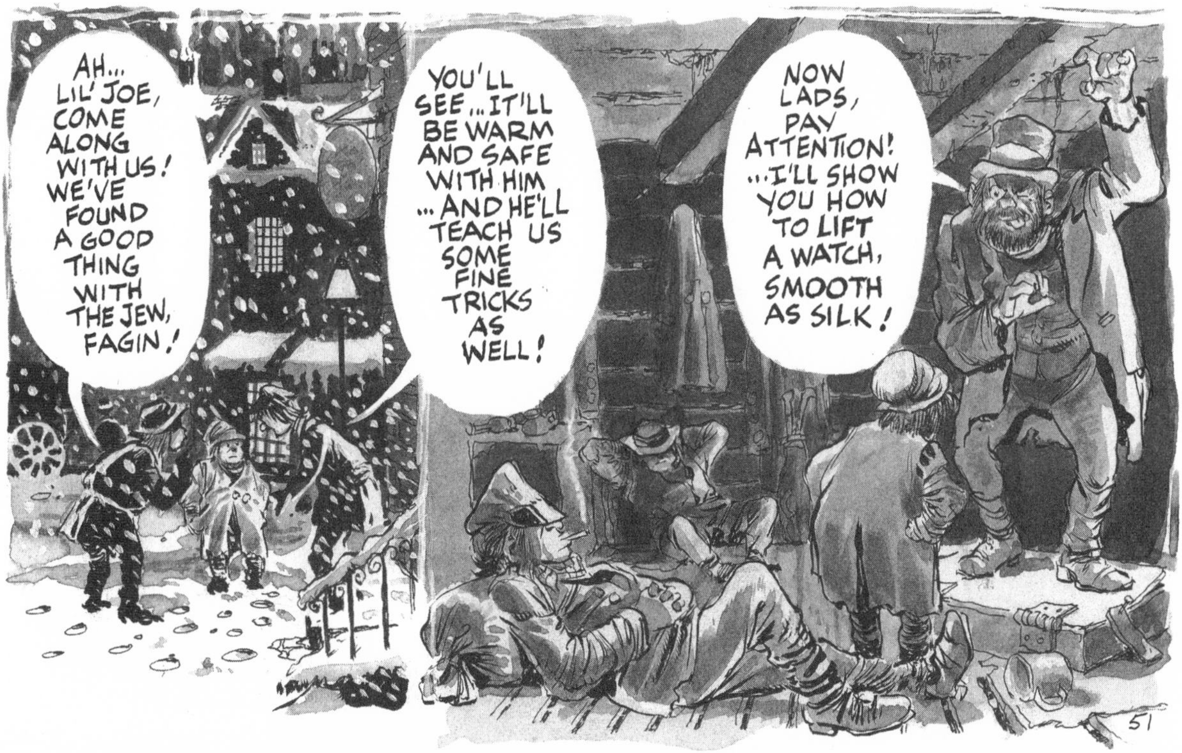
AH... LIL' JOE, COME ALONG WITH US! WE'VE FOUND A GOOD THING WITH THE JEW, FAGIN!
YOU'LL SEE... IT'LL BE WARM AND SAFE WITH HIM ... AND HE'LL TEACH US SOME FINE TRICKS AS WELL!
NOW LADS, PAY ATTENTION! ...I'LL SHOW YOU HOW TO LIFT A WATCH, SMOOTH AS SILK!

I bought and sold what I could from whatever my boys brought me. Ah, but they required a bit of discipline.

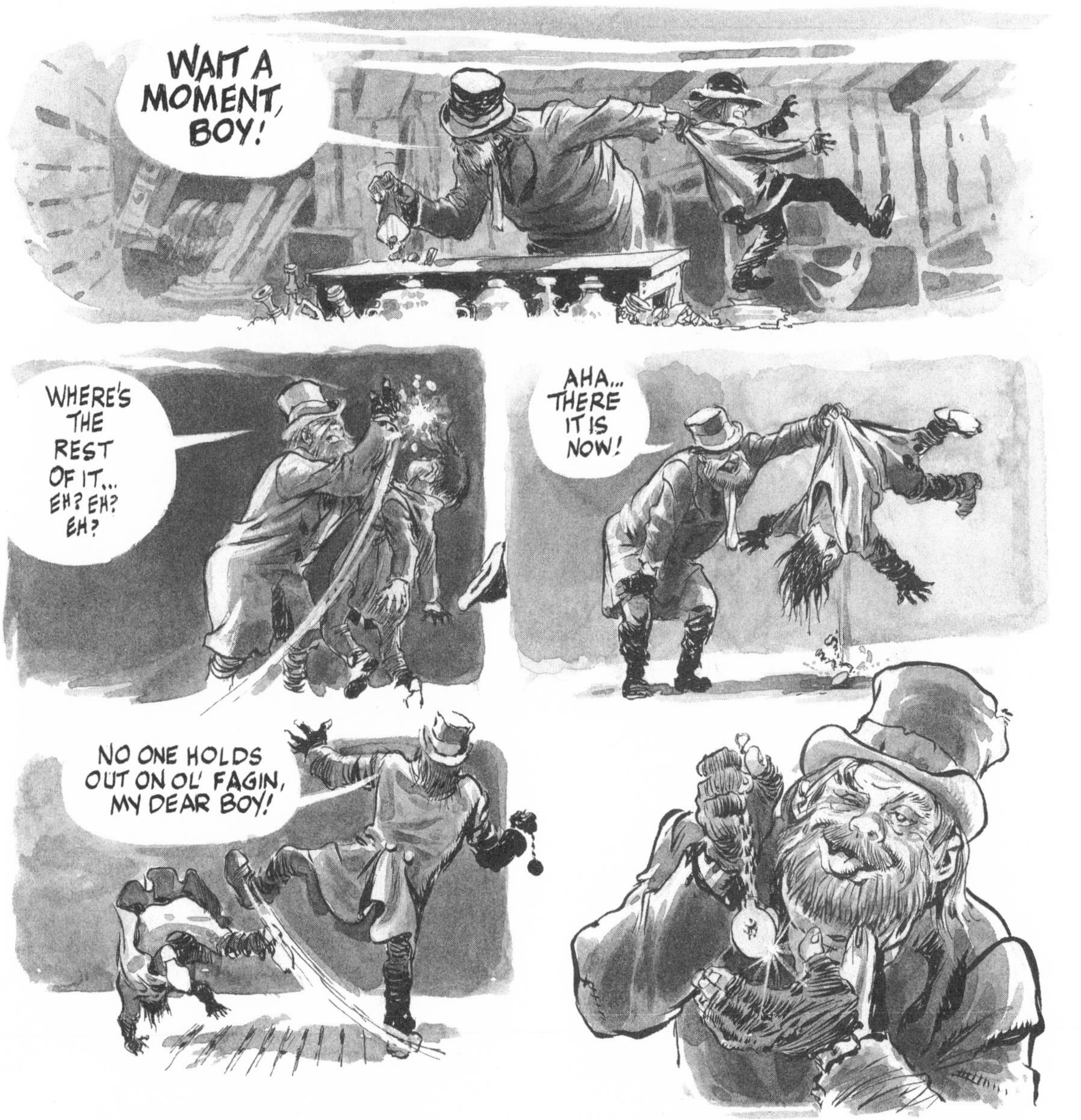
WAIT A MOMENT, BOY!
WHERE'S THE REST OF IT... EH? EH? EH?
AHA... THERE IT IS NOW!
NO ONE HOLDS OUT ON OL' FAGIN, MY DEAR BOY!

So the years went by. I never did prosper, nor was I able to advance beyond the grimy life on the streets of London. Still, I kept myself and my boys from the bitter refuge of workhouses.

It was in one of these houses of questionable charity that fate delivered a young companion for me in the last chapter of my life. He joined my "family" as usual, recruited by one of my steady boys. Years later, I learned of his origin from young Claypole, who was once employed with him at Sowerberry's. The rest came from hearsay and deduction. The boy was born out of grim circumstances not unusual for our society.

It was ten years ago. Late one evening a young woman appeared at the doorstep of one of these poorly maintained workhouses.

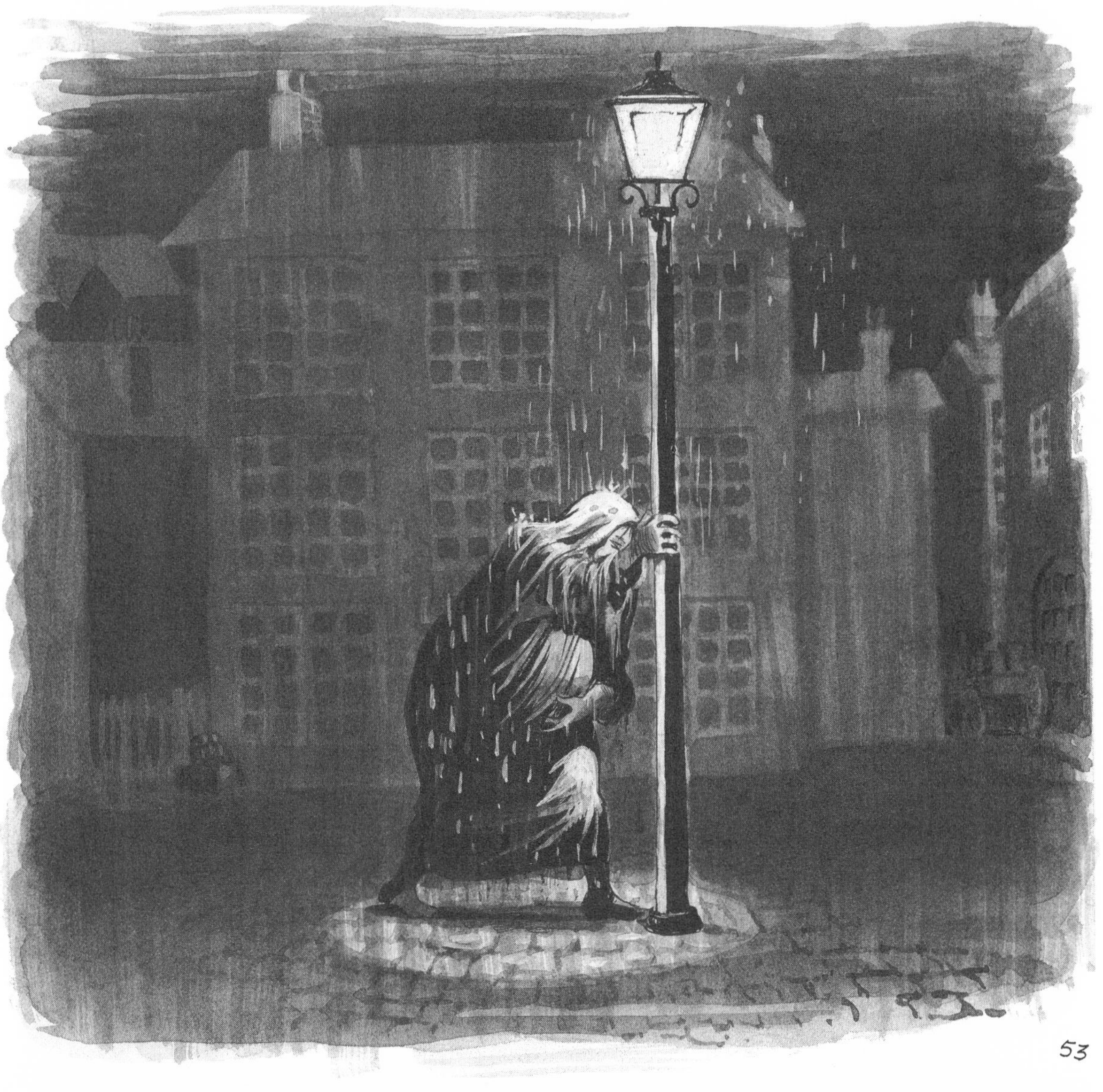

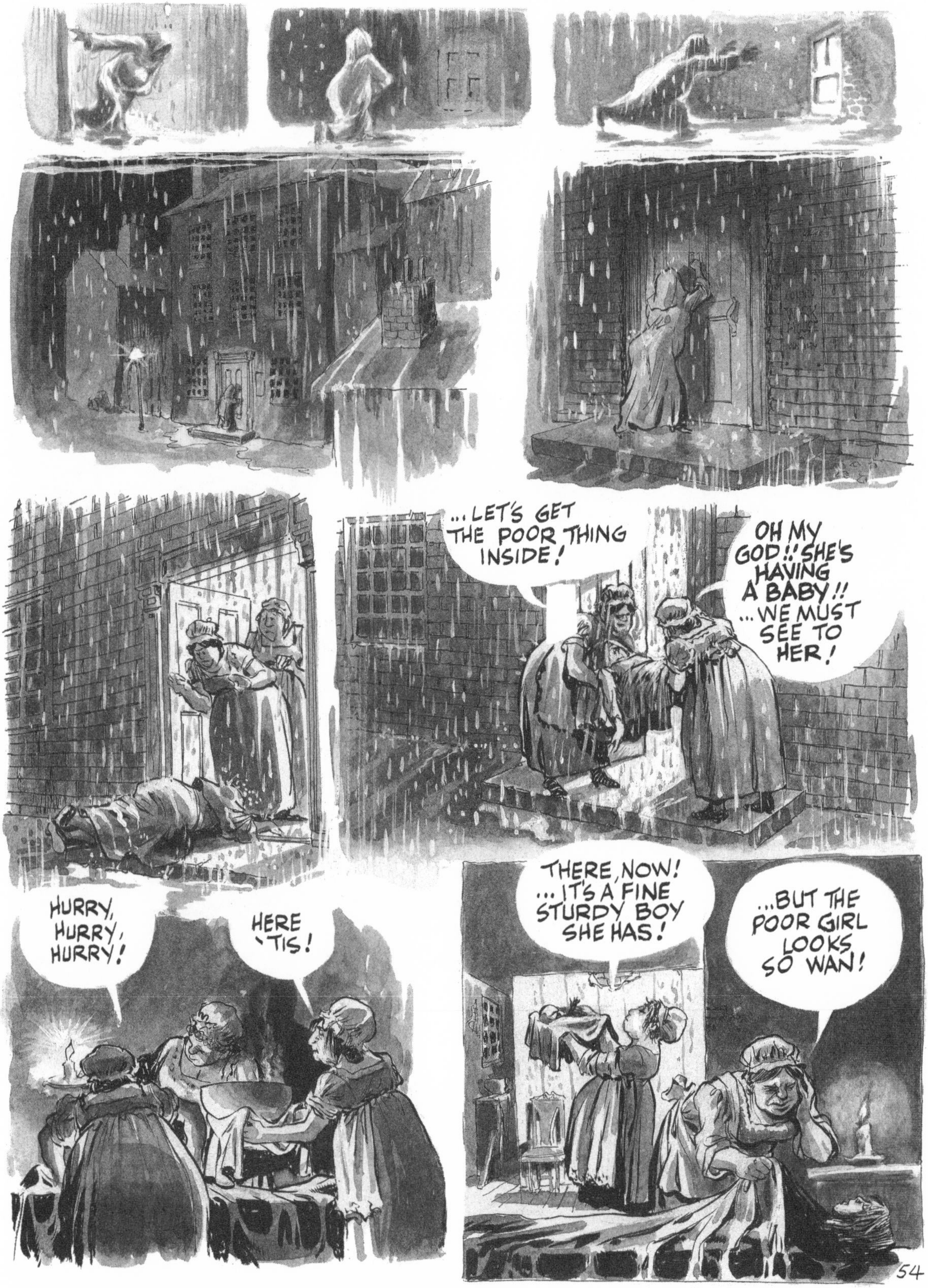
...LET'S GET THE POOR THING INSIDE!
OH MY GOD!! SHE'S HAVING A BABY!! ...WE MUST SEE TO HER!
HURRY, HURRY, HURRY!
HERE 'TIS!
THERE, NOW! ...IT'S A FINE STURDY BOY SHE HAS!
...BUT THE POOR GIRL LOOKS SO WAN!

Growing up in a workhouse, as you may have heard, is not easy. In these places, largesse or charity is doled out with a cruel economy by the people who operate them, for they seek to profit from the money they receive out of its management. Oh, I know well enough what Oliver's life was like there, and what he had to endure.

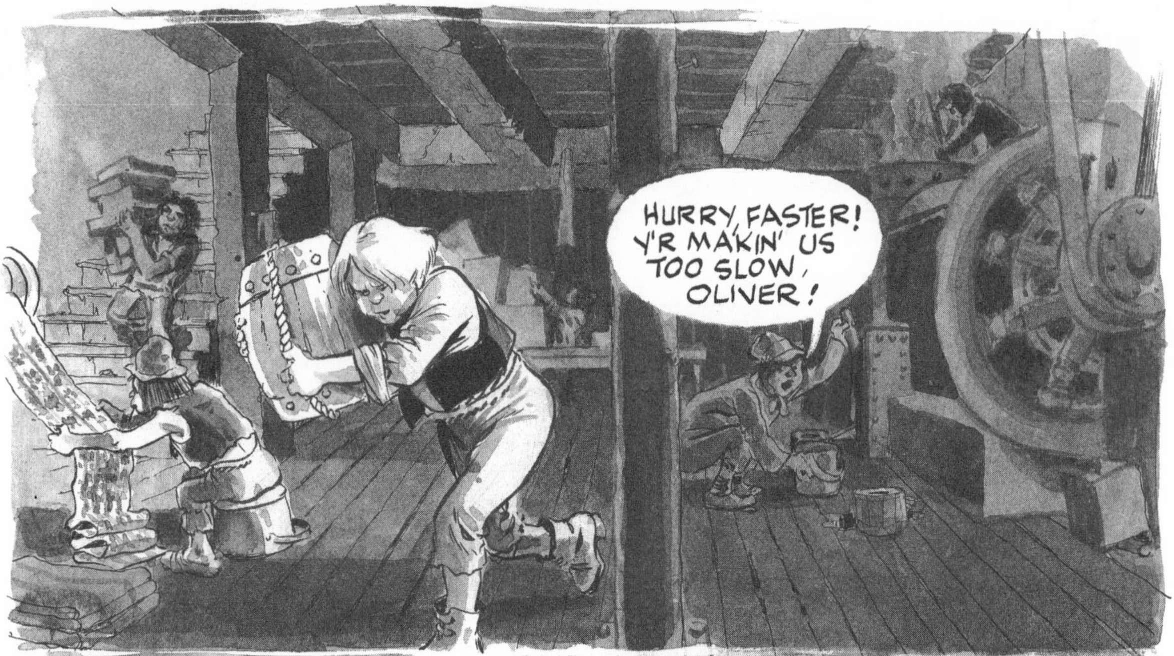
HURRY, FASTER! Y'R MAKIN' US TOO SLOW, OLIVER!

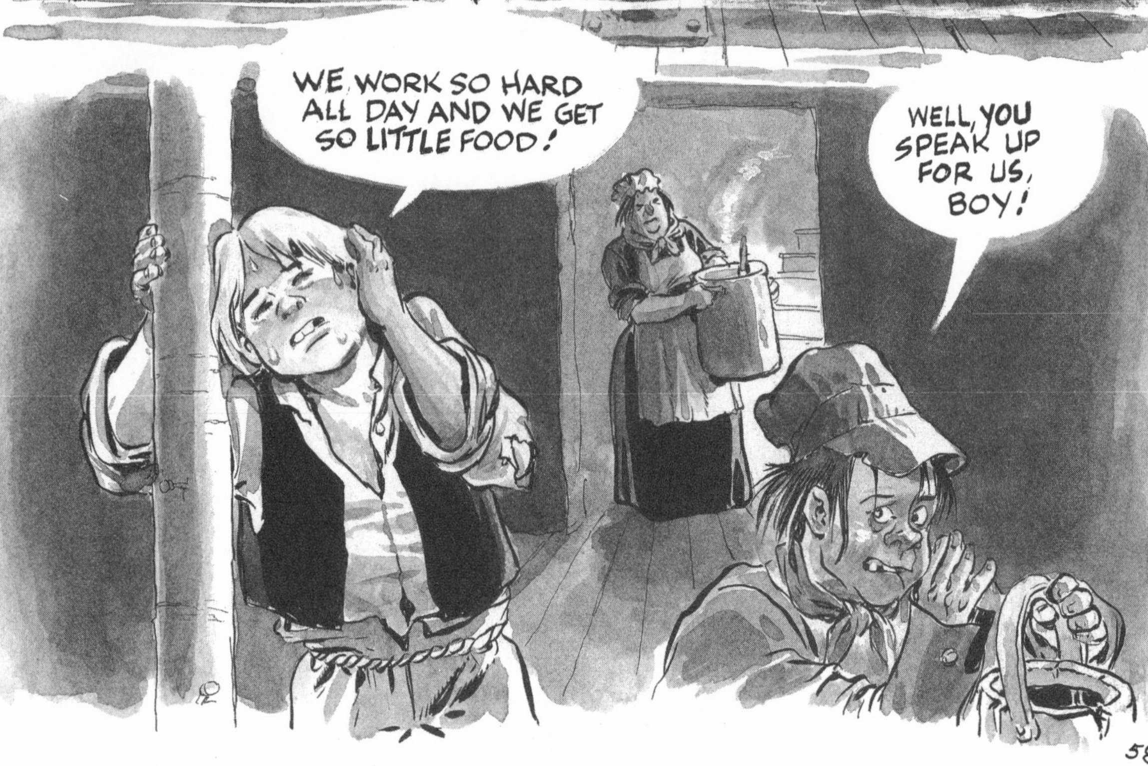
WE WORK SO HARD ALL DAY AND WE GET SO LITTLE FOOD!
WELL, YOU SPEAK UP FOR US, BOY!

60

The next day the trustees met again. It was their duty as custodians of this charitable institution to sit in judgment on all matters of discipline.

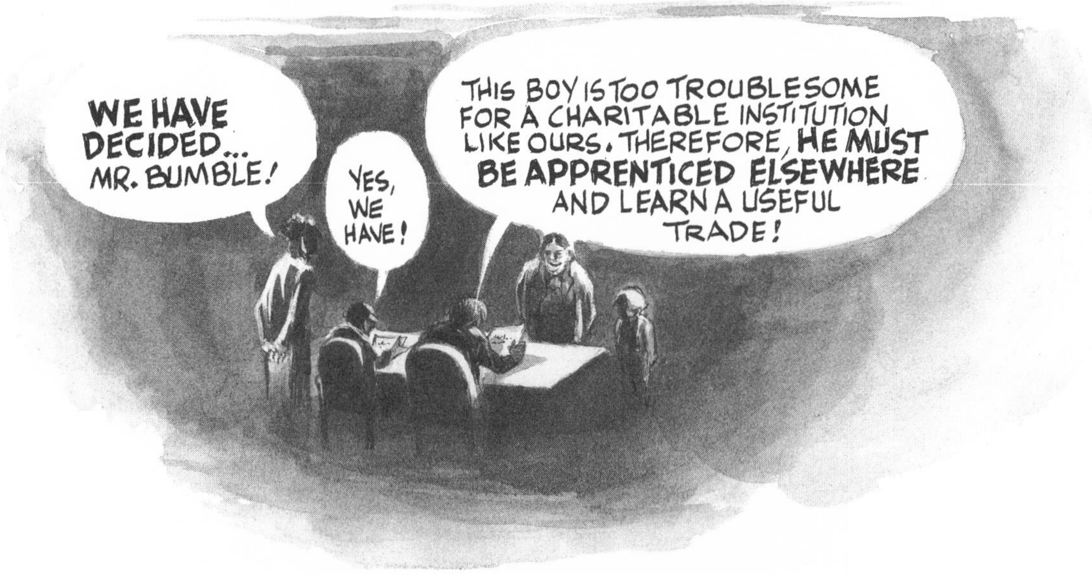

WE HAVE DECIDED... MR. BUMBLE!
YES, WE HAVE!
THIS BOY IS TOO TROUBLESOME FOR A CHARITABLE INSTITUTION LIKE OURS. THEREFORE, HE MUST BE APPRENTICED ELSEWHERE AND LEARN A USEFUL TRADE!

So Mr. Bumble undertook this task of finding a suitable apprenticeship for Oliver.

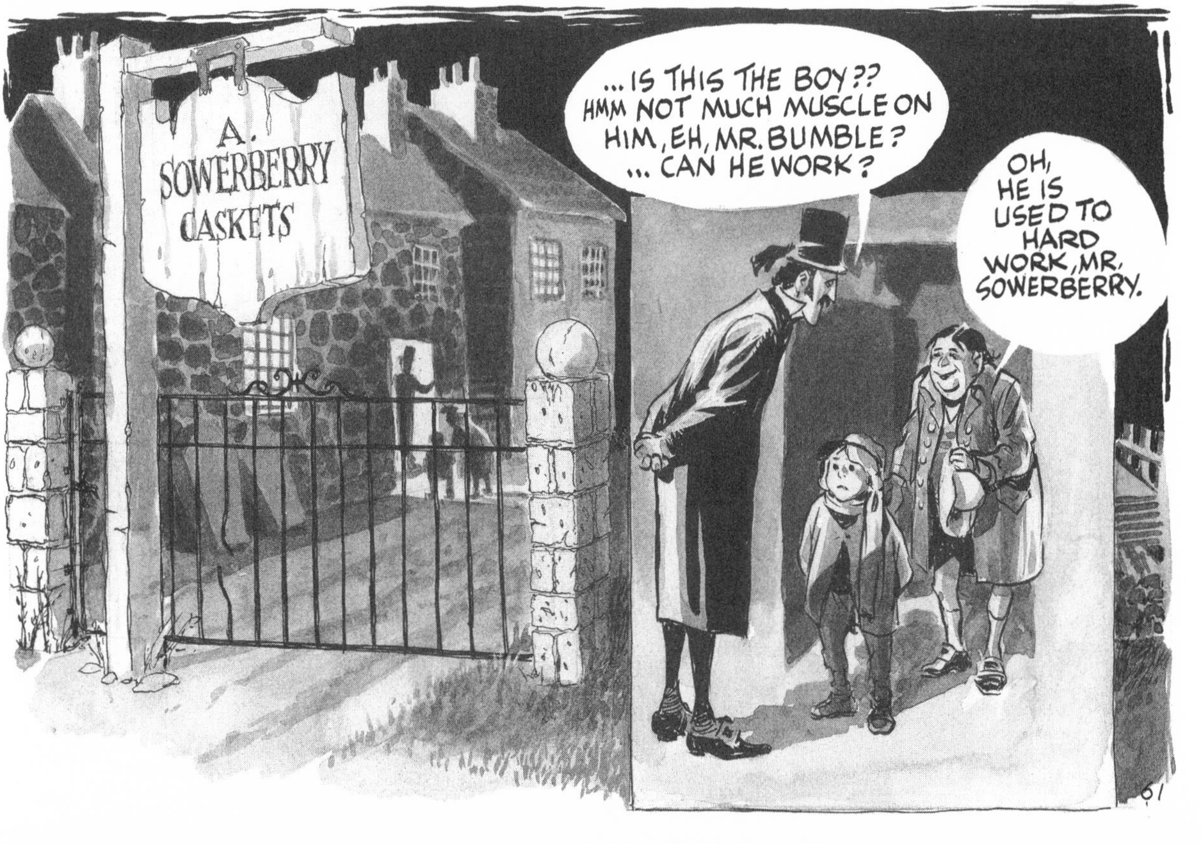

A. SOWERBERRY CASKETS
...IS THIS THE BOY?? HMM NOT MUCH MUSCLE ON HIM, EH, MR. BUMBLE? ... CAN HE WORK?
OH, HE IS USED TO HARD WORK, MR. SOWERBERRY.

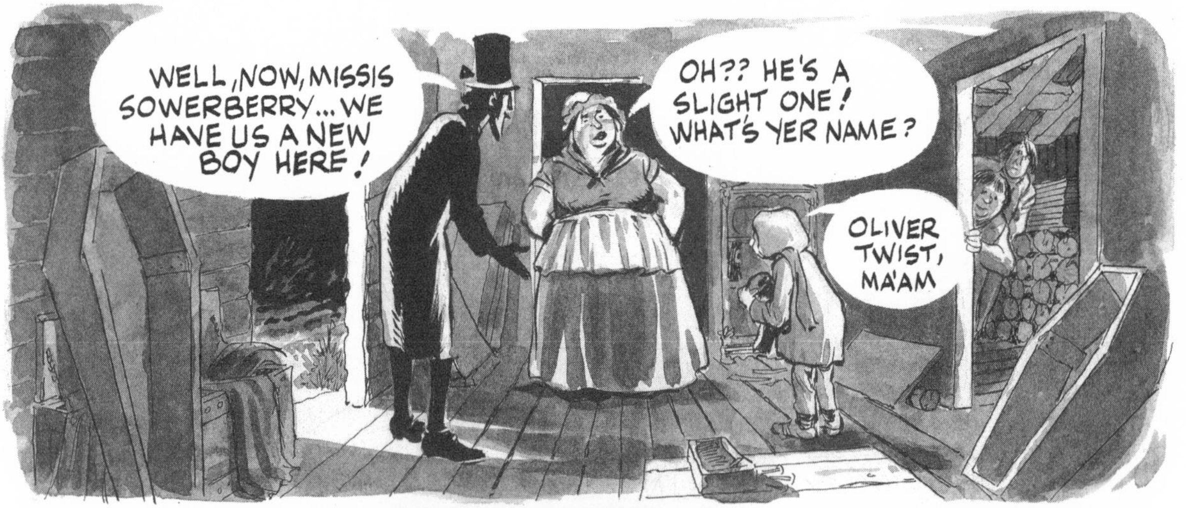
WELL, NOW, MISSIS SOWERBERRY... WE HAVE US A NEW BOY HERE!
OH?? HE'S A SLIGHT ONE! WHAT'S YER NAME?
OLIVER TWIST, MA'AM

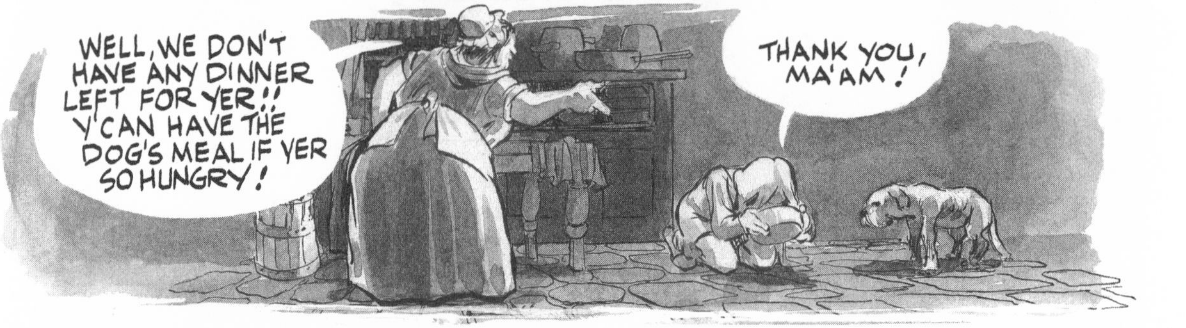
WELL, WE DON'T HAVE ANY DINNER LEFT FOR YER!! Y'CAN HAVE THE DOG'S MEAL IF YER SO HUNGRY!
THANK YOU, MA'AM!

As my boys who have also experienced employment in similar circumstances tell me, finding a place here is always a challenge.

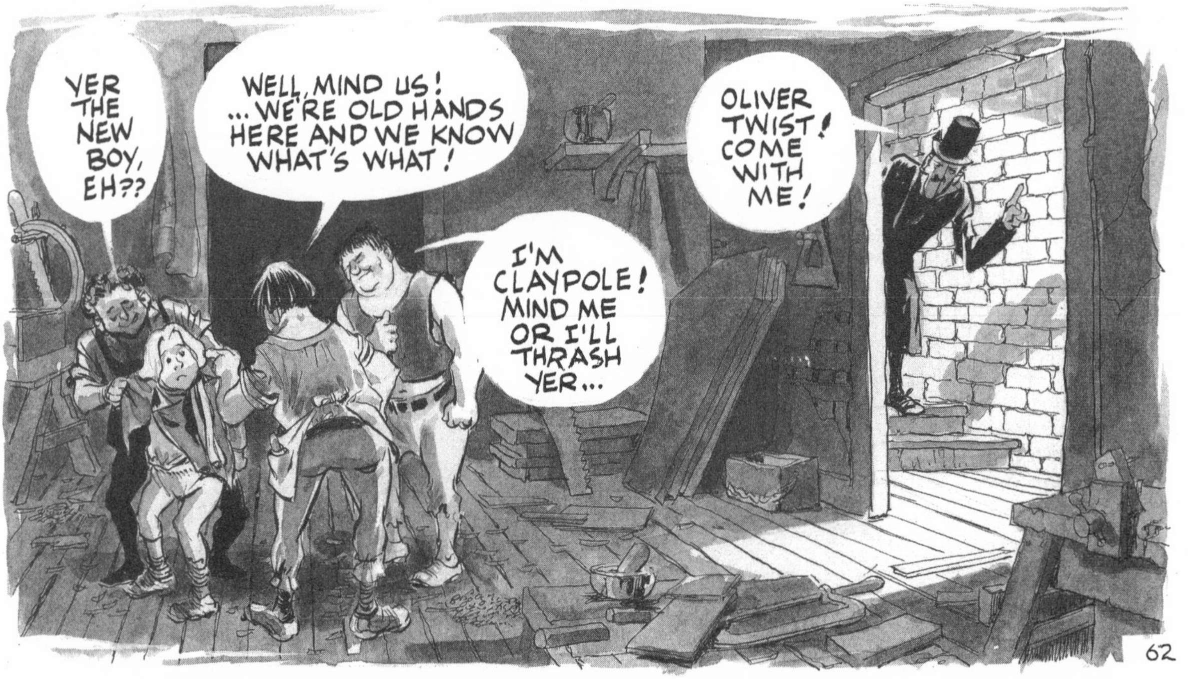
YER THE NEW BOY, EH??
WELL, MIND US! ...WE'RE OLD HANDS HERE AND WE KNOW WHAT'S WHAT!
I'M CLAYPOLE! MIND ME OR I'LL THRASH YER...
OLIVER TWIST! COME WITH ME!

A rise in position in such a place is a splendid opportunity, as I can tell you.

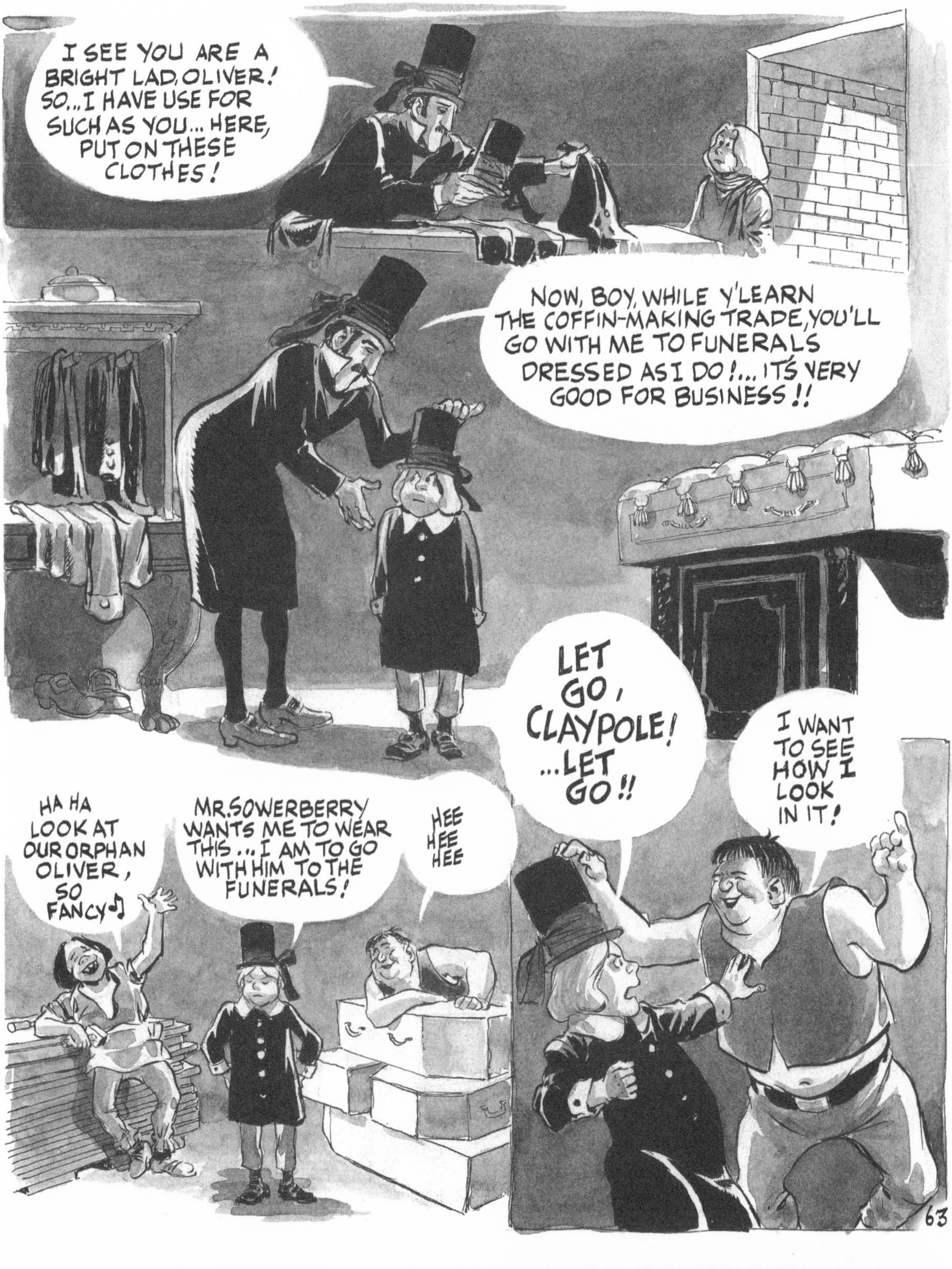

I SEE YOU ARE A BRIGHT LAD, OLIVER! SO...I HAVE USE FOR SUCH AS YOU... HERE, PUT ON THESE CLOTHES!
NOW, BOY, WHILE Y'LEARN THE COFFIN-MAKING TRADE, YOU'LL GO WITH ME TO FUNERALS DRESSED AS I DO!... IT'S VERY GOOD FOR BUSINESS!!
HA HA LOOK AT OUR ORPHAN OLIVER, SO FANCY♪
MR. SOWERBERRY WANTS ME TO WEAR THIS... I AM TO GO WITH HIM TO THE FUNERALS!
HEE HEE HEE
LET GO, CLAYPOLE! ...LET GO!!
I WANT TO SEE HOW I LOOK IN IT!

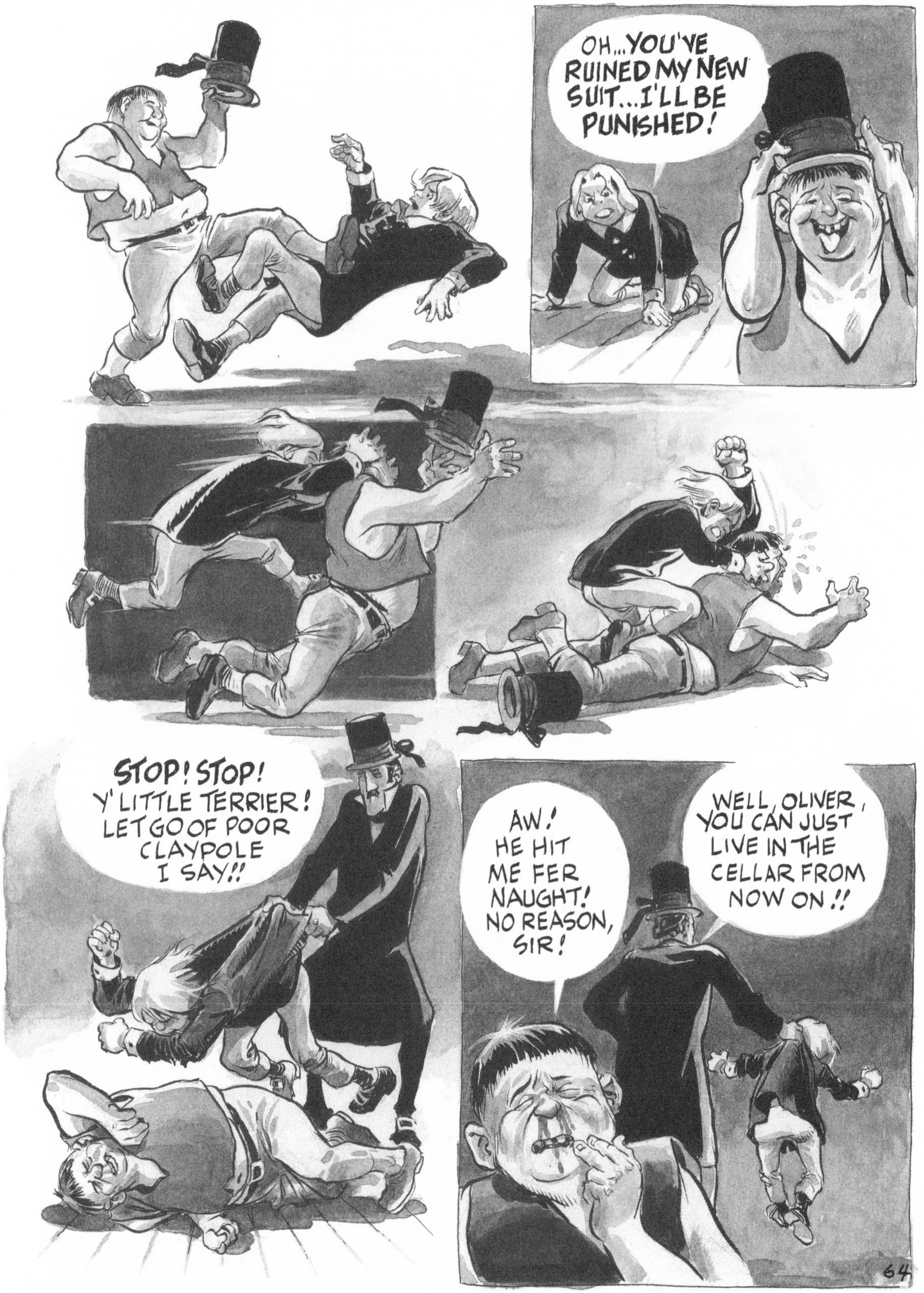
OH...YOU'VE RUINED MY NEW SUIT...I'LL BE PUNISHED!
STOP! STOP! Y' LITTLE TERRIER! LET GO OF POOR CLAYPOLE I SAY!!
AW! HE HIT ME FER NAUGHT! NO REASON, SIR!
WELL, OLIVER, YOU CAN JUST LIVE IN THE CELLAR FROM NOW ON!!

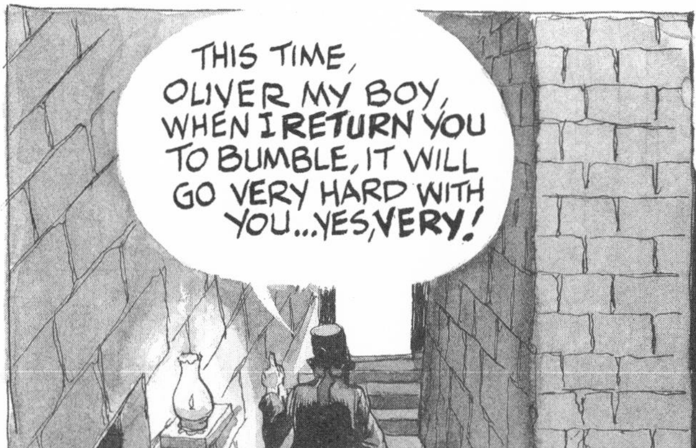
THIS TIME, OLIVER MY BOY, WHEN I RETURN YOU TO BUMBLE, IT WILL GO VERY HARD WITH YOU...YES, VERY!

That night Oliver decided he must escape at last.

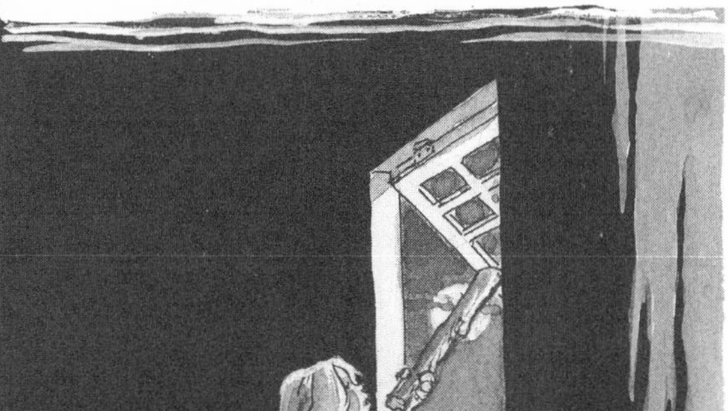

And he walked to the center of London, for want of a better place to go.

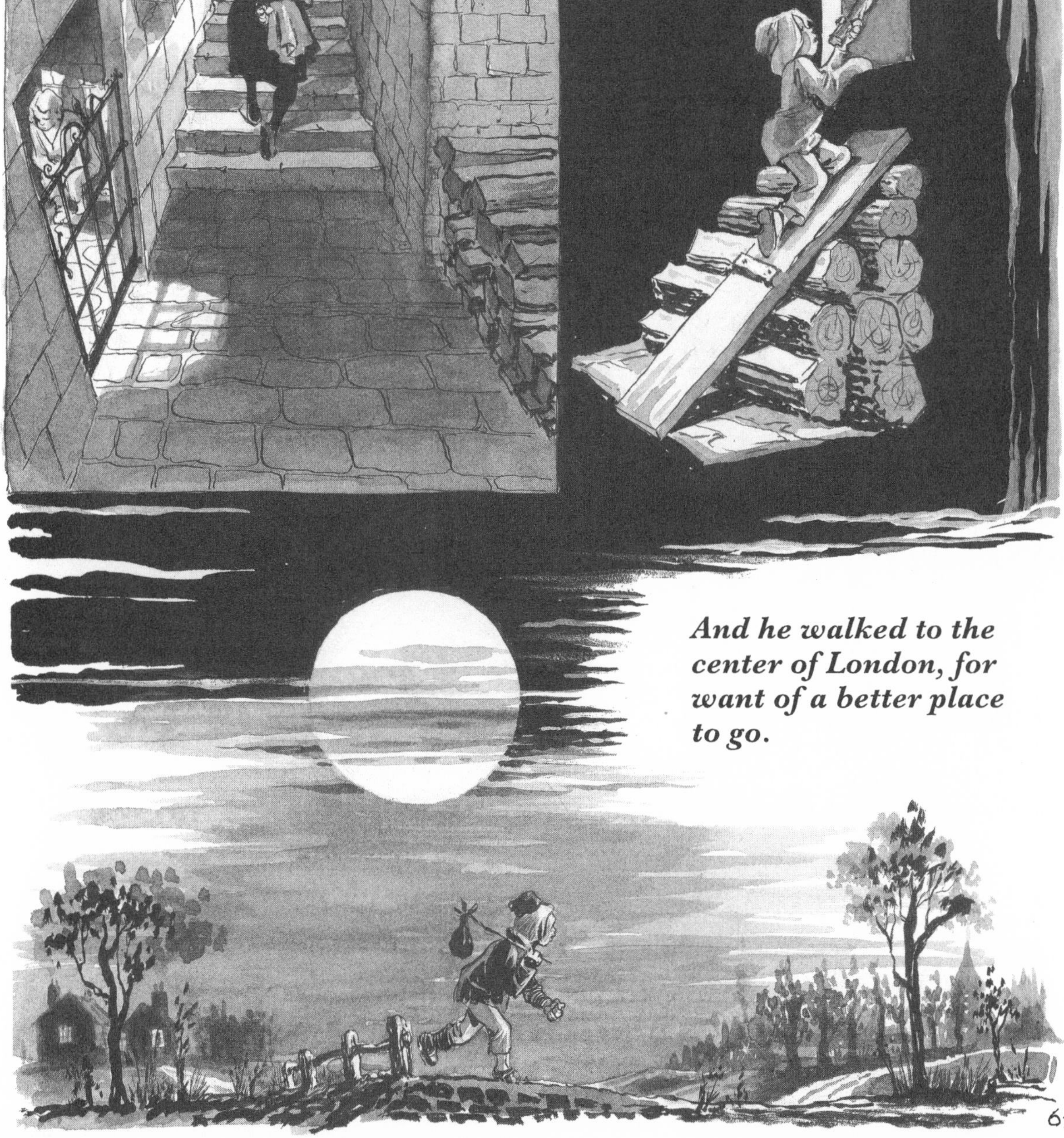

So began my relationship with a child of destiny, as they say...and with it the circumstances that defined my own encounter with fate. My affairs were taking a troubling turn and I had a meeting with my best boy, Jack Dawkins.

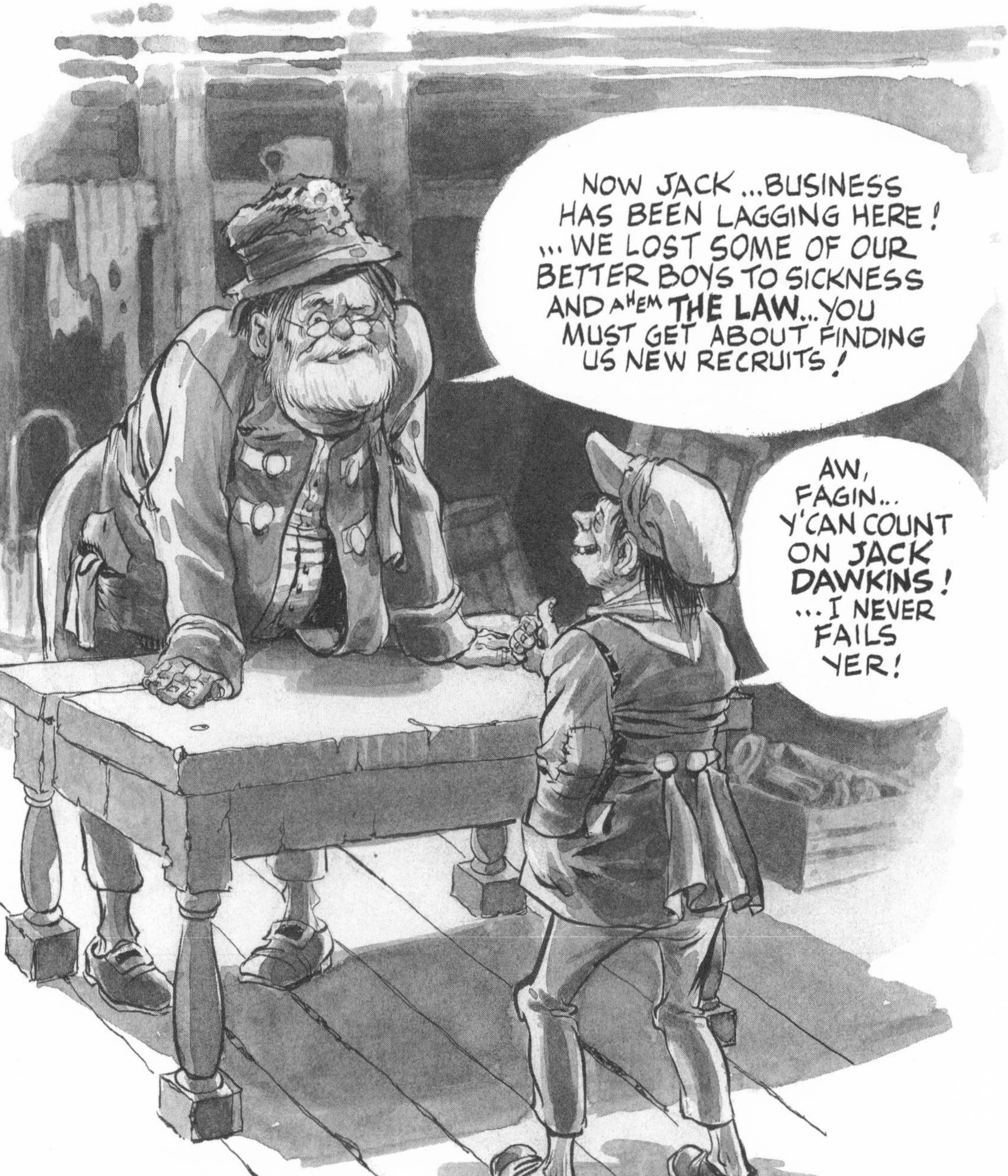
NOW JACK ...BUSINESS HAS BEEN LAGGING HERE! ...WE LOST SOME OF OUR BETTER BOYS TO SICKNESS AND AHEM THE LAW...YOU MUST GET ABOUT FINDING US NEW RECRUITS!
AW, FAGIN... Y'CAN COUNT ON JACK DAWKINS! ...I NEVER FAILS YER!

And as fate would have it, that was the very day young Oliver arrived in London.

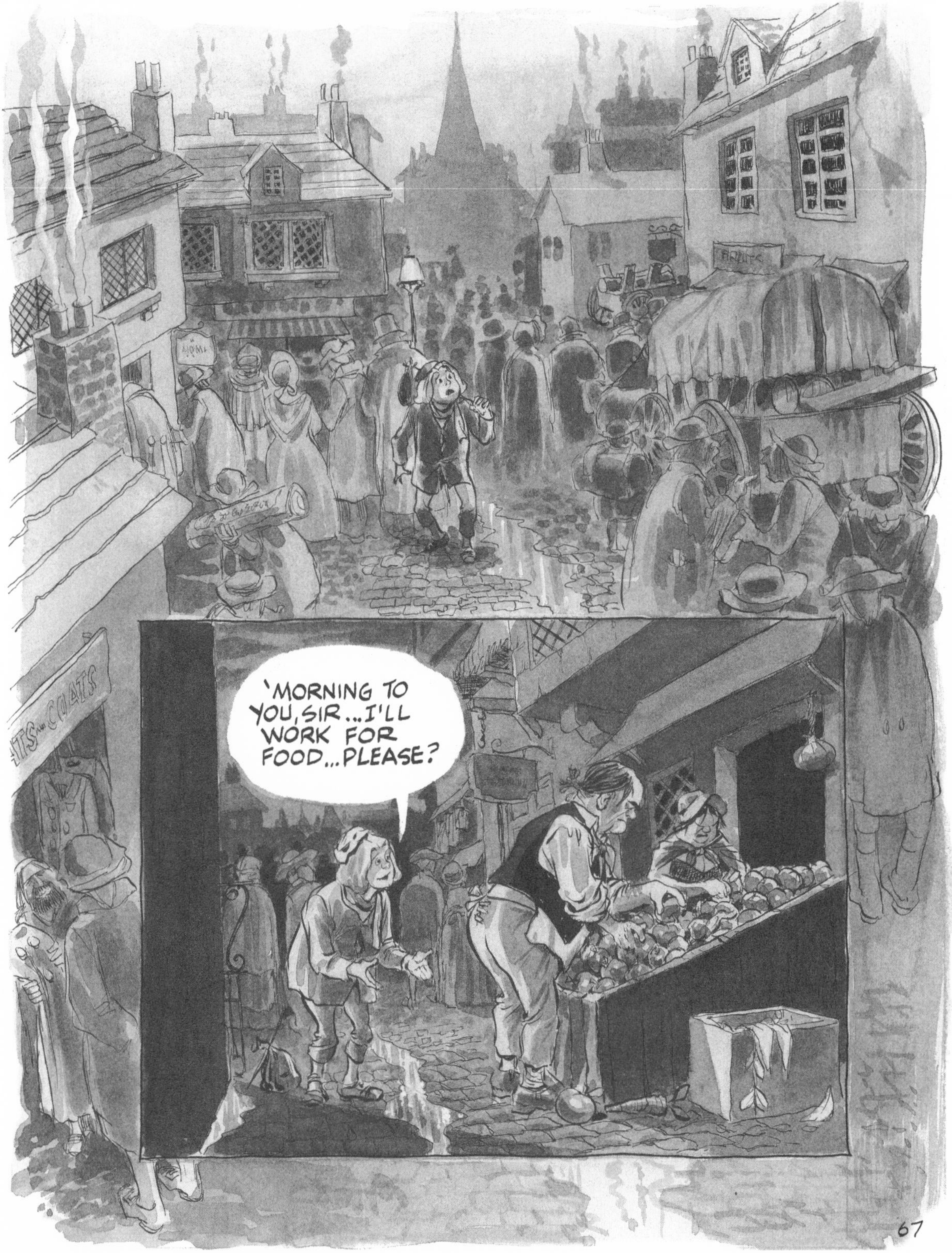
'MORNING TO YOU, SIR...I'LL WORK FOR FOOD...PLEASE?

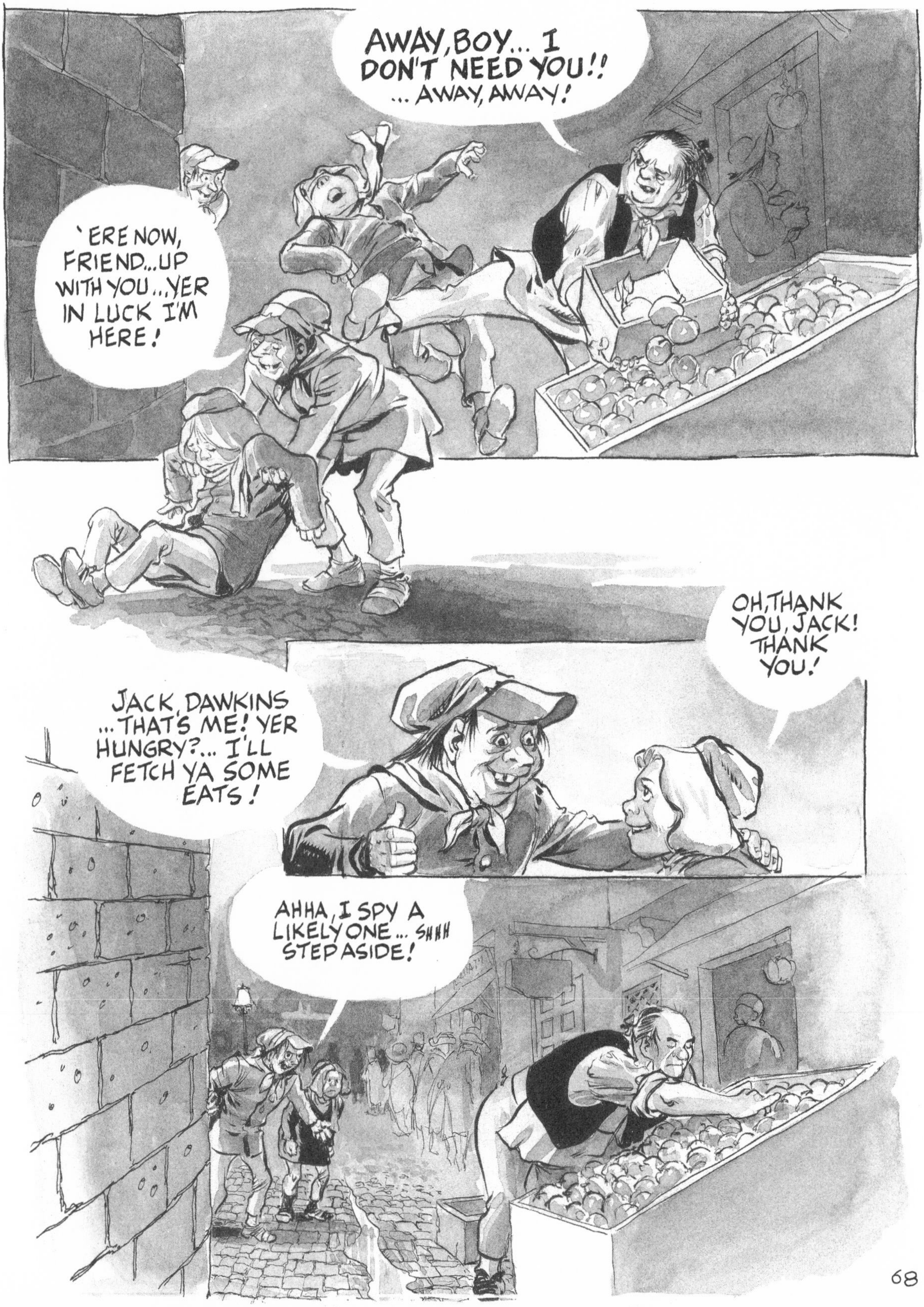
AWAY, BOY... I DON'T NEED YOU!! ...AWAY, AWAY!
`ERE NOW, FRIEND...UP WITH YOU...YER IN LUCK I'M HERE!
JACK, DAWKINS ...THAT'S ME! YER HUNGRY?... I'LL FETCH YA SOME EATS!
OH, THANK YOU, JACK! THANK YOU!
AHHA, I SPY A LIKELY ONE... SHHH STEP ASIDE!

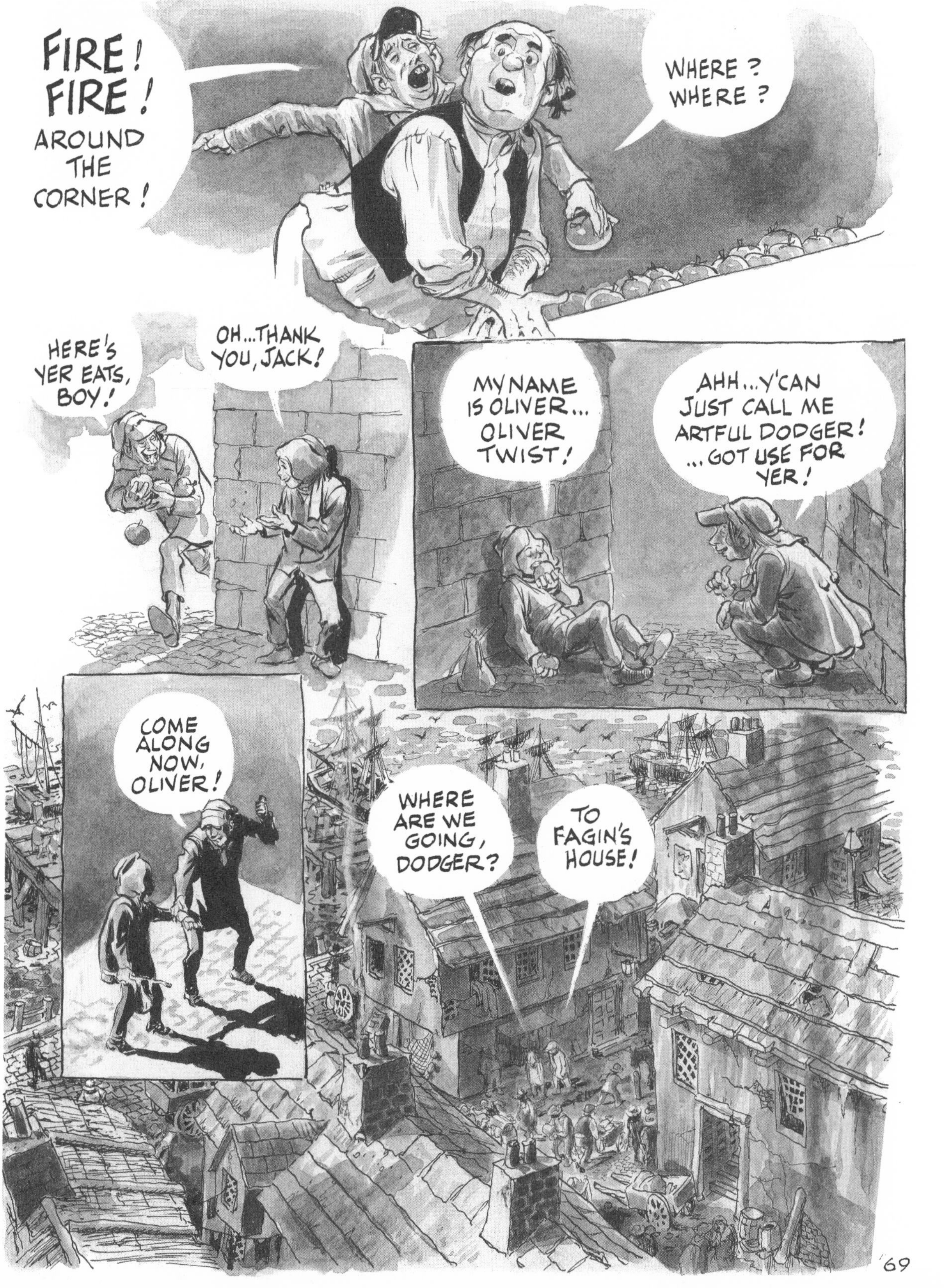
FIRE! FIRE! AROUND THE CORNER!
WHERE? WHERE?
HERE'S YER EATS, BOY!
OH...THANK YOU, JACK!
MY NAME IS OLIVER... OLIVER TWIST!
AHH...Y'CAN JUST CALL ME ARTFUL DODGER! ...GOT USE FOR YER!
COME ALONG NOW, OLIVER!
WHERE ARE WE GOING, DODGER?
TO FAGIN'S HOUSE!

Ah, well do I remember him ... clearly a lad of quality ... rare indeed in those days, I can assure you.

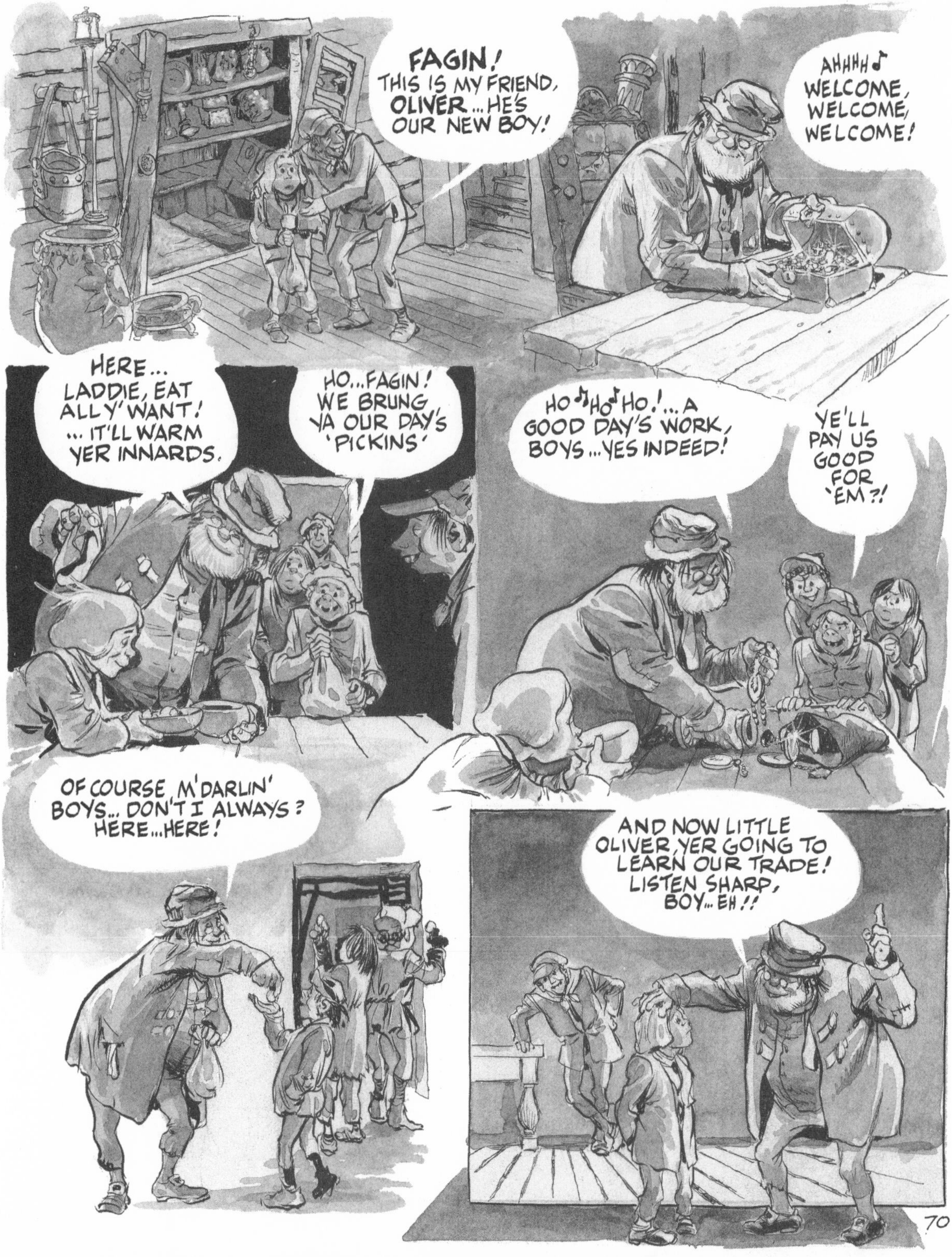
FAGIN! THIS IS MY FRIEND, OLIVER ... HE'S OUR NEW BOY!
AHHHH ♪ WELCOME, WELCOME, WELCOME!
HERE... LADDIE, EAT ALL Y' WANT! ... IT'LL WARM YER INNARDS.
HO... FAGIN! WE BRUNG YA OUR DAY'S 'PICKINS'
HO ♪ HO ♪ HO! ... A GOOD DAY'S WORK, BOYS ... YES INDEED!
YE'LL PAY US GOOD FOR 'EM?!
OF COURSE M'DARLIN' BOYS... DON'T I ALWAYS? HERE...HERE!
AND NOW LITTLE OLIVER, YER GOING TO LEARN OUR TRADE! LISTEN SHARP, BOY... EH!!

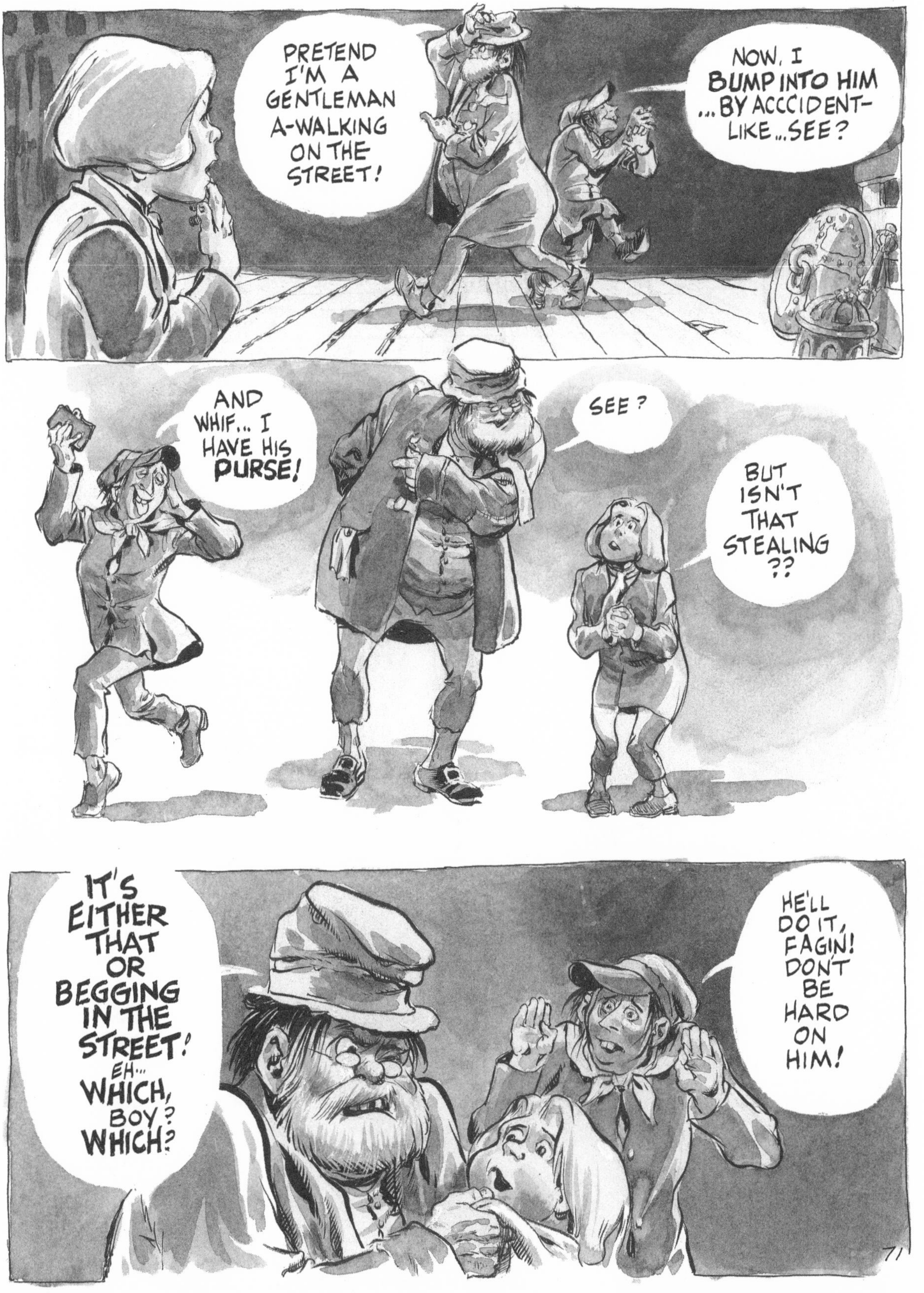
PRETEND I'M A GENTLEMAN A-WALKING ON THE STREET!
NOW, I BUMP INTO HIM ...BY ACCCIDENT-LIKE...SEE?
AND WHIF... I HAVE HIS PURSE!
SEE?
BUT ISN'T THAT STEALING ??
IT'S EITHER THAT OR BEGGING IN THE STREET! EH... WHICH, BOY? WHICH?
HE'LL DO IT, FAGIN! DON'T BE HARD ON HIM!

Well, Oliver was recruited ... oh yes! In just a week he was working the street with the Artful Dodger.

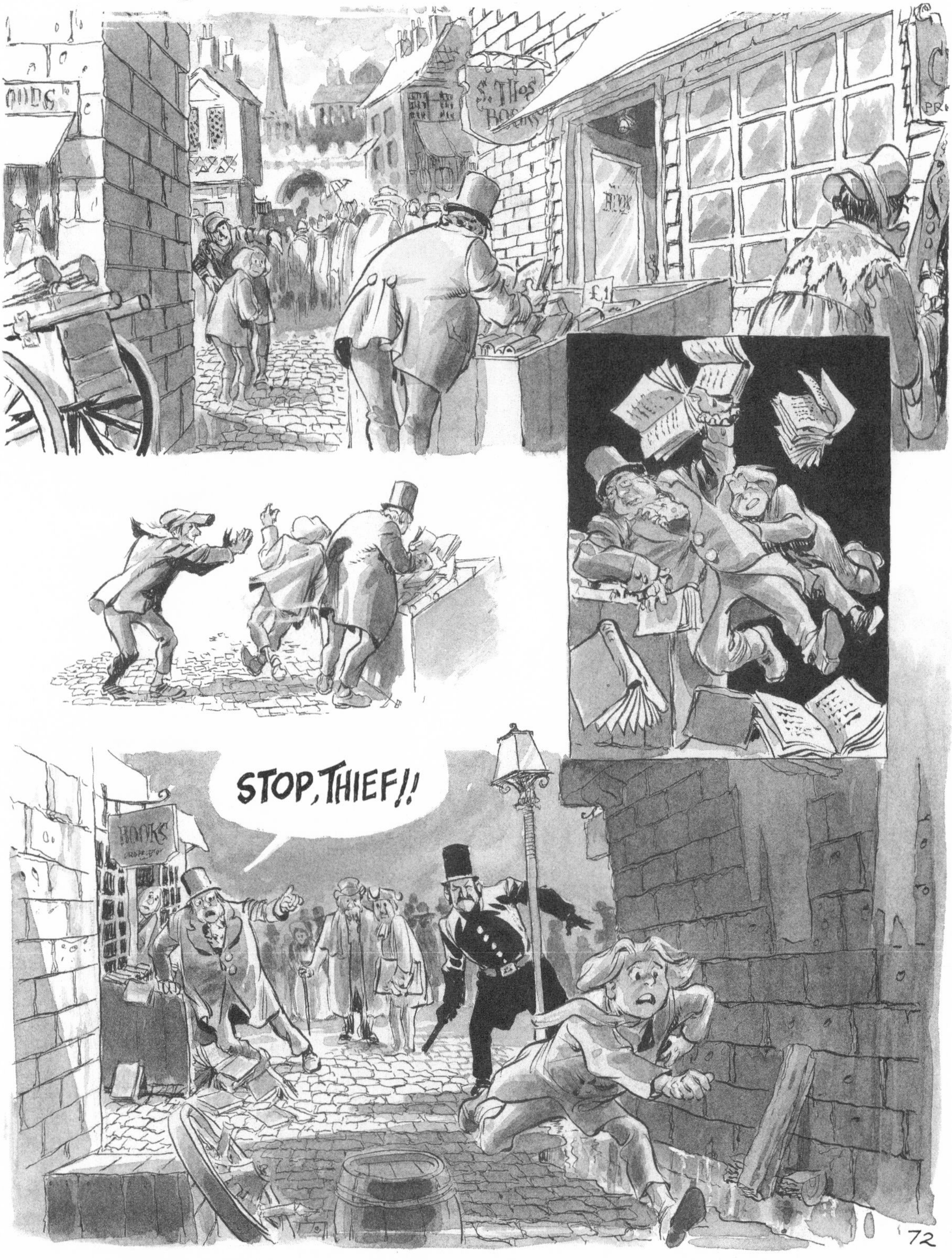
STOP, THIEF!!
BOOKS

74

Oliver was out of our hands. I knew not where until later, when I found out he was at the Brownlows, quite safe. Then my partner, Sikes, returned. He was always in fear of betrayal.

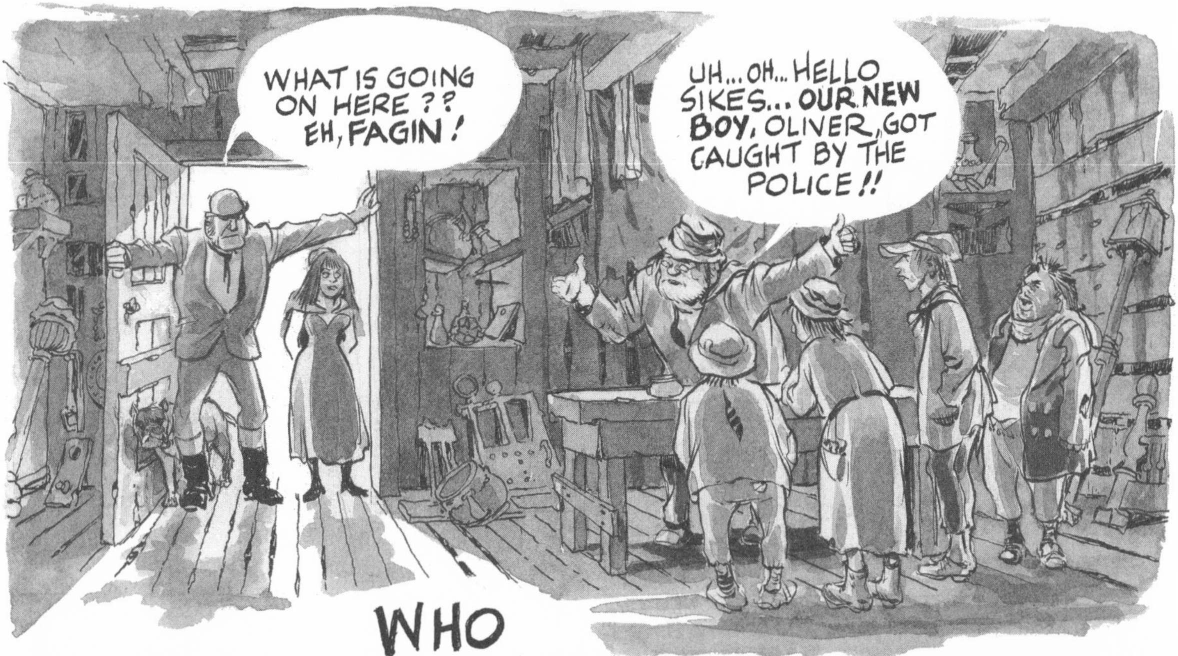
WHAT IS GOING ON HERE ?? EH, FAGIN !
UH... OH... HELLO SIKES... OUR NEW BOY, OLIVER, GOT CAUGHT BY THE POLICE !!

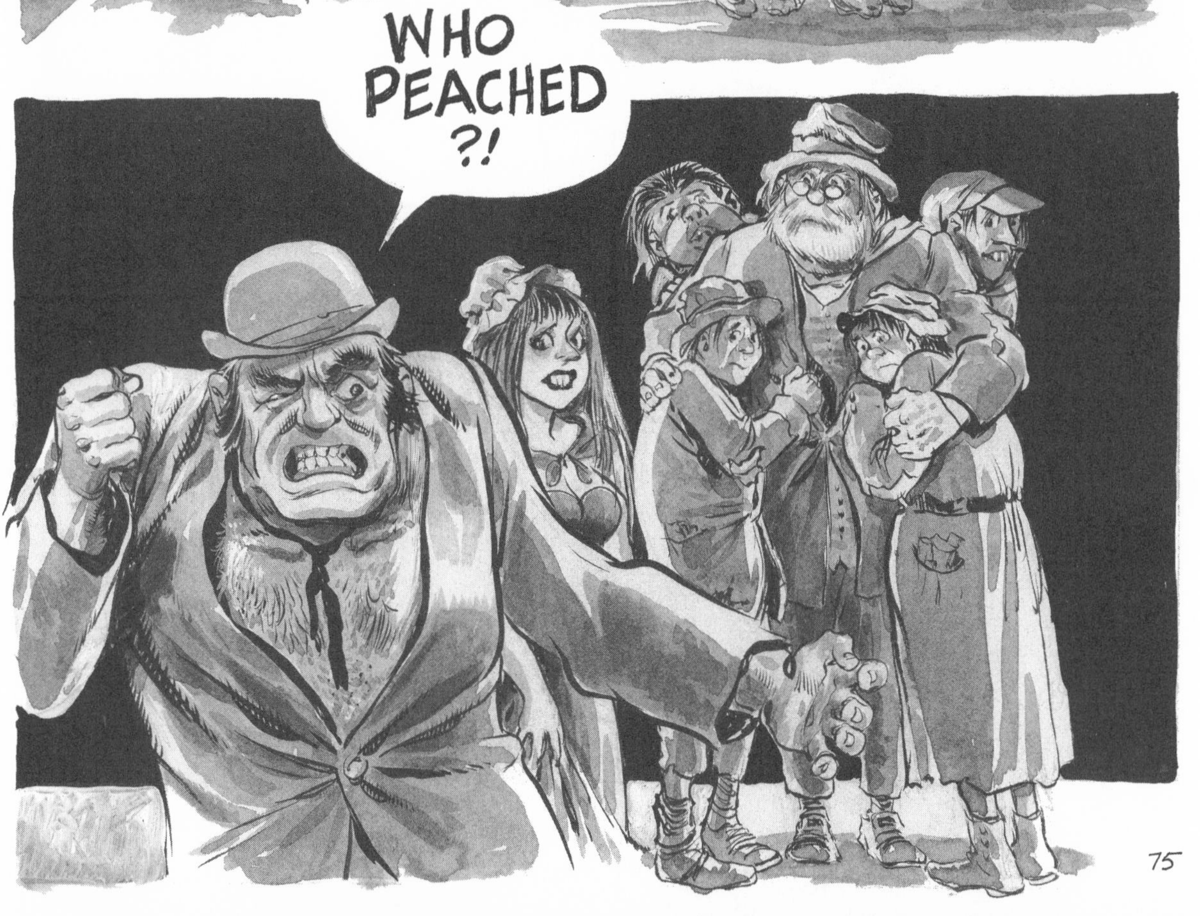
WHO PEACHED ?!

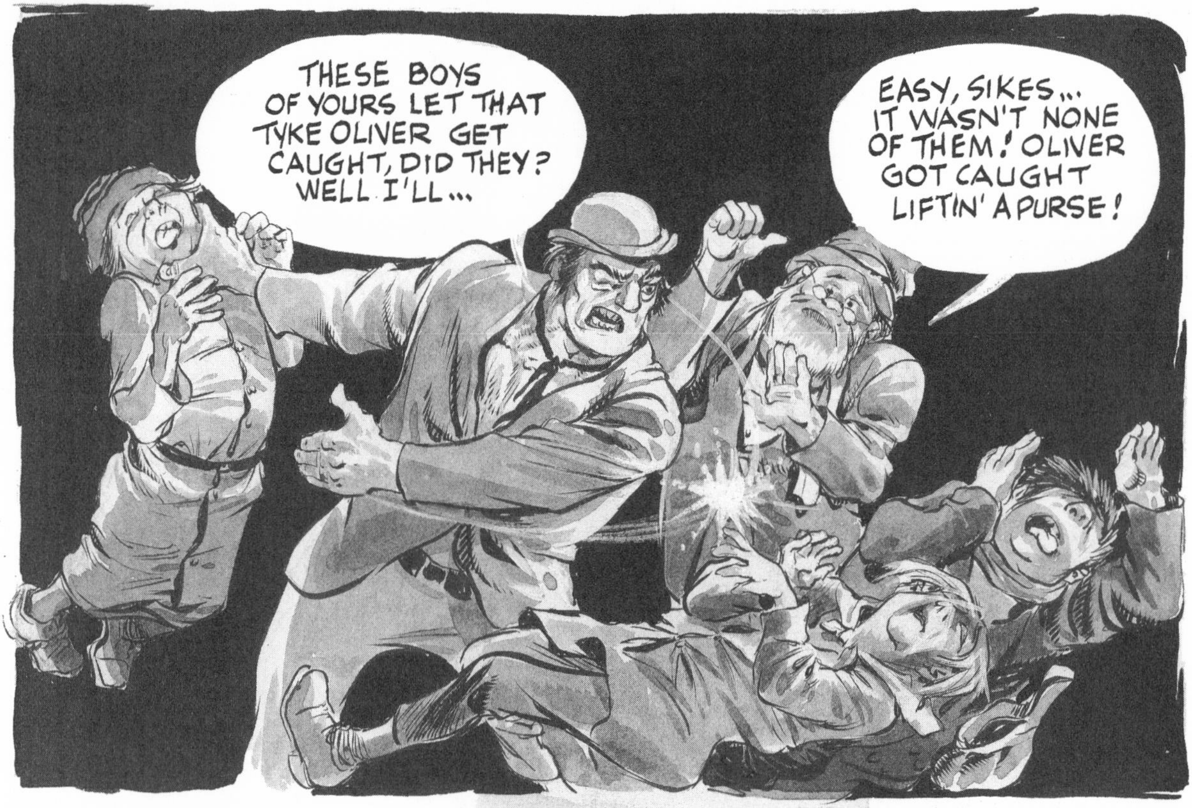
THESE BOYS OF YOURS LET THAT TYKE OLIVER GET CAUGHT, DID THEY? WELL I'LL...
EASY, SIKES... IT WASN'T NONE OF THEM! OLIVER GOT CAUGHT LIFTIN' A PURSE!

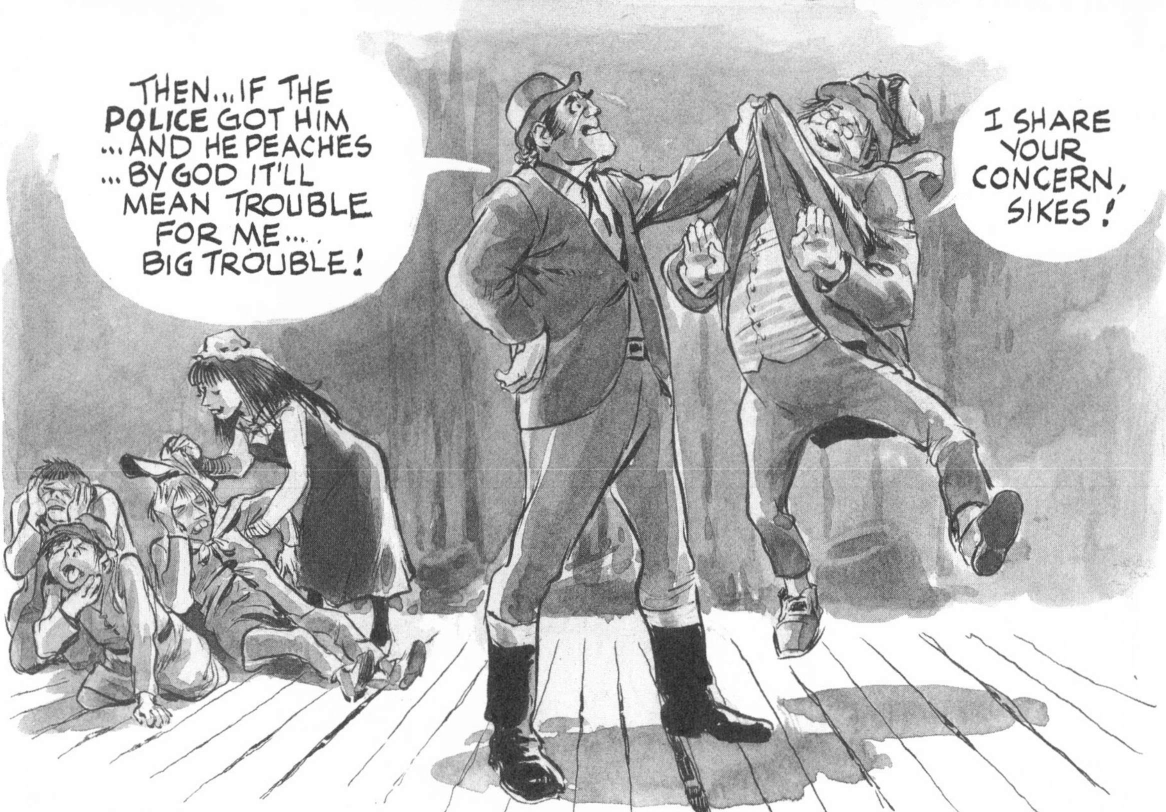
THEN... IF THE POLICE GOT HIM ...AND HE PEACHES ...BY GOD IT'LL MEAN TROUBLE FOR ME.... BIG TROUBLE!
I SHARE YOUR CONCERN, SIKES!

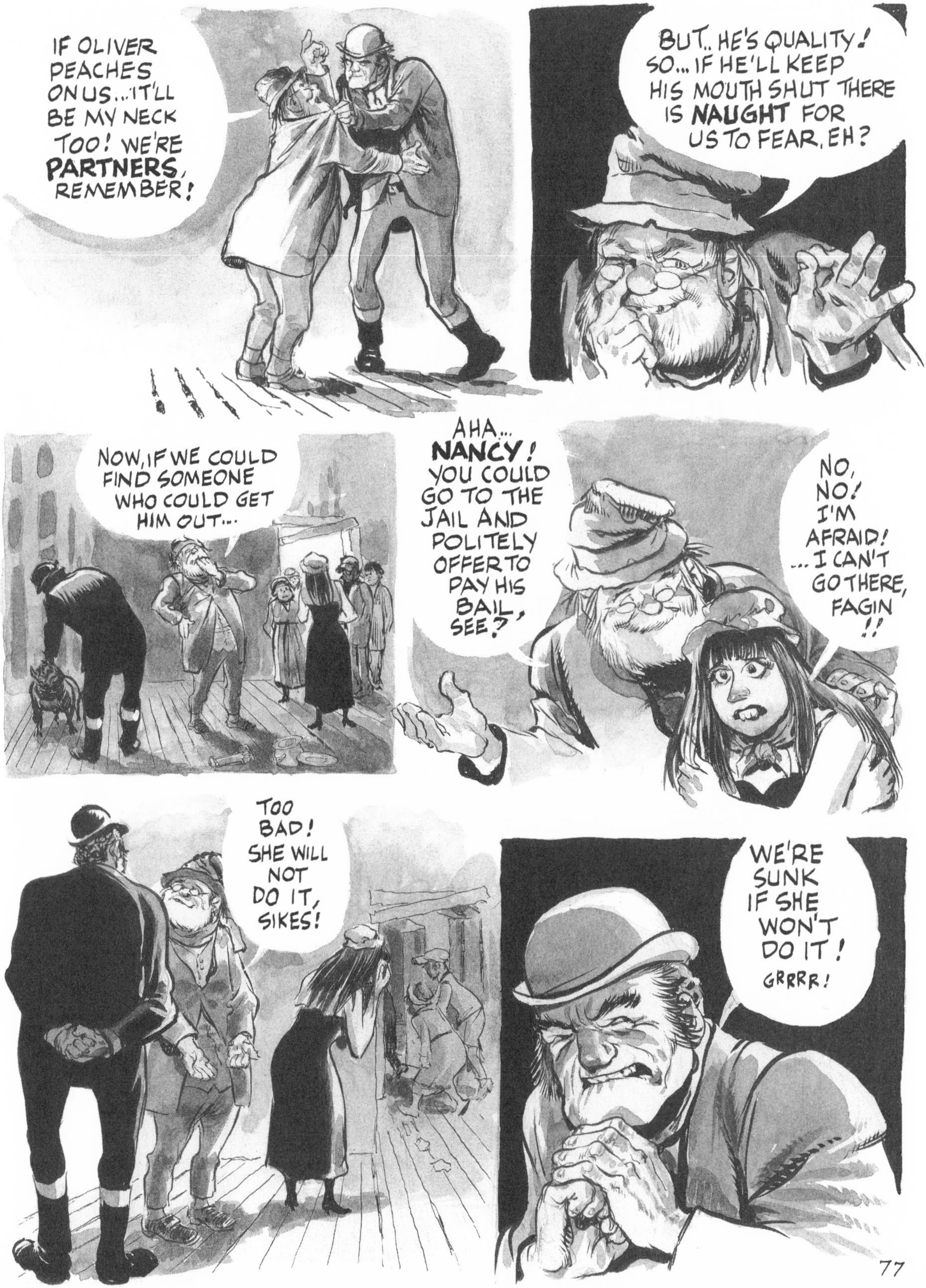
IF OLIVER PEACHES ON US...IT'LL BE MY NECK TOO! WE'RE **PARTNERS**, REMEMBER!
BUT.. HE'S QUALITY! SO... IF HE'LL KEEP HIS MOUTH SHUT THERE IS **NAUGHT** FOR US TO FEAR, EH?
NOW, IF WE COULD FIND SOMEONE WHO COULD GET HIM OUT...
AHA... **NANCY**! YOU COULD GO TO THE JAIL AND POLITELY OFFER TO PAY HIS BAIL, SEE?
NO, NO! I'M AFRAID! ...I CAN'T GO THERE, FAGIN!!
TOO BAD! SHE WILL NOT DO IT, SIKES!
WE'RE SUNK IF SHE WON'T DO IT! GRRRR!

78

But Nancy had bad news for us.

At the Brownlows' home, Oliver soon recovered from his fainting in the magistrate's office.

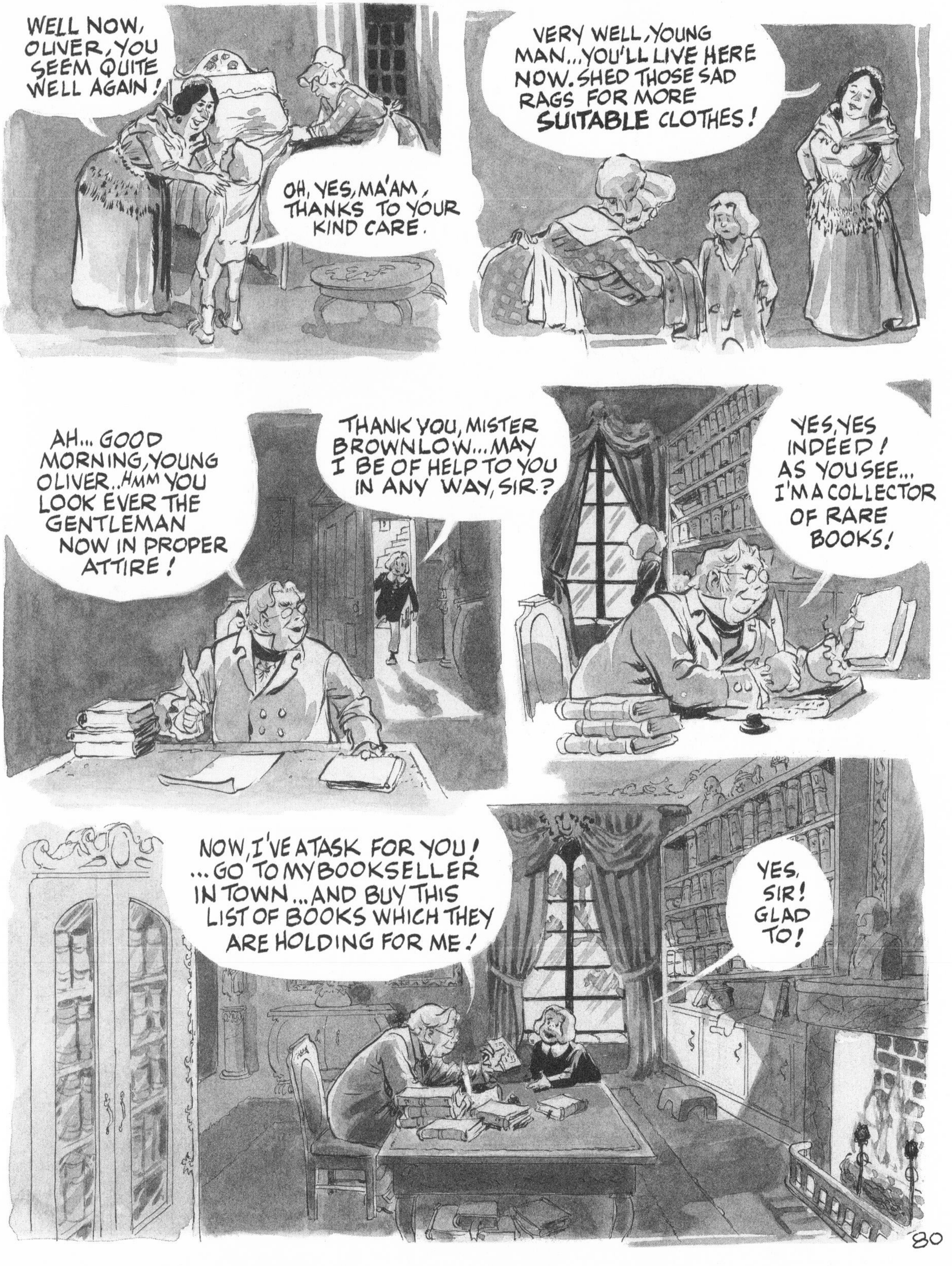

WELL NOW, OLIVER, YOU SEEM QUITE WELL AGAIN!
OH, YES, MA'AM, THANKS TO YOUR KIND CARE.
VERY WELL, YOUNG MAN...YOU'LL LIVE HERE NOW. SHED THOSE SAD RAGS FOR MORE SUITABLE CLOTHES!
AH... GOOD MORNING, YOUNG OLIVER.. HMM YOU LOOK EVER THE GENTLEMAN NOW IN PROPER ATTIRE!
THANK YOU, MISTER BROWNLOW...MAY I BE OF HELP TO YOU IN ANY WAY, SIR?
YES, YES INDEED! AS YOU SEE... I'M A COLLECTOR OF RARE BOOKS!
NOW, I'VE A TASK FOR YOU! ...GO TO MY BOOKSELLER IN TOWN...AND BUY THIS LIST OF BOOKS WHICH THEY ARE HOLDING FOR ME!
YES, SIR! GLAD TO!

In London's streets, Sikes and my boys were persistently searching for Oliver.

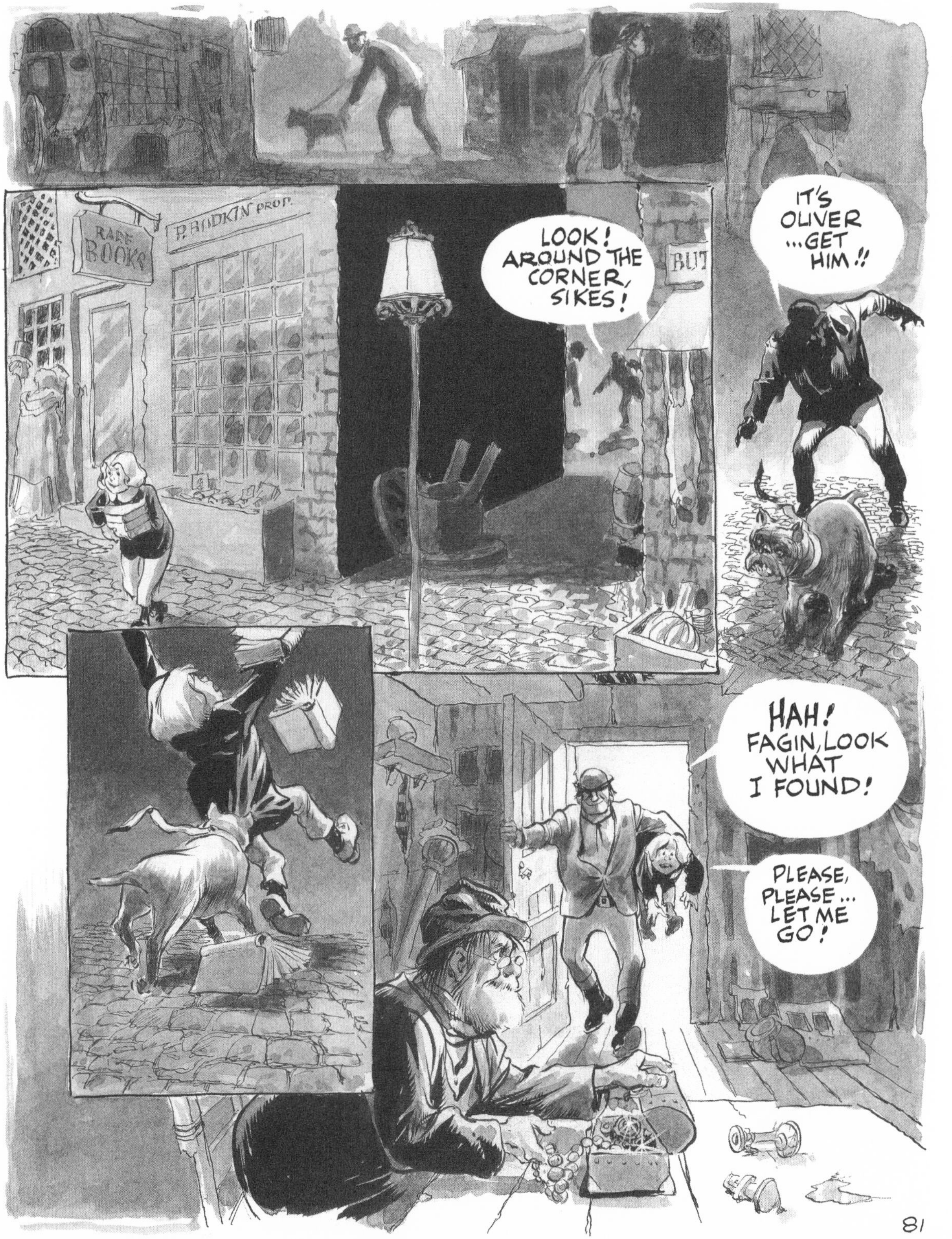
RARE BOOKS
R. BODKIN PROP.
BUT
LOOK! AROUND THE CORNER, SIKES!
IT'S OLIVER ...GET HIM!!
HAH! FAGIN, LOOK WHAT I FOUND!
PLEASE, PLEASE... LET ME GO!

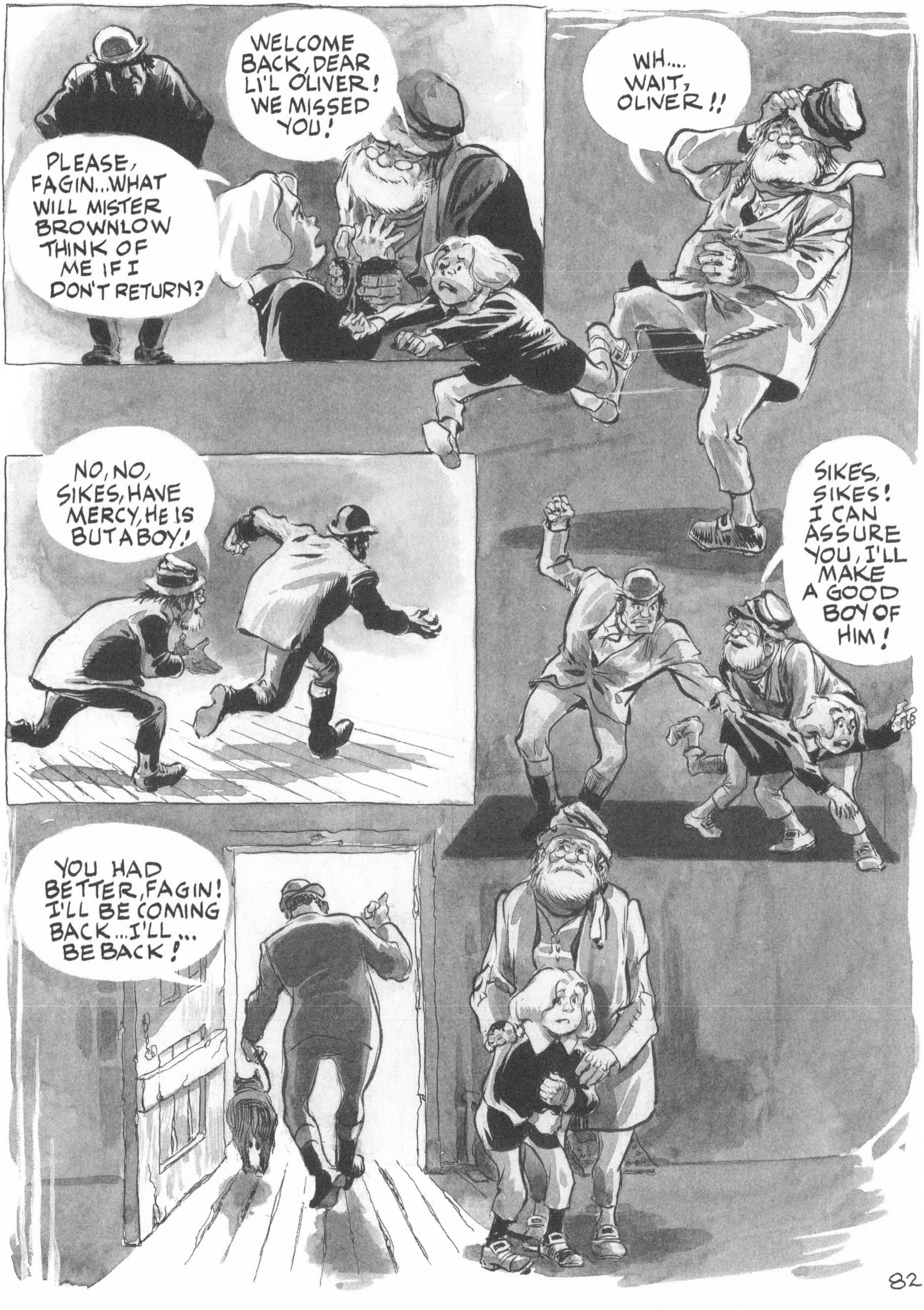
WELCOME BACK, DEAR LI'L OLIVER! WE MISSED YOU!
PLEASE, FAGIN...WHAT WILL MISTER BROWNLOW THINK OF ME IF I DON'T RETURN?
WH.... WAIT, OLIVER!!
NO, NO, SIKES, HAVE MERCY, HE IS BUT A BOY!
SIKES, SIKES! I CAN ASSURE YOU, I'LL MAKE A GOOD BOY OF HIM!
YOU HAD BETTER, FAGIN! I'LL BE COMING BACK...I'LL... BE BACK!

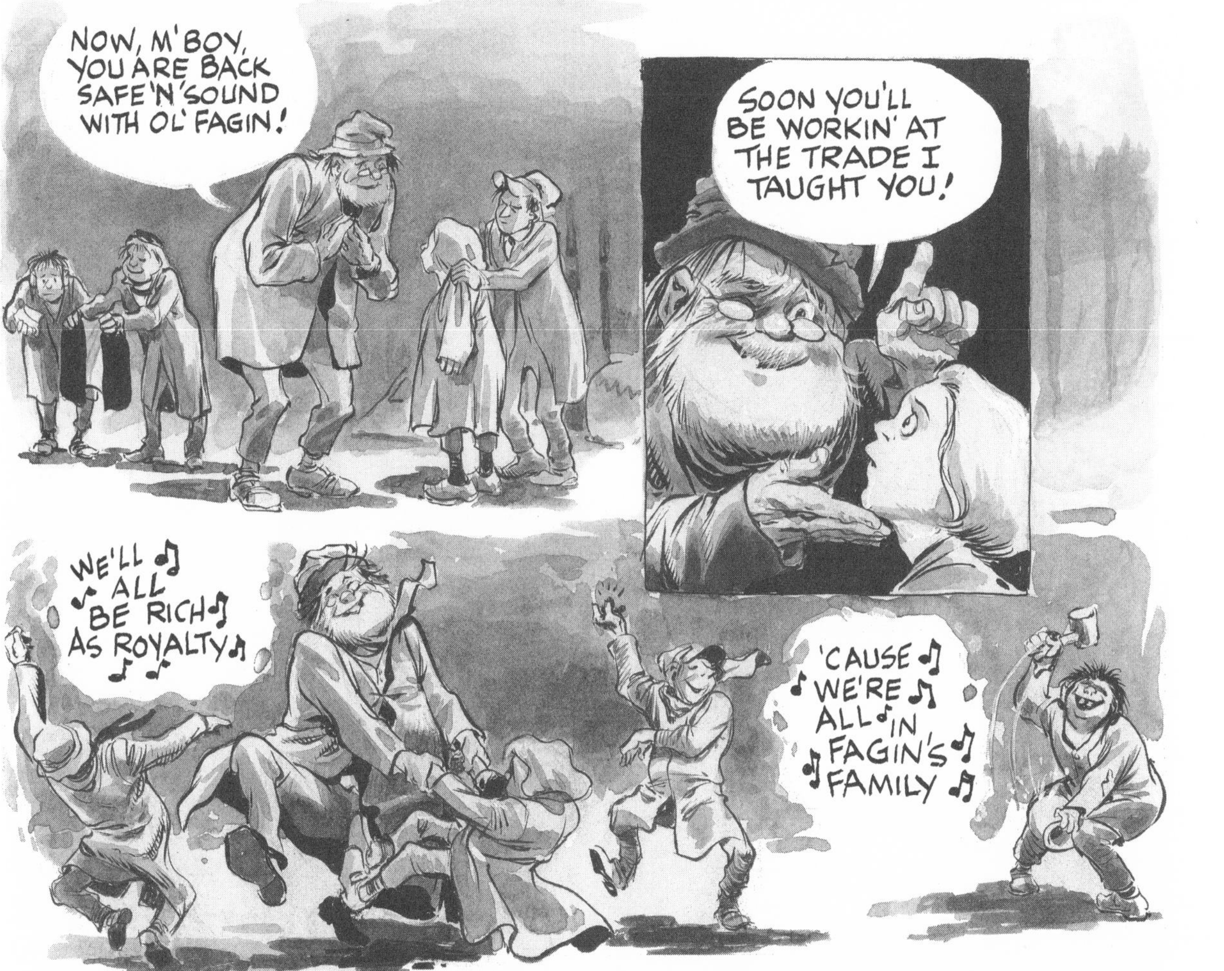
NOW, M'BOY, YOU ARE BACK SAFE 'N' SOUND WITH OL' FAGIN!
SOON YOU'LL BE WORKIN' AT THE TRADE I TAUGHT YOU!
WE'LL ALL BE RICH AS ROYALTY
'CAUSE WE'RE ALL IN FAGIN'S FAMILY

So, once more we had our Oliver back on the streets.

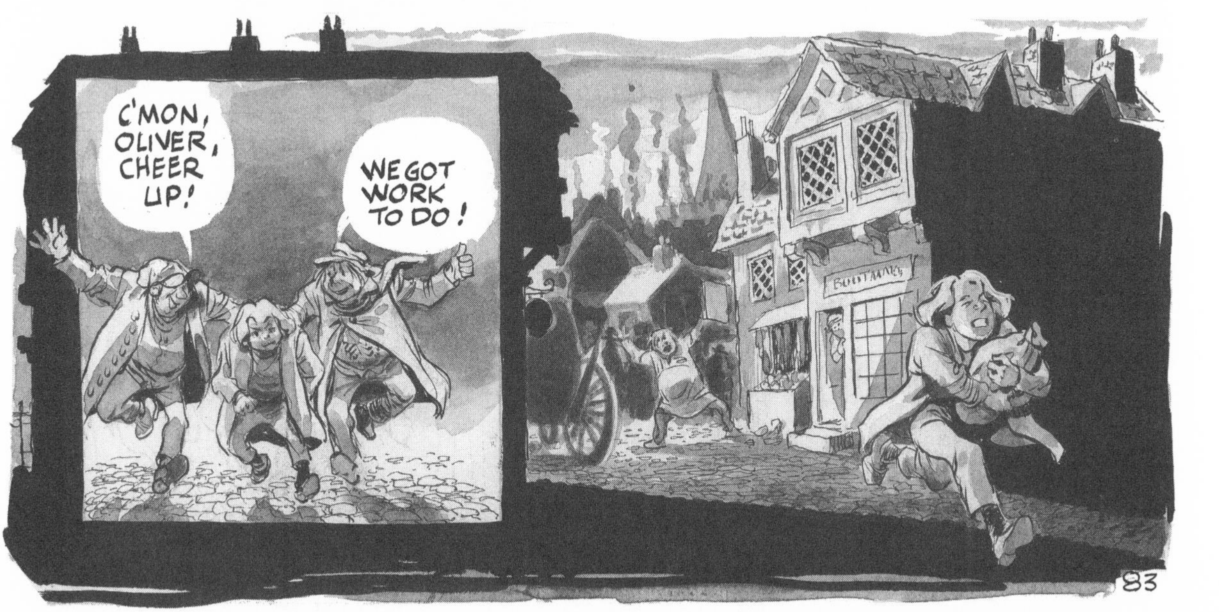
C'MON, OLIVER, CHEER UP!
WE GOT WORK TO DO!

Things was going very well again for me … until Sikes showed up.

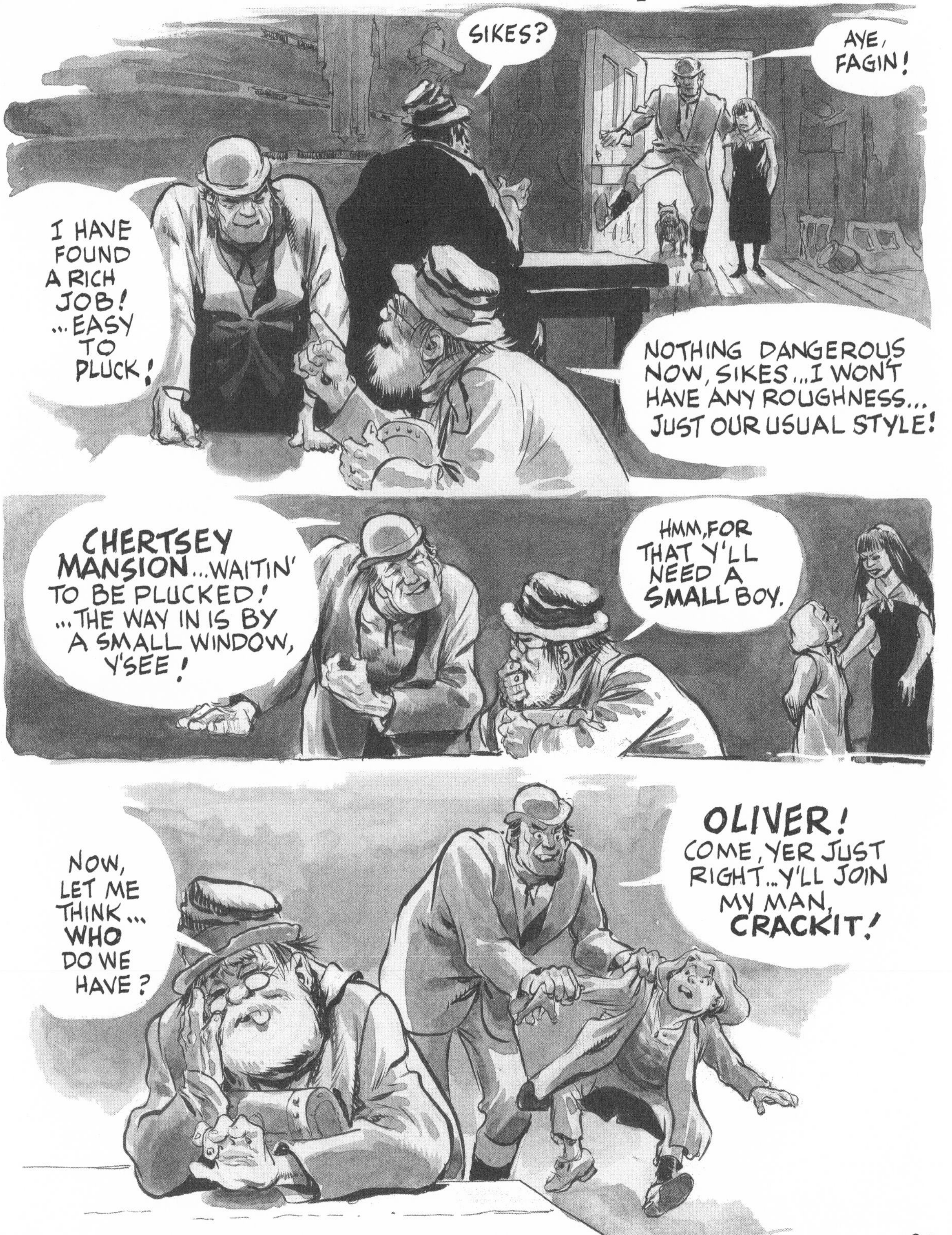

SIKES?
AYE, FAGIN!
I HAVE FOUND A RICH JOB! ...EASY TO PLUCK!
NOTHING DANGEROUS NOW, SIKES...I WON'T HAVE ANY ROUGHNESS... JUST OUR USUAL STYLE!
CHERTSEY MANSION...WAITIN' TO BE PLUCKED! ...THE WAY IN IS BY A SMALL WINDOW, Y'SEE!
HMM, FOR THAT Y'LL NEED A SMALL BOY.
NOW, LET ME THINK... WHO DO WE HAVE?
OLIVER! COME, YER JUST RIGHT...Y'LL JOIN MY MAN, CRACKIT!

That night outside the Chertsey mansion ...

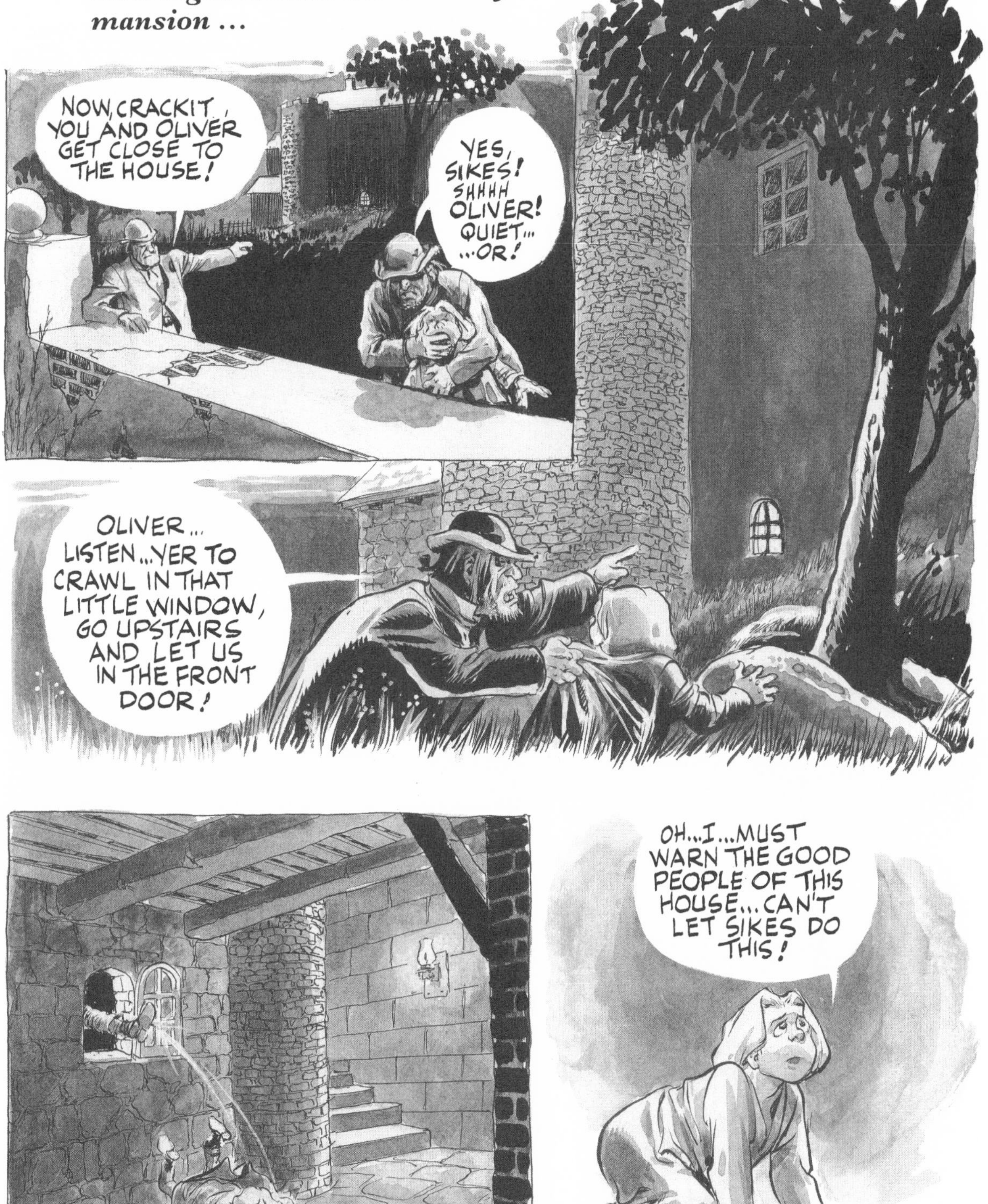
NOW, CRACKIT, YOU AND OLIVER GET CLOSE TO THE HOUSE!
YES, SIKES! SHHHH OLIVER! QUIET... ...OR!
OLIVER... LISTEN...YER TO CRAWL IN THAT LITTLE WINDOW, GO UPSTAIRS AND LET US IN THE FRONT DOOR!
OH...I...MUST WARN THE GOOD PEOPLE OF THIS HOUSE...CAN'T LET SIKES DO THIS!

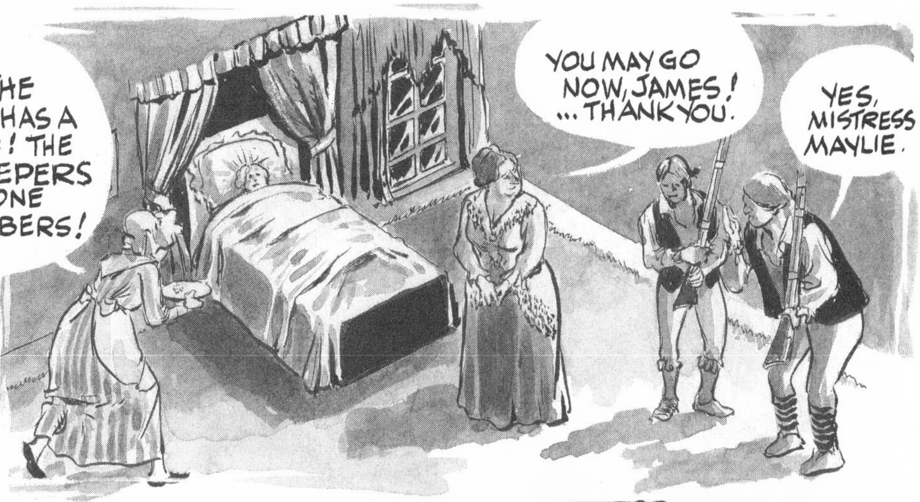
OH DEAR... THE POOR CHILD HAS A FLESH WOUND! THE GROUNDSKEEPERS SAY HE WAS ONE OF THE ROBBERS!
YOU MAY GO NOW, JAMES! ... THANK YOU.
YES, MISTRESS MAYLIE.

It so happened that Mr. Maylie was Mr. Brownlow's lawyer.

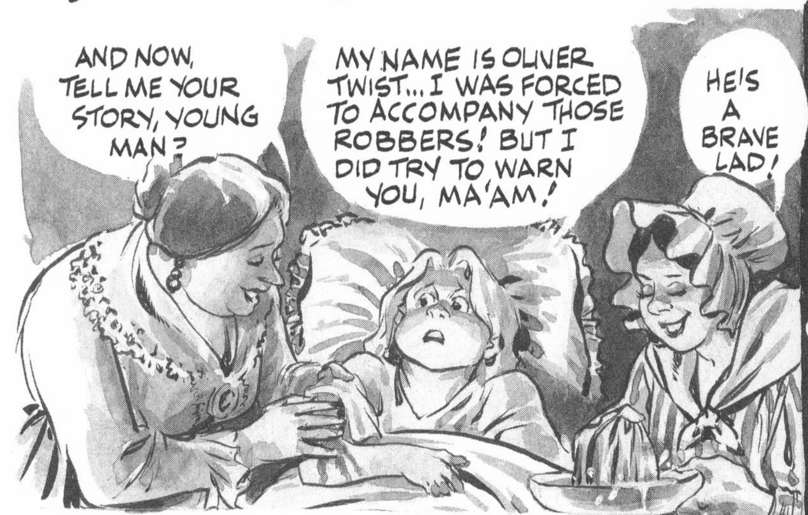
AND NOW, TELL ME YOUR STORY, YOUNG MAN?
MY NAME IS OLIVER TWIST... I WAS FORCED TO ACCOMPANY THOSE ROBBERS! BUT I DID TRY TO WARN YOU, MA'AM!
HE'S A BRAVE LAD!

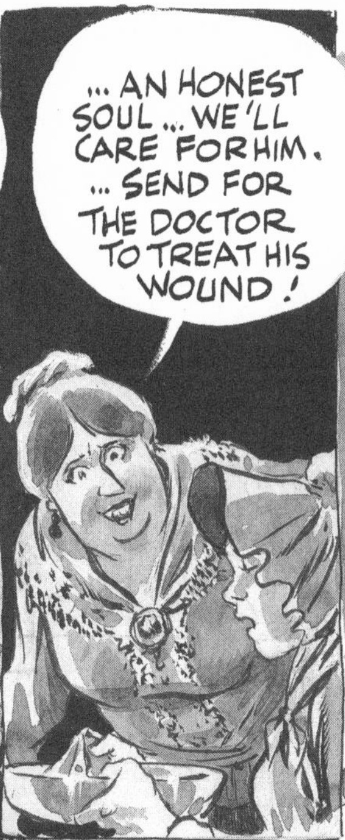
... AN HONEST SOUL... WE'LL CARE FOR HIM. ... SEND FOR THE DOCTOR TO TREAT HIS WOUND!

So Oliver found a new home with the Maylies in Chertsey, to Mr. Brownlow's relief.

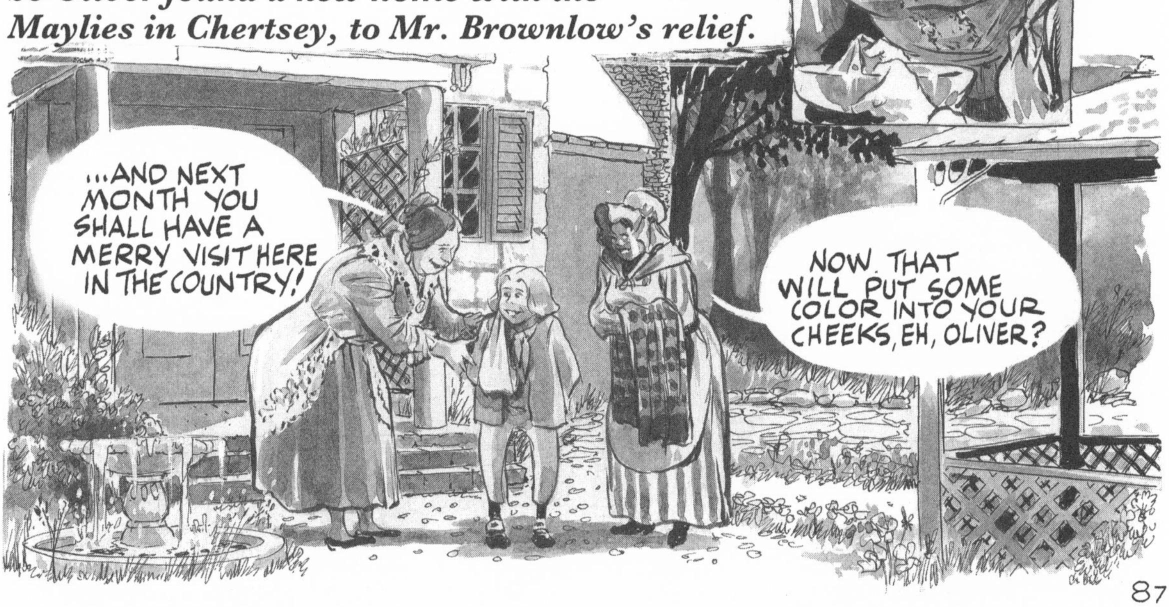
...AND NEXT MONTH YOU SHALL HAVE A MERRY VISIT HERE IN THE COUNTRY!
NOW. THAT WILL PUT SOME COLOR INTO YOUR CHEEKS, EH, OLIVER?

Later I learned that Monks made his way to a tavern frequented by the beadle who was at the workhouse where Oliver was born.

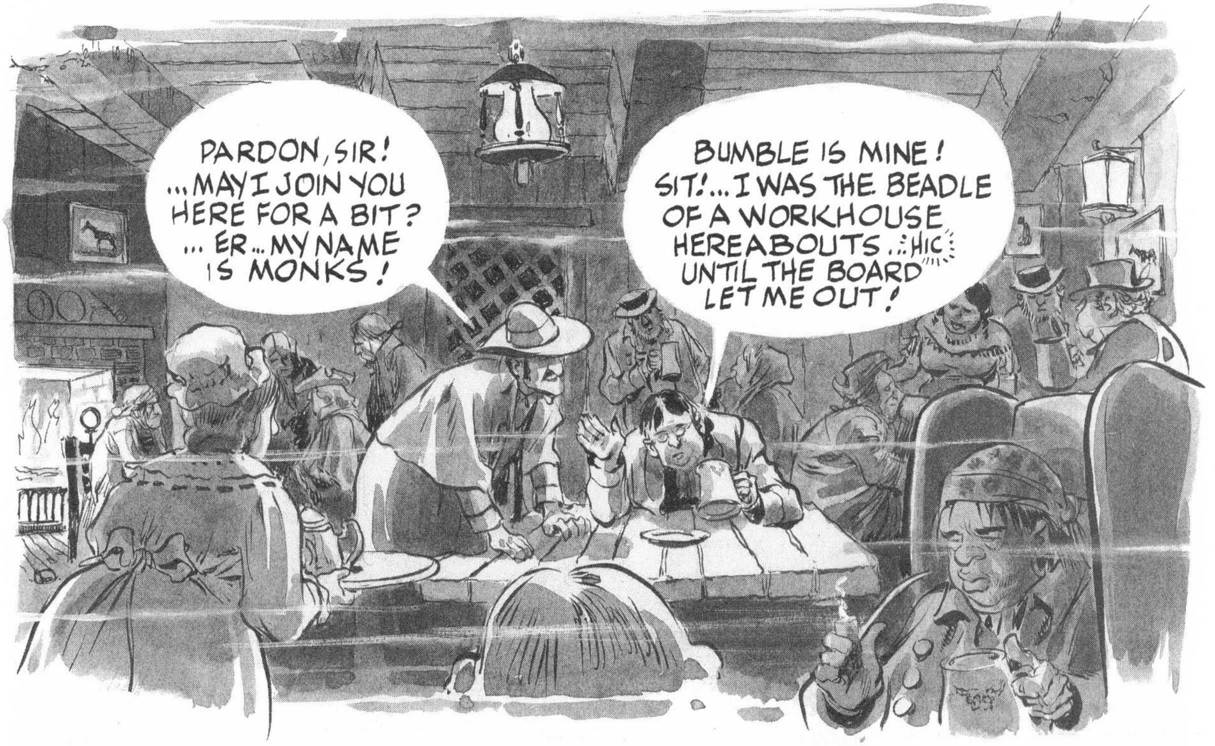
PARDON, SIR! ...MAY I JOIN YOU HERE FOR A BIT? ... ER... MY NAME IS MONKS!
BUMBLE IS MINE! SIT! ...I WAS THE BEADLE OF A WORKHOUSE HEREABOUTS ... HIC UNTIL THE BOARD LET ME OUT!

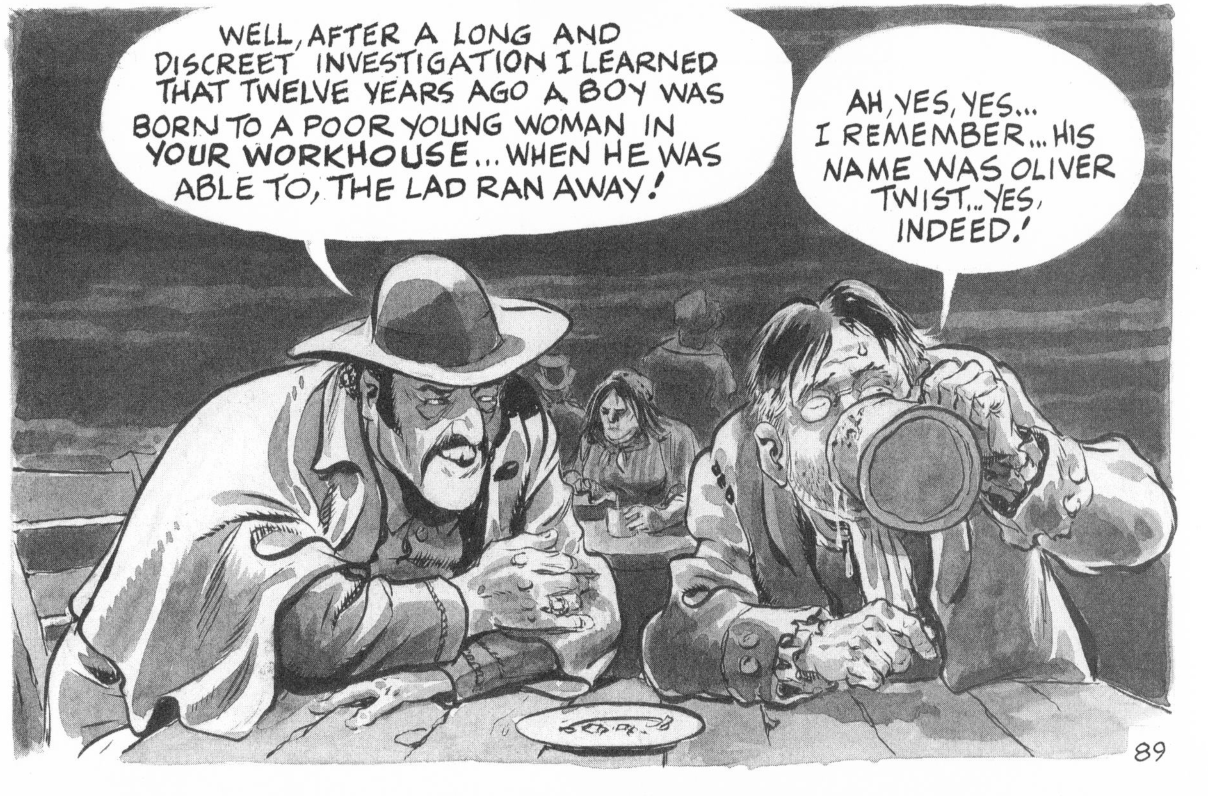
WELL, AFTER A LONG AND DISCREET INVESTIGATION I LEARNED THAT TWELVE YEARS AGO A BOY WAS BORN TO A POOR YOUNG WOMAN IN YOUR WORKHOUSE... WHEN HE WAS ABLE TO, THE LAD RAN AWAY!
AH, YES, YES... I REMEMBER... HIS NAME WAS OLIVER TWIST... YES, INDEED!

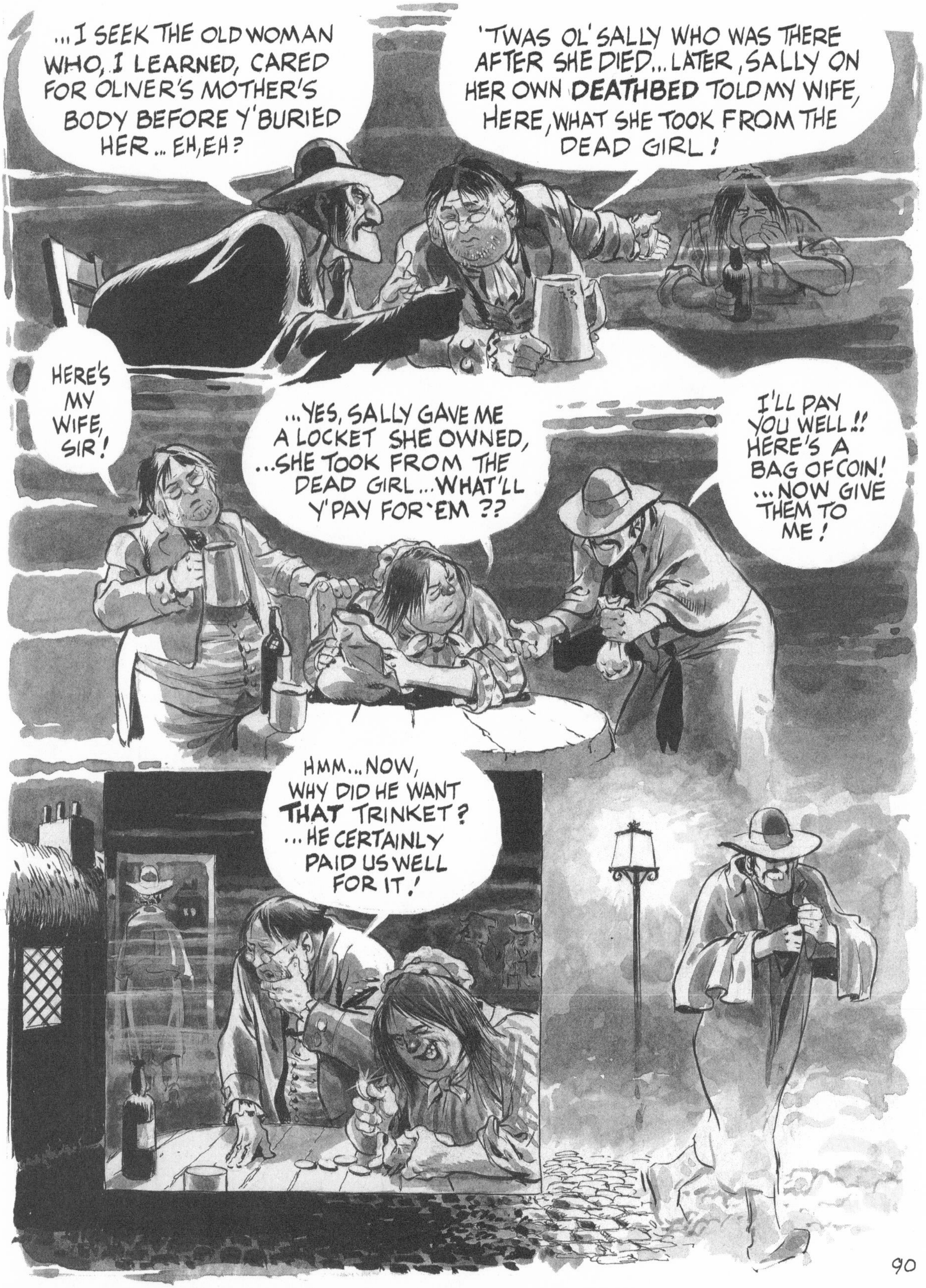
...I SEEK THE OLD WOMAN WHO, I LEARNED, CARED FOR OLIVER'S MOTHER'S BODY BEFORE Y'BURIED HER... EH, EH?
'TWAS OL' SALLY WHO WAS THERE AFTER SHE DIED... LATER, SALLY ON HER OWN **DEATHBED** TOLD MY WIFE, HERE, WHAT SHE TOOK FROM THE DEAD GIRL!
HERE'S MY WIFE, SIR!
...YES, SALLY GAVE ME A LOCKET SHE OWNED, ...SHE TOOK FROM THE DEAD GIRL... WHAT'LL Y'PAY FOR 'EM??
I'LL PAY YOU WELL!! HERE'S A BAG OF COIN! ...NOW GIVE THEM TO ME!
HMM... NOW, WHY DID HE WANT **THAT** TRINKET? ...HE CERTAINLY PAID US WELL FOR IT!

The next day I had another visit from Monks.

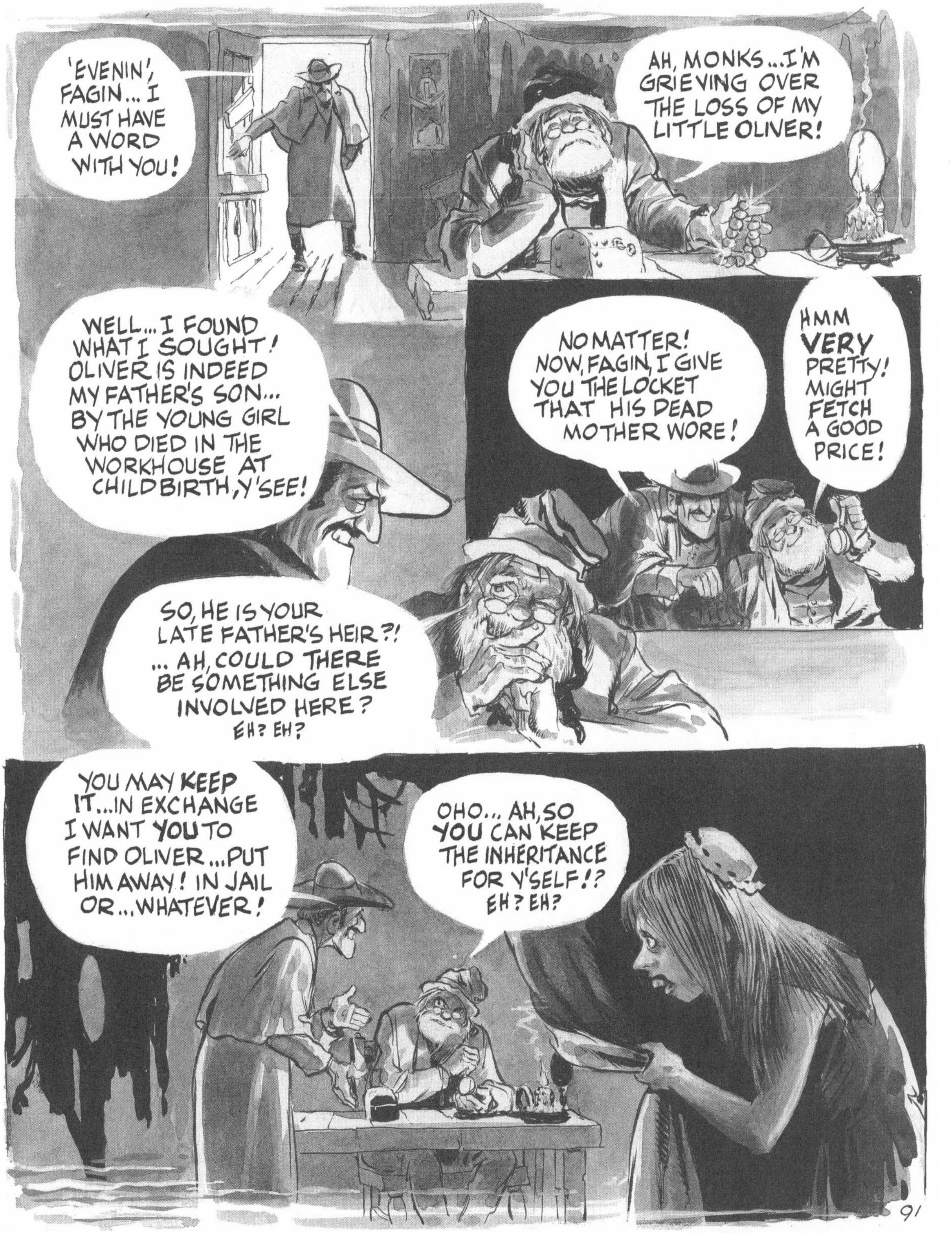
'EVENIN', FAGIN... I MUST HAVE A WORD WITH YOU!
AH, MONKS...I'M GRIEVING OVER THE LOSS OF MY LITTLE OLIVER!
WELL... I FOUND WHAT I SOUGHT! OLIVER IS INDEED MY FATHER'S SON... BY THE YOUNG GIRL WHO DIED IN THE WORKHOUSE AT CHILDBIRTH, Y'SEE!
NO MATTER! NOW, FAGIN, I GIVE YOU THE LOCKET THAT HIS DEAD MOTHER WORE!
HMM VERY PRETTY! MIGHT FETCH A GOOD PRICE!
SO, HE IS YOUR LATE FATHER'S HEIR?! ... AH, COULD THERE BE SOMETHING ELSE INVOLVED HERE? EH? EH?
YOU MAY KEEP IT...IN EXCHANGE I WANT YOU TO FIND OLIVER...PUT HIM AWAY! IN JAIL OR...WHATEVER!
OHO... AH, SO YOU CAN KEEP THE INHERITANCE FOR Y'SELF!? EH? EH?

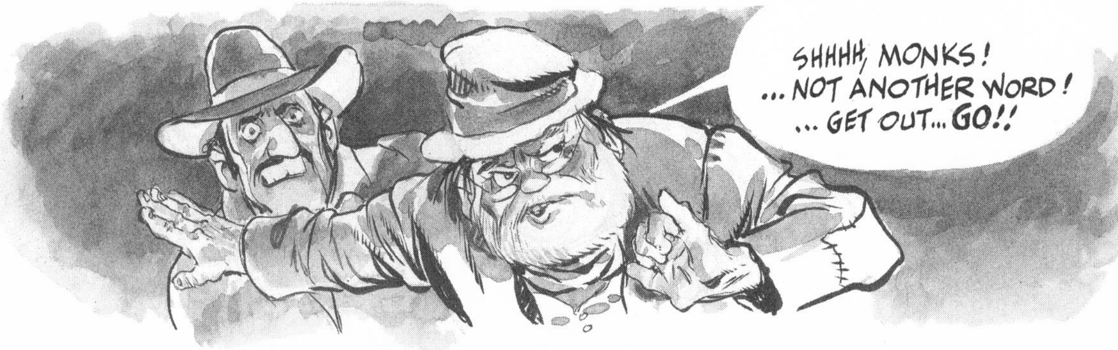
SHHHH, MONKS! ... NOT ANOTHER WORD! ... GET OUT... GO!!

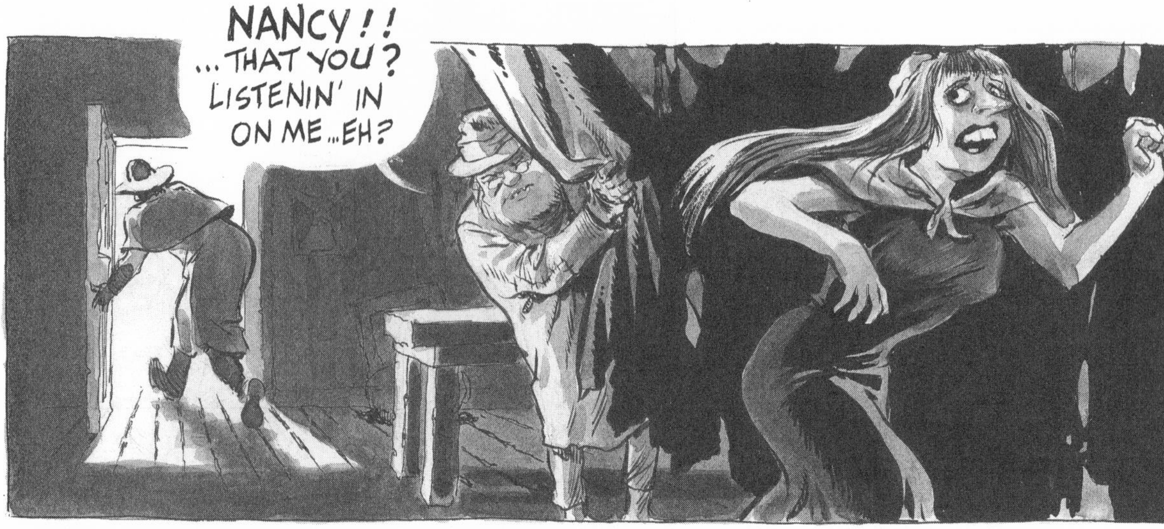
NANCY!! ... THAT YOU? LISTENIN' IN ON ME... EH?

Nancy ran off to the Maylie family. I reckon that she learned from Sikes' boasting where they were sheltering Oliver.

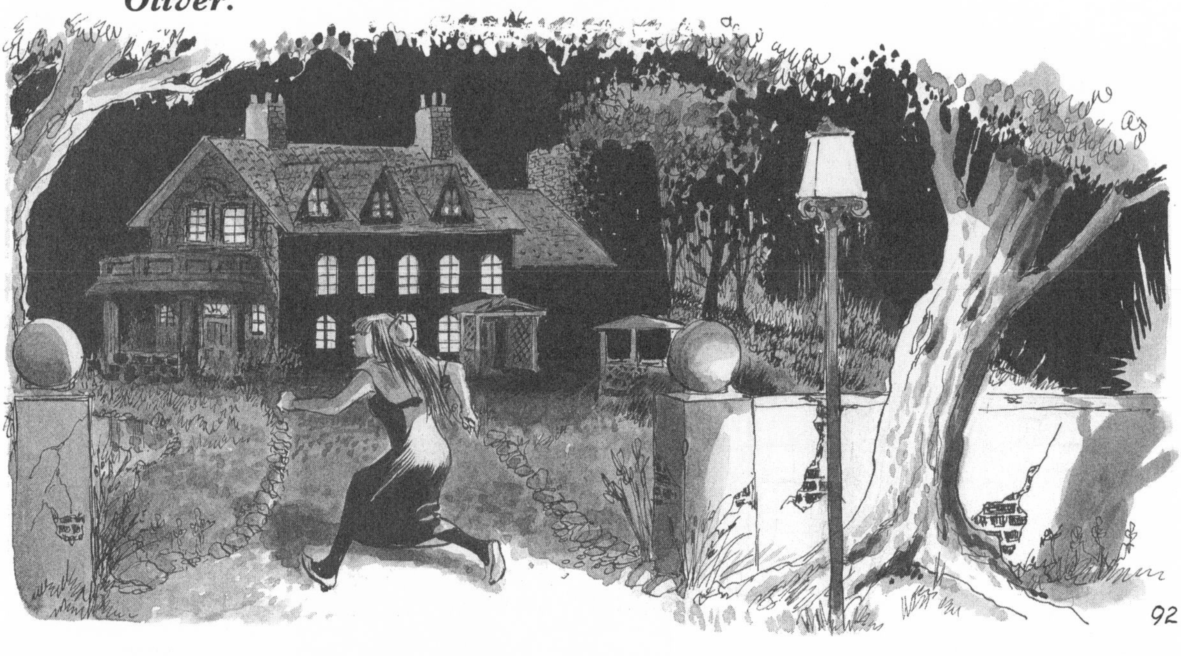

It was not hard to guess that Nancy told the Maylies what she overheard.

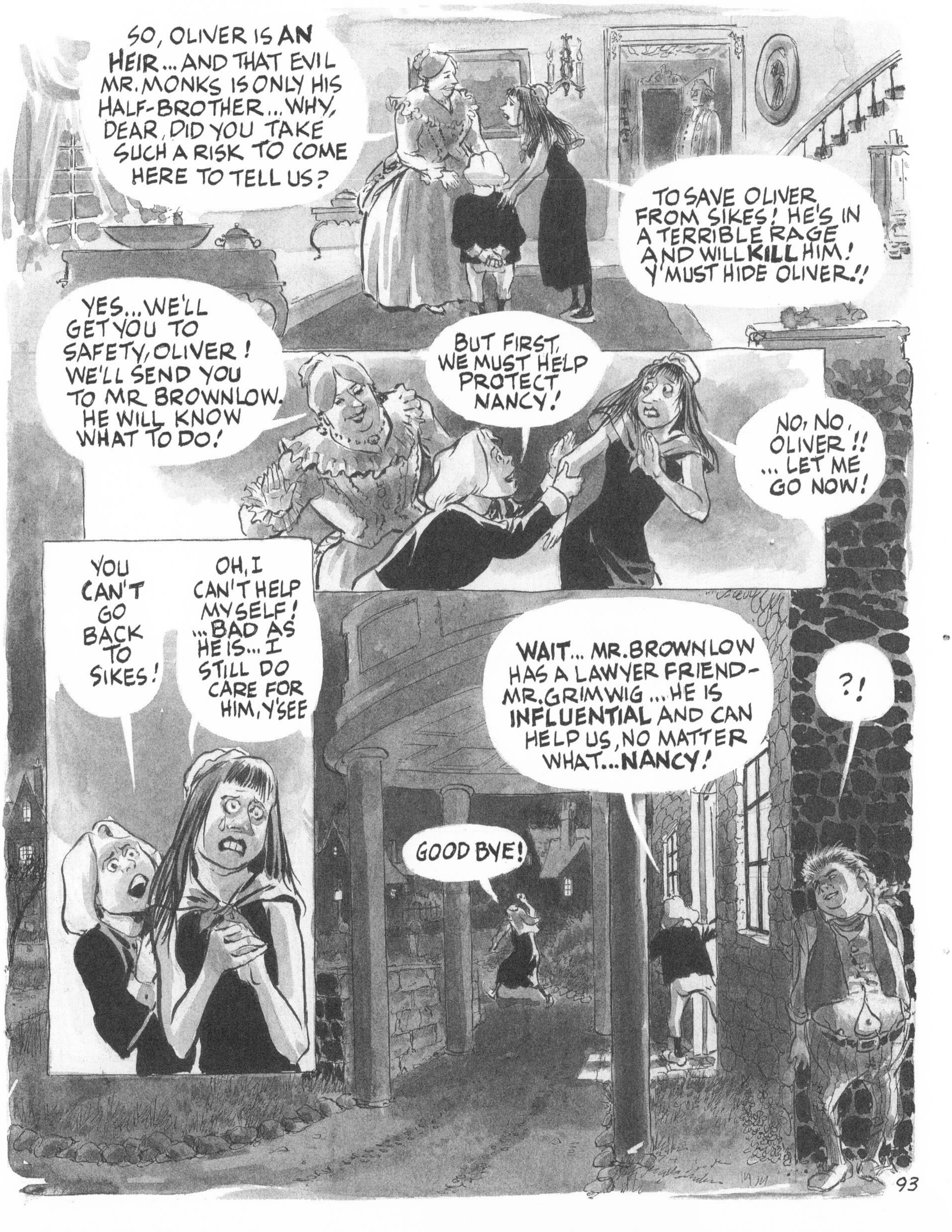

SO, OLIVER IS AN HEIR... AND THAT EVIL MR. MONKS IS ONLY HIS HALF-BROTHER... WHY, DEAR, DID YOU TAKE SUCH A RISK TO COME HERE TO TELL US?
TO SAVE OLIVER FROM SIKES! HE'S IN A TERRIBLE RAGE AND WILL KILL HIM! Y'MUST HIDE OLIVER!!
YES... WE'LL GET YOU TO SAFETY, OLIVER! WE'LL SEND YOU TO MR BROWNLOW. HE WILL KNOW WHAT TO DO!
BUT FIRST, WE MUST HELP PROTECT NANCY!
NO, NO, OLIVER!! ... LET ME GO NOW!
YOU CAN'T GO BACK TO SIKES!
OH, I CAN'T HELP MYSELF! ... BAD AS HE IS... I STILL DO CARE FOR HIM, Y'SEE
WAIT... MR. BROWNLOW HAS A LAWYER FRIEND- MR. GRIMWIG ... HE IS INFLUENTIAL AND CAN HELP US, NO MATTER WHAT... NANCY!
?!
GOOD BYE!

94

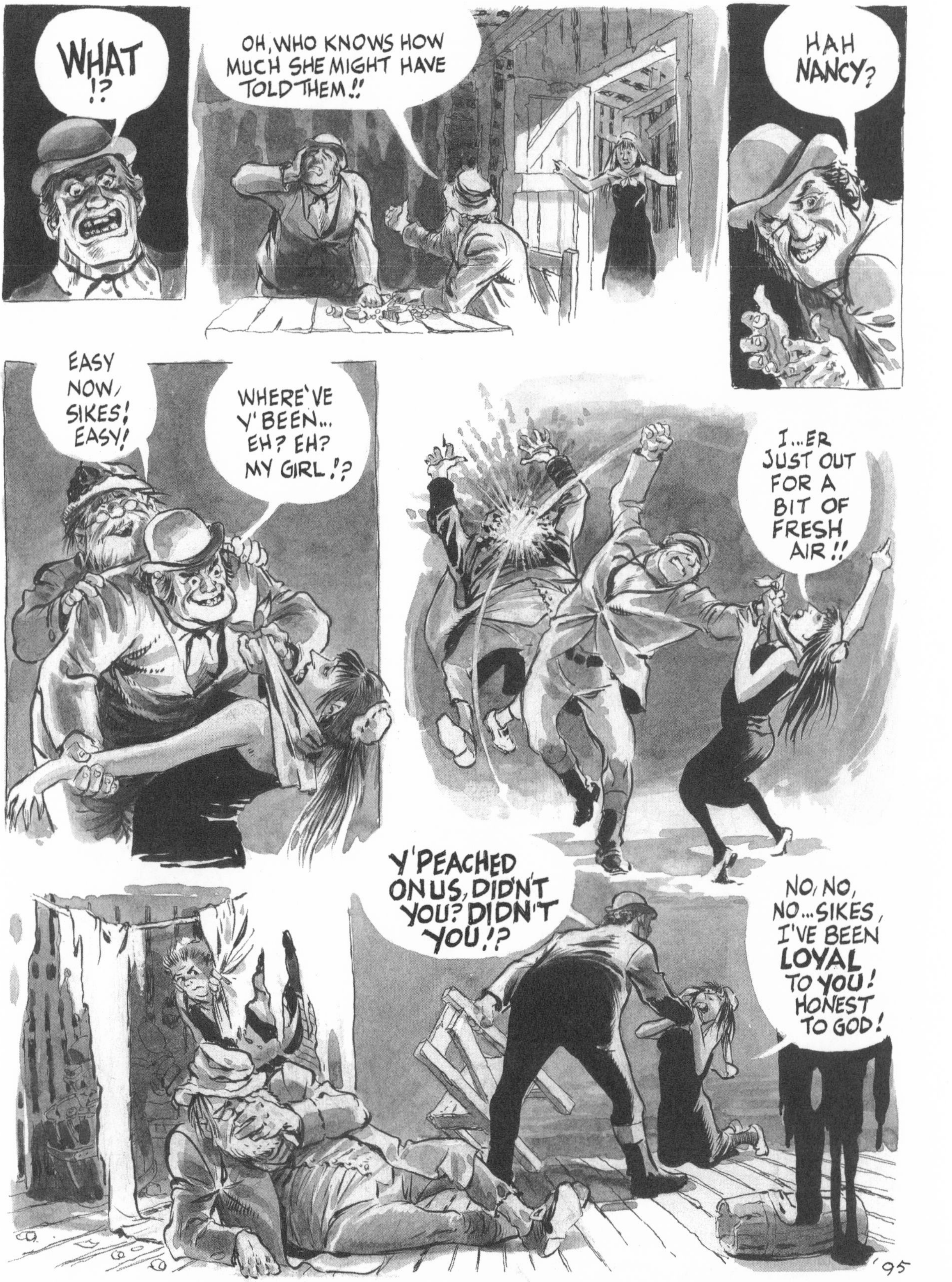
WHAT !?
OH, WHO KNOWS HOW MUCH SHE MIGHT HAVE TOLD THEM !!
HAH NANCY?
EASY NOW, SIKES! EASY!
WHERE'VE Y' BEEN... EH? EH? MY GIRL !?
I...ER JUST OUT FOR A BIT OF FRESH AIR !!
Y'PEACHED ON US, DIDN'T YOU? DIDN'T YOU !?
NO, NO, NO...SIKES, I'VE BEEN LOYAL TO YOU! HONEST TO GOD!
'95

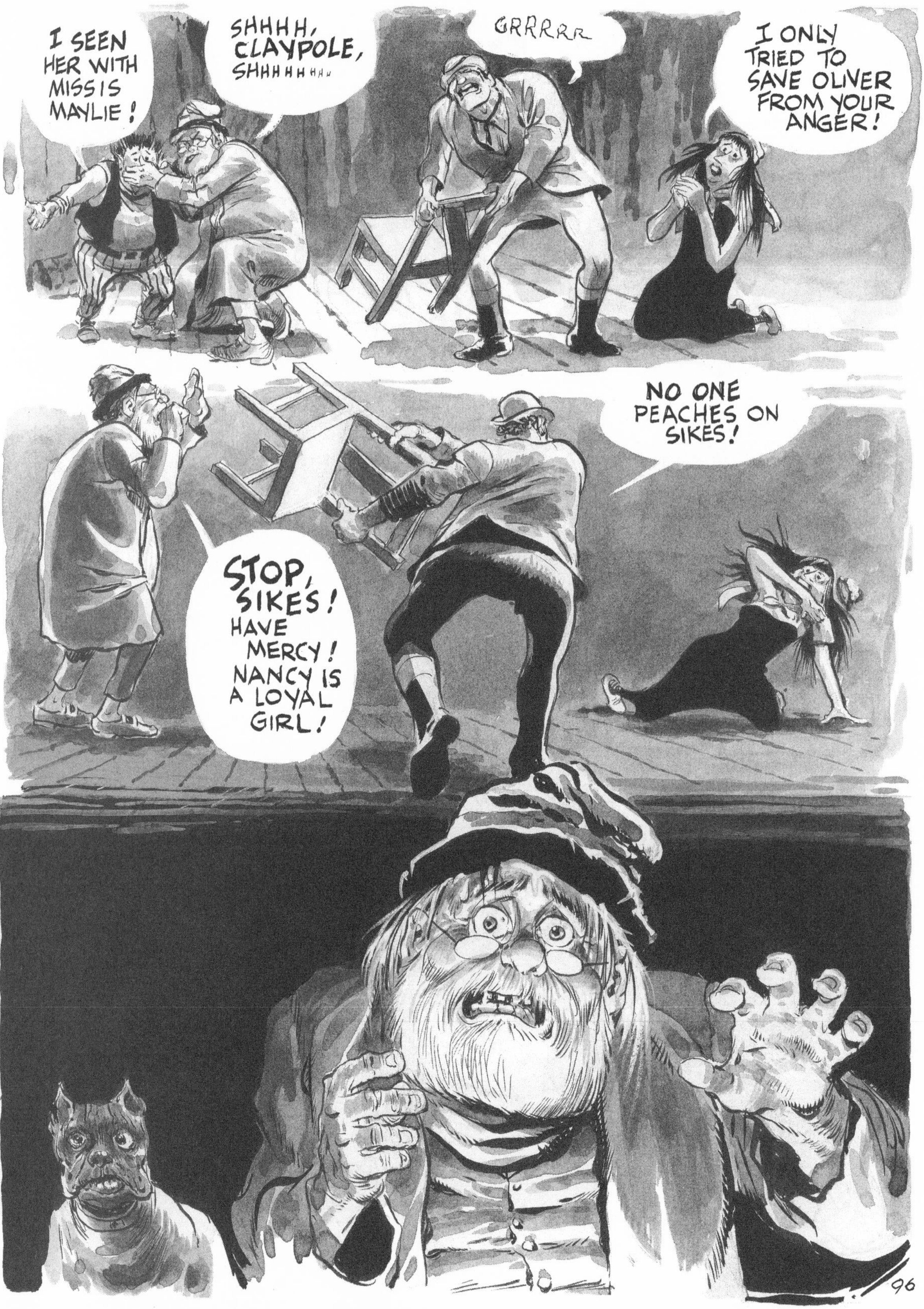
I SEEN HER WITH MISSIS MAYLIE!
SHHHH, CLAYPOLE, SHHHHHHH
GRRRRRR
I ONLY TRIED TO SAVE OLIVER FROM YOUR ANGER!
NO ONE PEACHES ON SIKES!
STOP, SIKES! HAVE MERCY! NANCY IS A LOYAL GIRL!

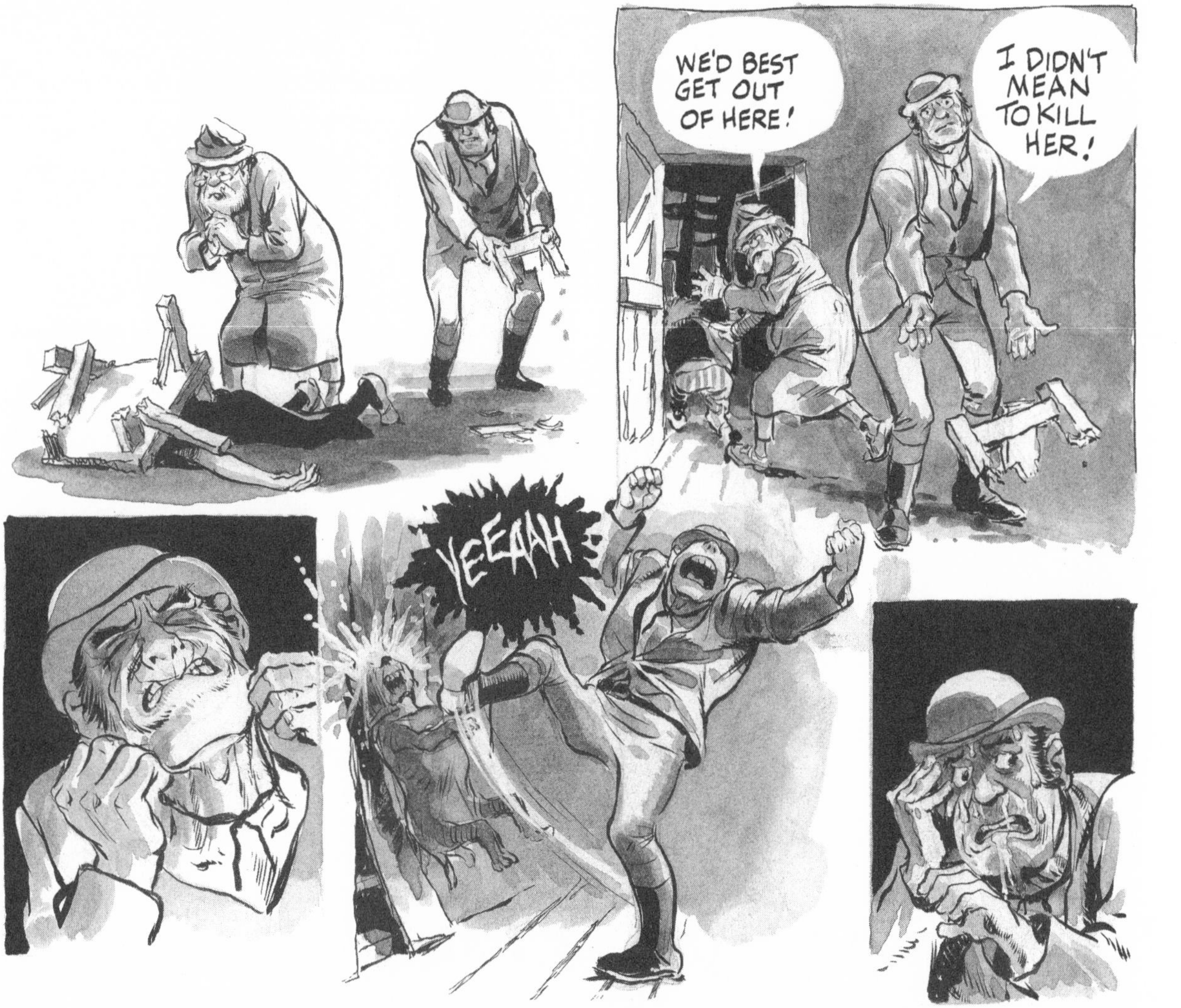
WE'D BEST GET OUT OF HERE!
I DIDN'T MEAN TO KILL HER!
YEEAAH

I knew, of course, where the brute would go. In a mortal panic, Sikes ran to the docks. There he hoped to hide among old thieves he knew.

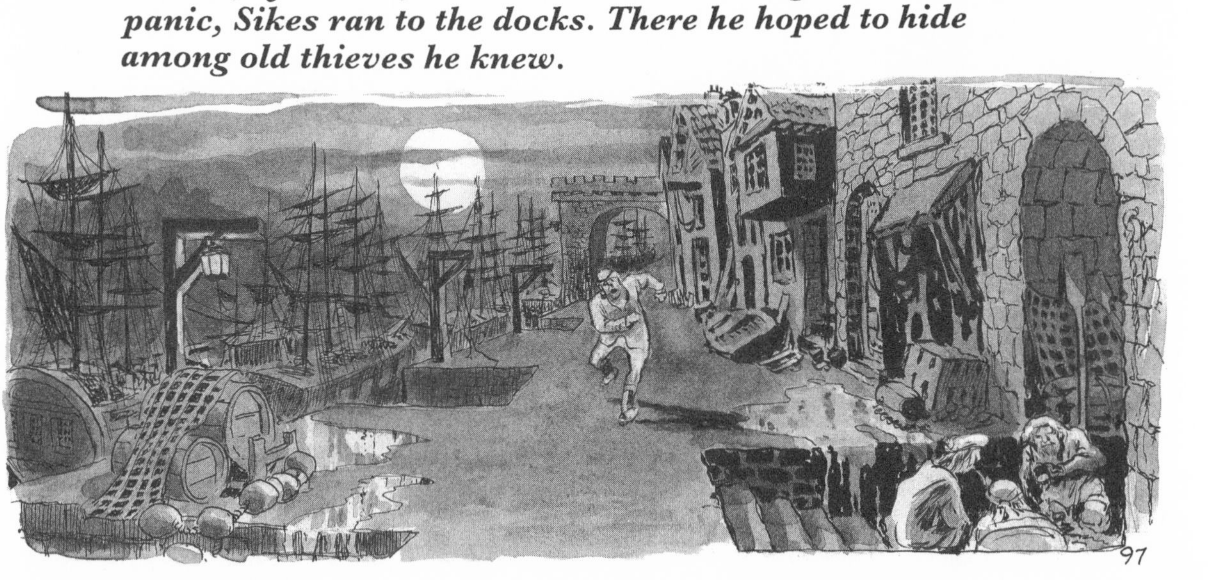

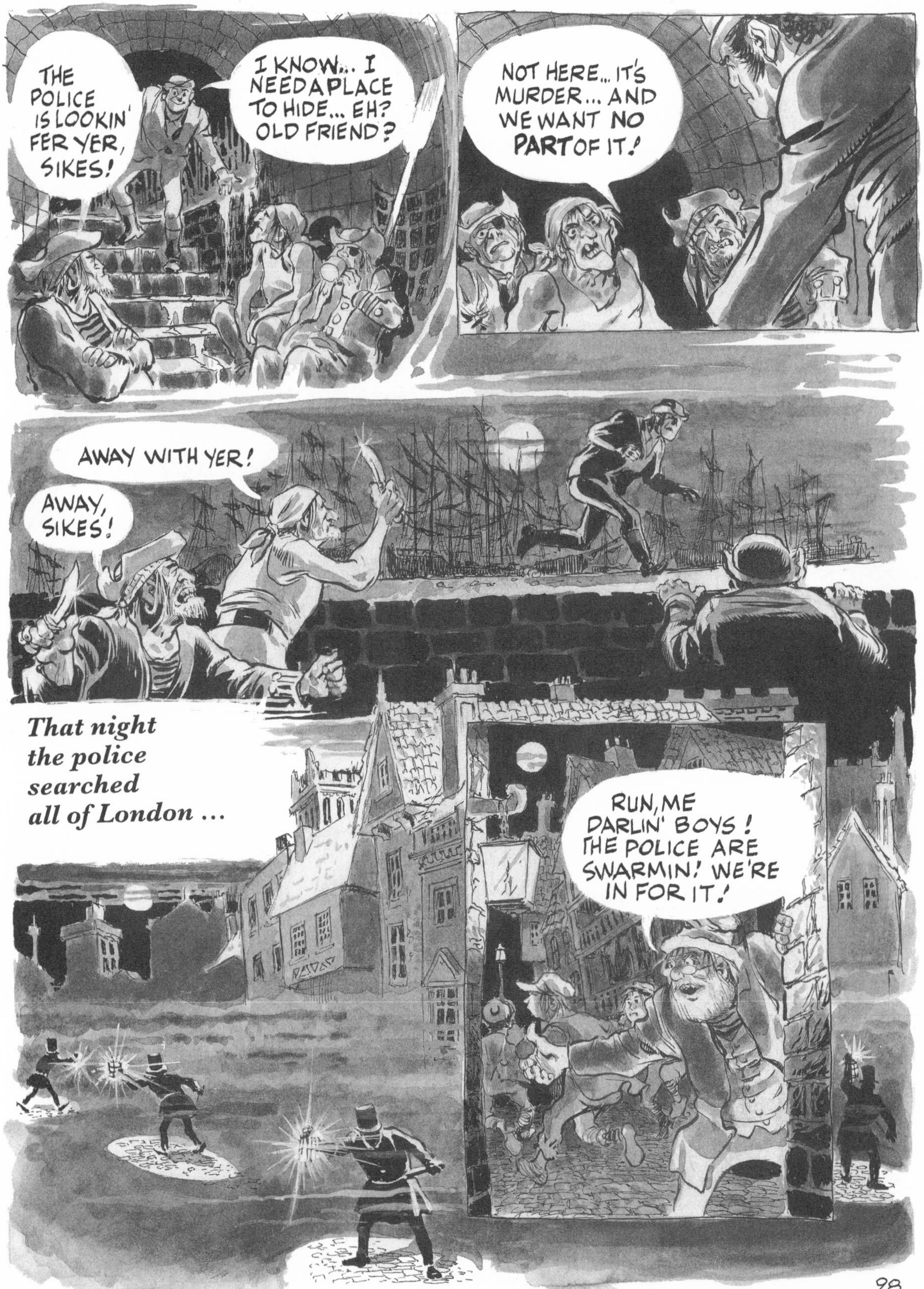
THE POLICE IS LOOKIN' FER YER, SIKES!
I KNOW... I NEED A PLACE TO HIDE... EH? OLD FRIEND?
NOT HERE... IT'S MURDER... AND WE WANT NO PART OF IT!
AWAY WITH YER!
AWAY, SIKES!
That night the police searched all of London ...
RUN, ME DARLIN' BOYS! THE POLICE ARE SWARMIN'! WE'RE IN FOR IT!

Oh, I ran…on tired legs…but not quick enough…

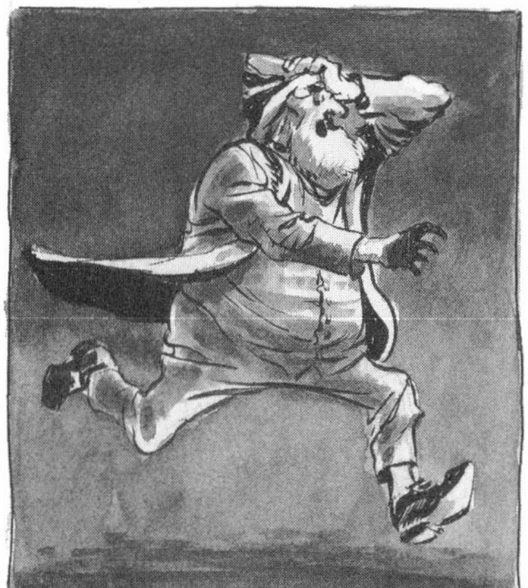

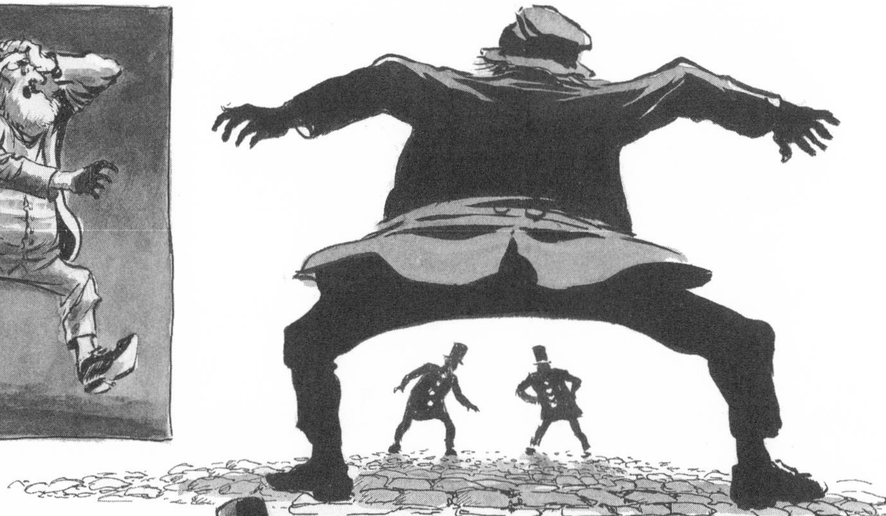

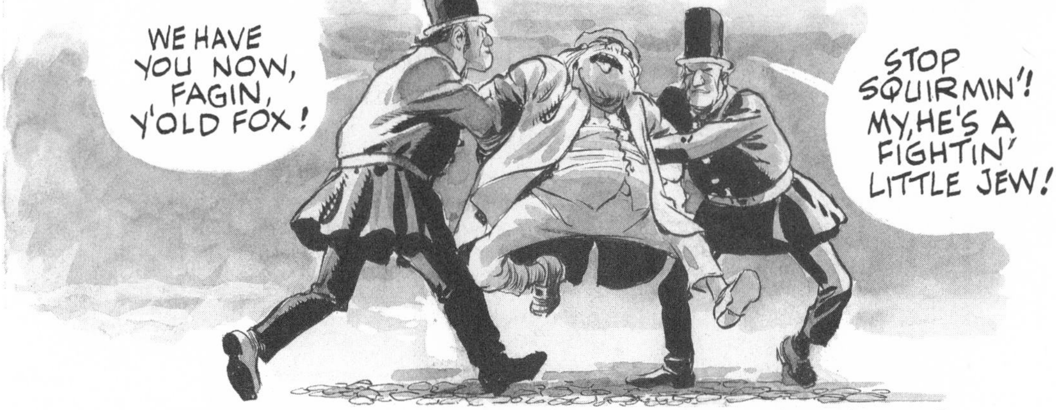
WE HAVE YOU NOW, FAGIN, Y'OLD FOX!
STOP SQUIRMIN'! MY, HE'S A FIGHTIN' LITTLE JEW!

Meanwhile, Sikes was running through the alleys … now haunted by a ghost…

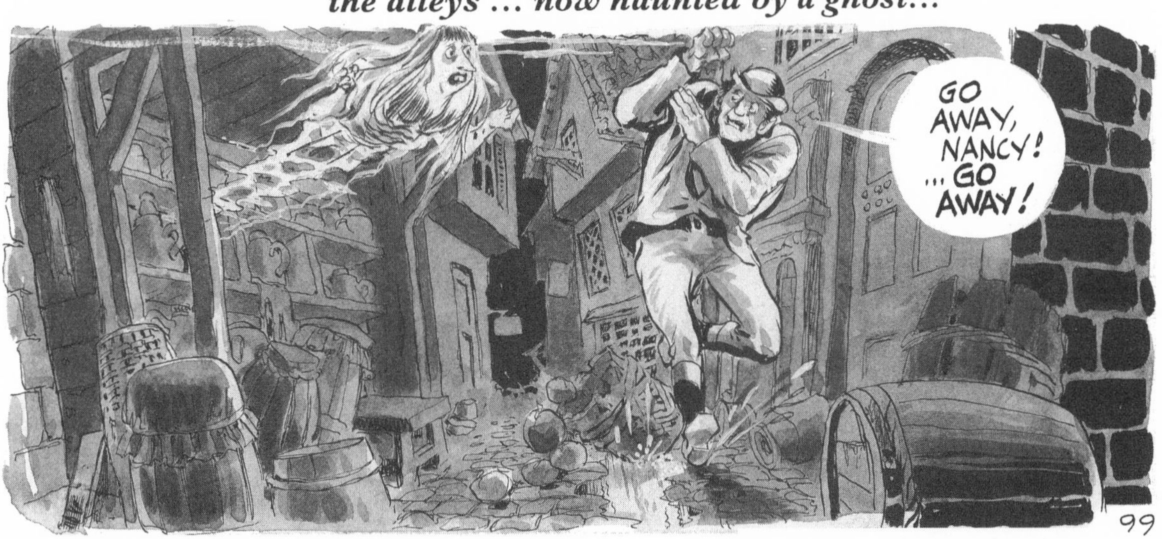
GO AWAY, NANCY! …GO AWAY!

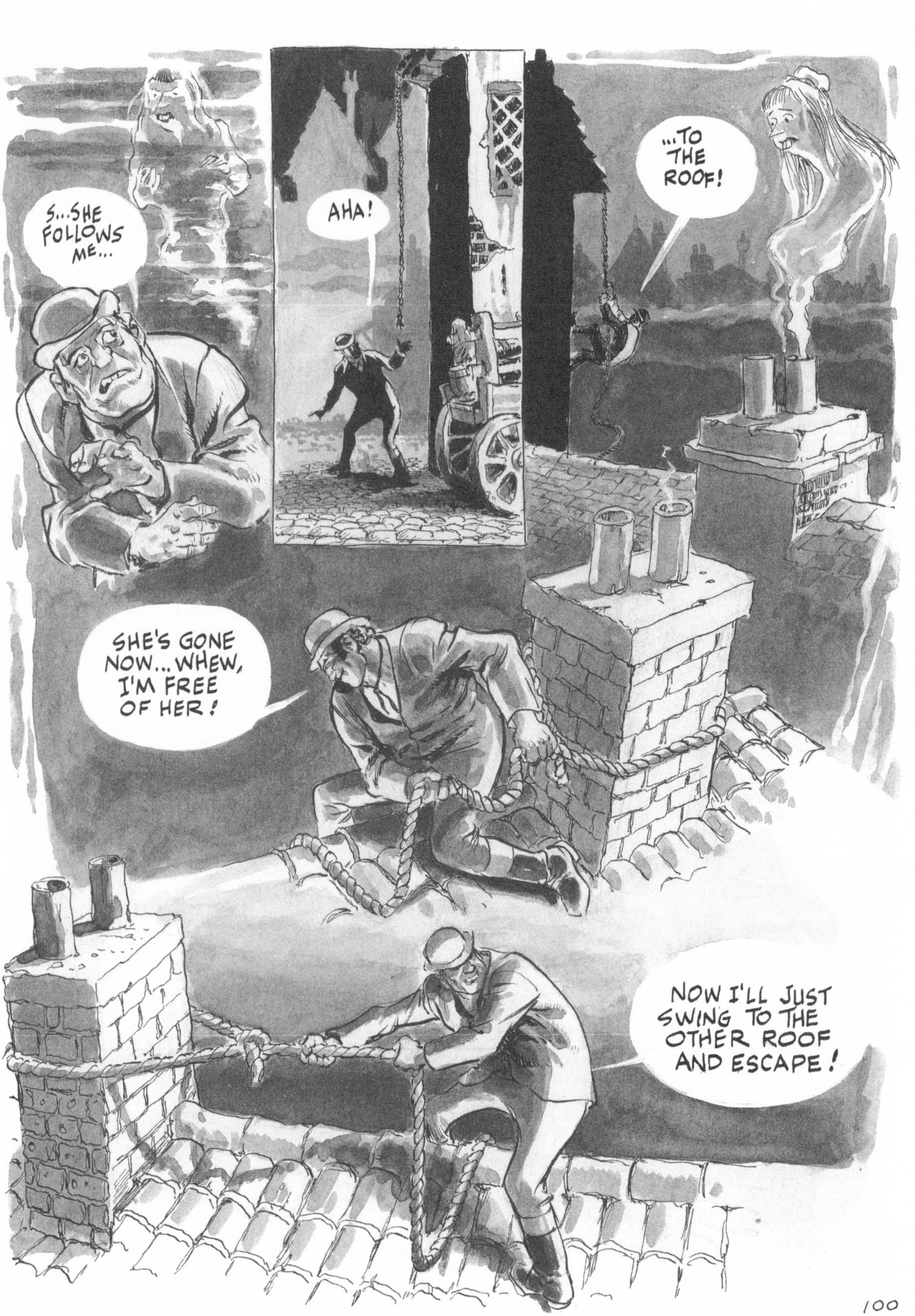
S...SHE FOLLOWS ME...
AHA!
...TO THE ROOF!
SHE'S GONE NOW... WHEW, I'M FREE OF HER!
NOW I'LL JUST SWING TO THE OTHER ROOF AND ESCAPE!

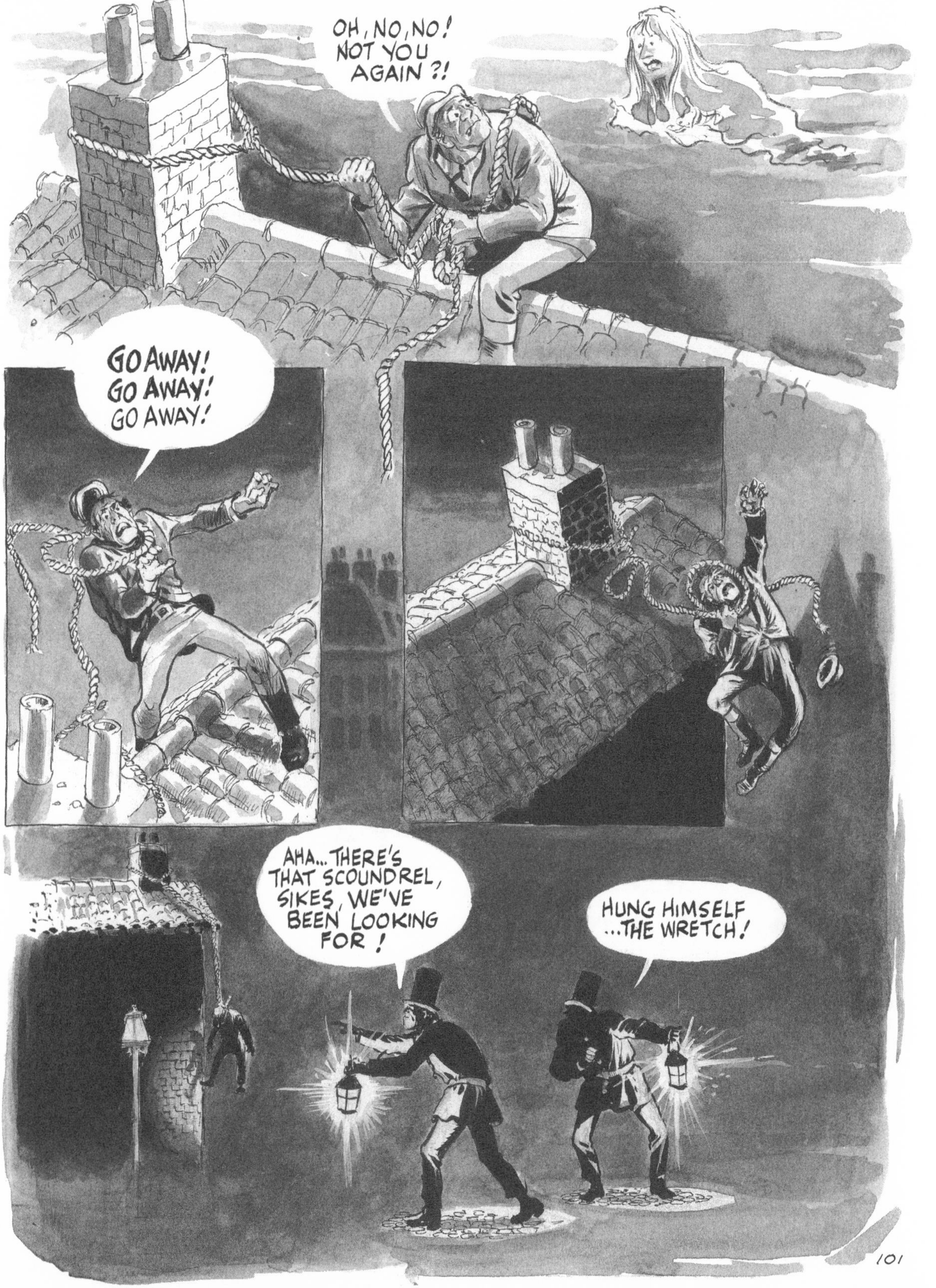
OH, NO, NO! NOT YOU AGAIN ?!
GO AWAY! GO AWAY! GO AWAY!
AHA... THERE'S THAT SCOUNDREL, SIKES, WE'VE BEEN LOOKING FOR!
HUNG HIMSELF ...THE WRETCH!

With Sikes dead there was no one to testify to my innocence. Well, I was locked up in Newgate Prison, where I was tried and sentenced in short order.

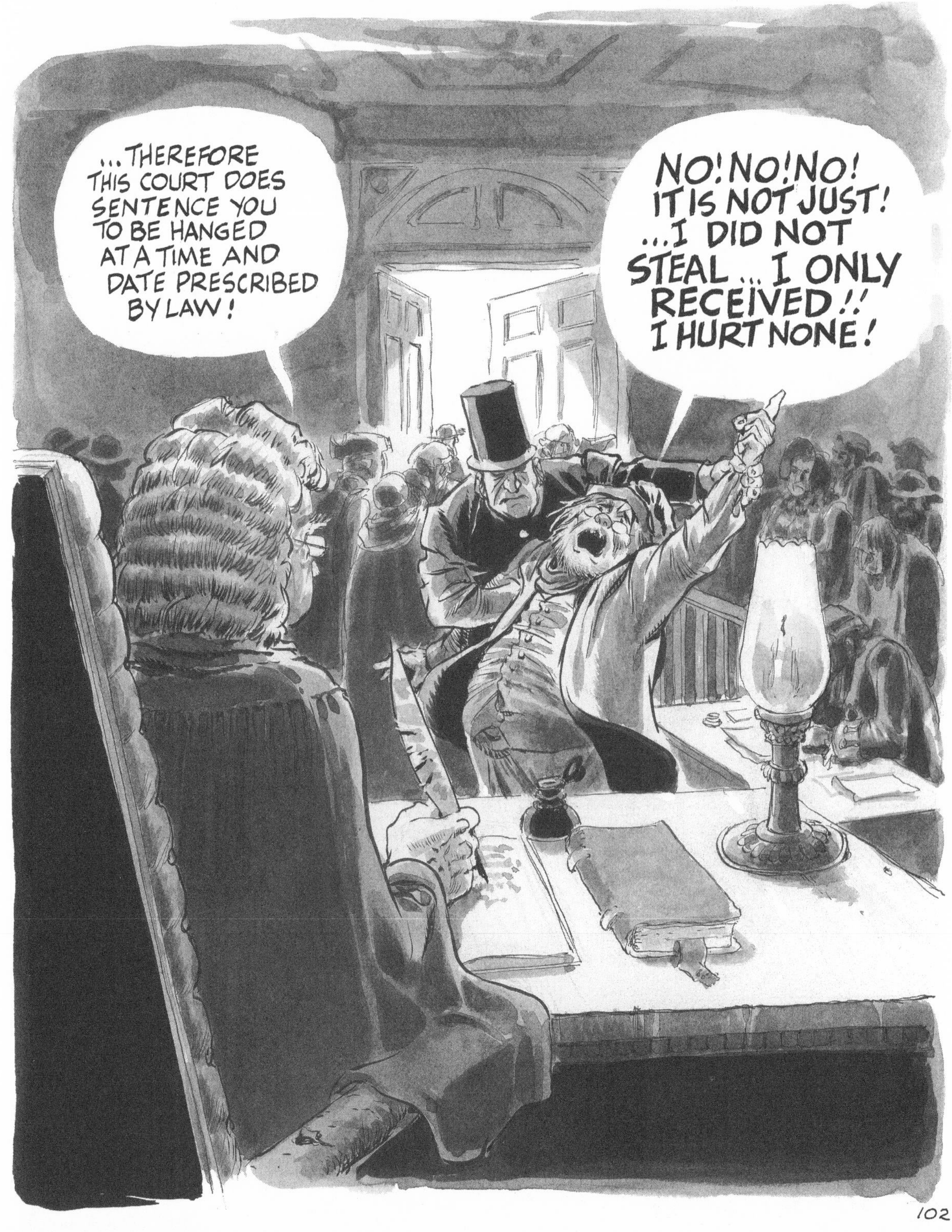
...THEREFORE THIS COURT DOES SENTENCE YOU TO BE HANGED AT A TIME AND DATE PRESCRIBED BY LAW!
NO! NO! NO! IT IS NOT JUST! ...I DID NOT STEAL... I ONLY RECEIVED!! I HURT NONE!

I lay in my cell exhausted from writhing and flailing against my sorry fate... Aided by his influential new benefactor and patron Mr. Brownlow, Oliver was allowed to visit me here. His visit added to my comfort and helped me endure the agony of an undeserved fate.

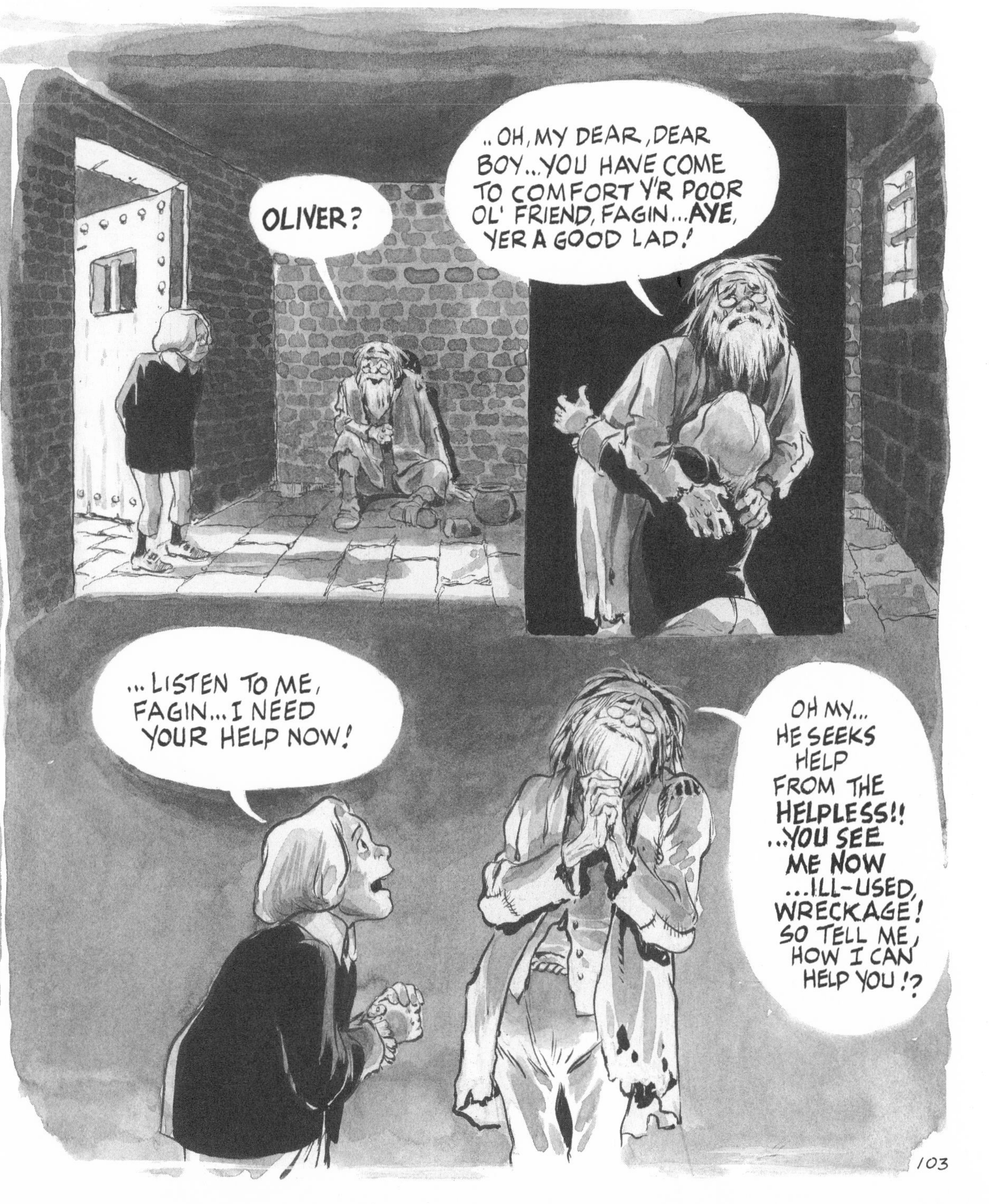
OLIVER?
..OH, MY DEAR, DEAR BOY...YOU HAVE COME TO COMFORT Y'R POOR OL' FRIEND, FAGIN...AYE, YER A GOOD LAD!
...LISTEN TO ME, FAGIN...I NEED YOUR HELP NOW!
OH MY... HE SEEKS HELP FROM THE HELPLESS!! ..YOU SEE ME NOW ...ILL-USED, WRECKAGE! SO TELL ME, HOW I CAN HELP YOU!?

104

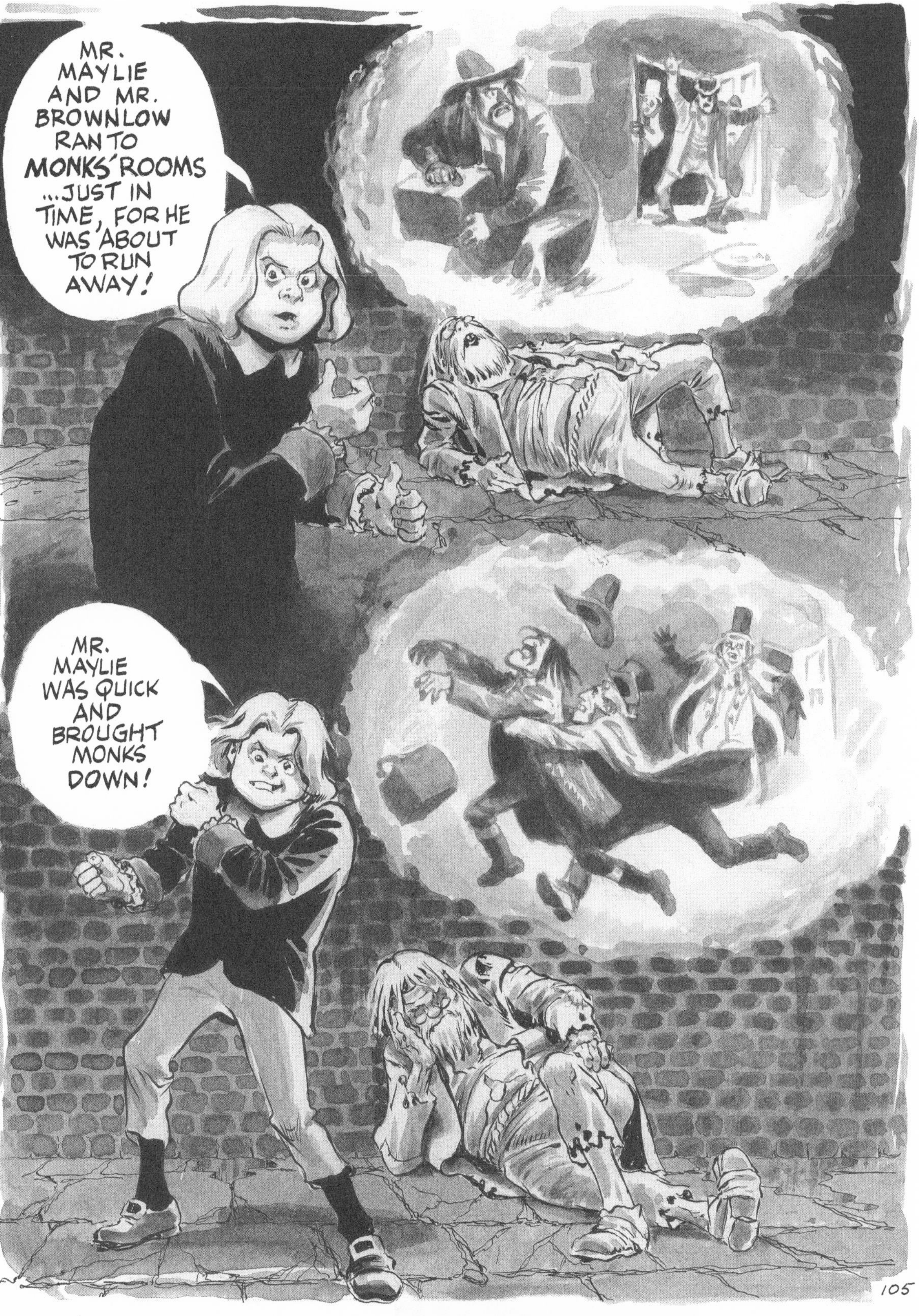
MR. MAYLIE AND MR. BROWNLOW RAN TO MONKS' ROOMS ...JUST IN TIME, FOR HE WAS ABOUT TO RUN AWAY!
MR. MAYLIE WAS QUICK AND BROUGHT MONKS DOWN!

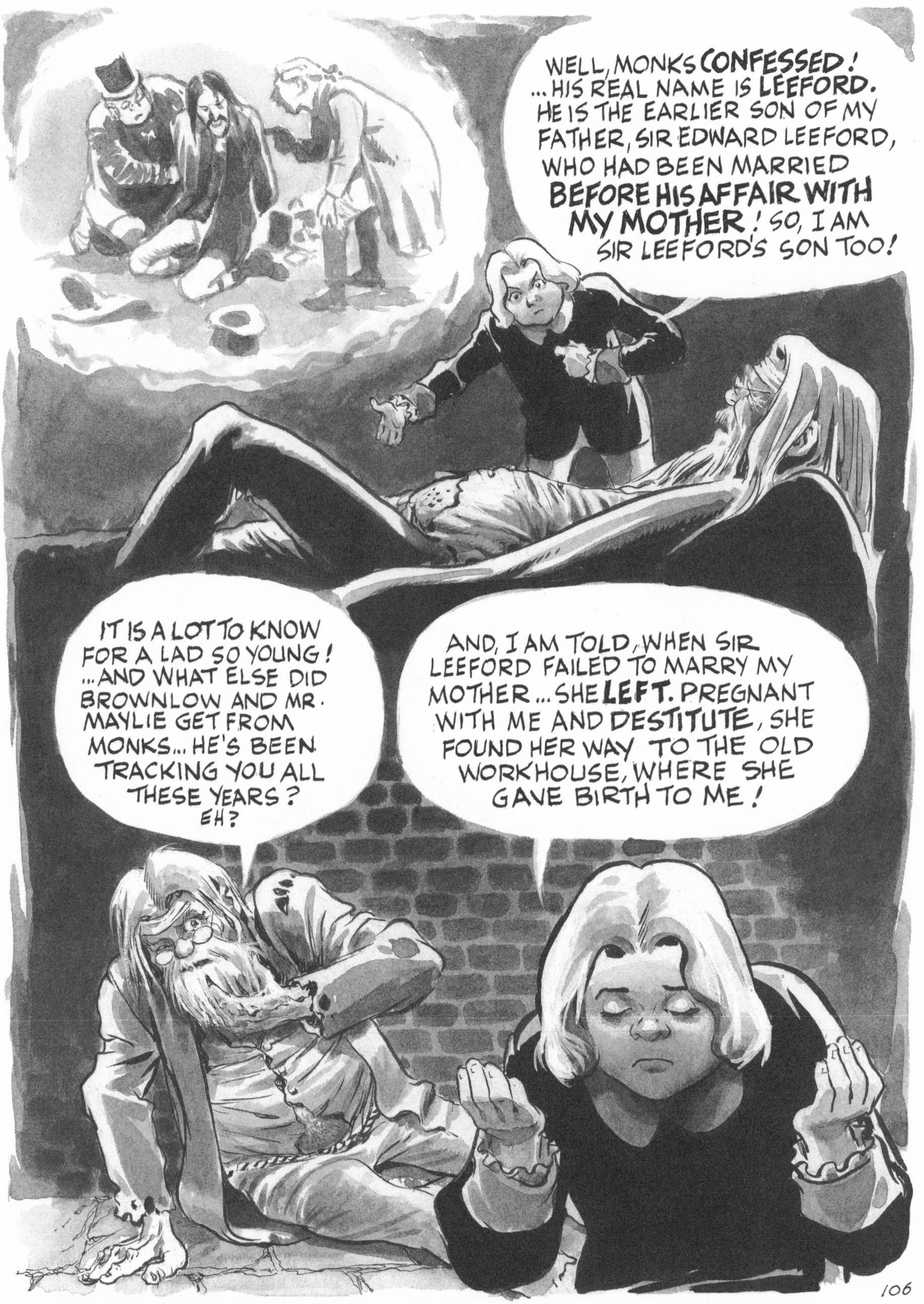
WELL, MONKS CONFESSED! ...HIS REAL NAME IS LEEFORD. HE IS THE EARLIER SON OF MY FATHER, SIR EDWARD LEEFORD, WHO HAD BEEN MARRIED BEFORE HIS AFFAIR WITH MY MOTHER! SO, I AM SIR LEEFORD'S SON TOO!
IT IS A LOT TO KNOW FOR A LAD SO YOUNG! ...AND WHAT ELSE DID BROWNLOW AND MR. MAYLIE GET FROM MONKS... HE'S BEEN TRACKING YOU ALL THESE YEARS? EH?
AND, I AM TOLD, WHEN SIR LEEFORD FAILED TO MARRY MY MOTHER... SHE LEFT. PREGNANT WITH ME AND DESTITUTE, SHE FOUND HER WAY TO THE OLD WORKHOUSE, WHERE SHE GAVE BIRTH TO ME!

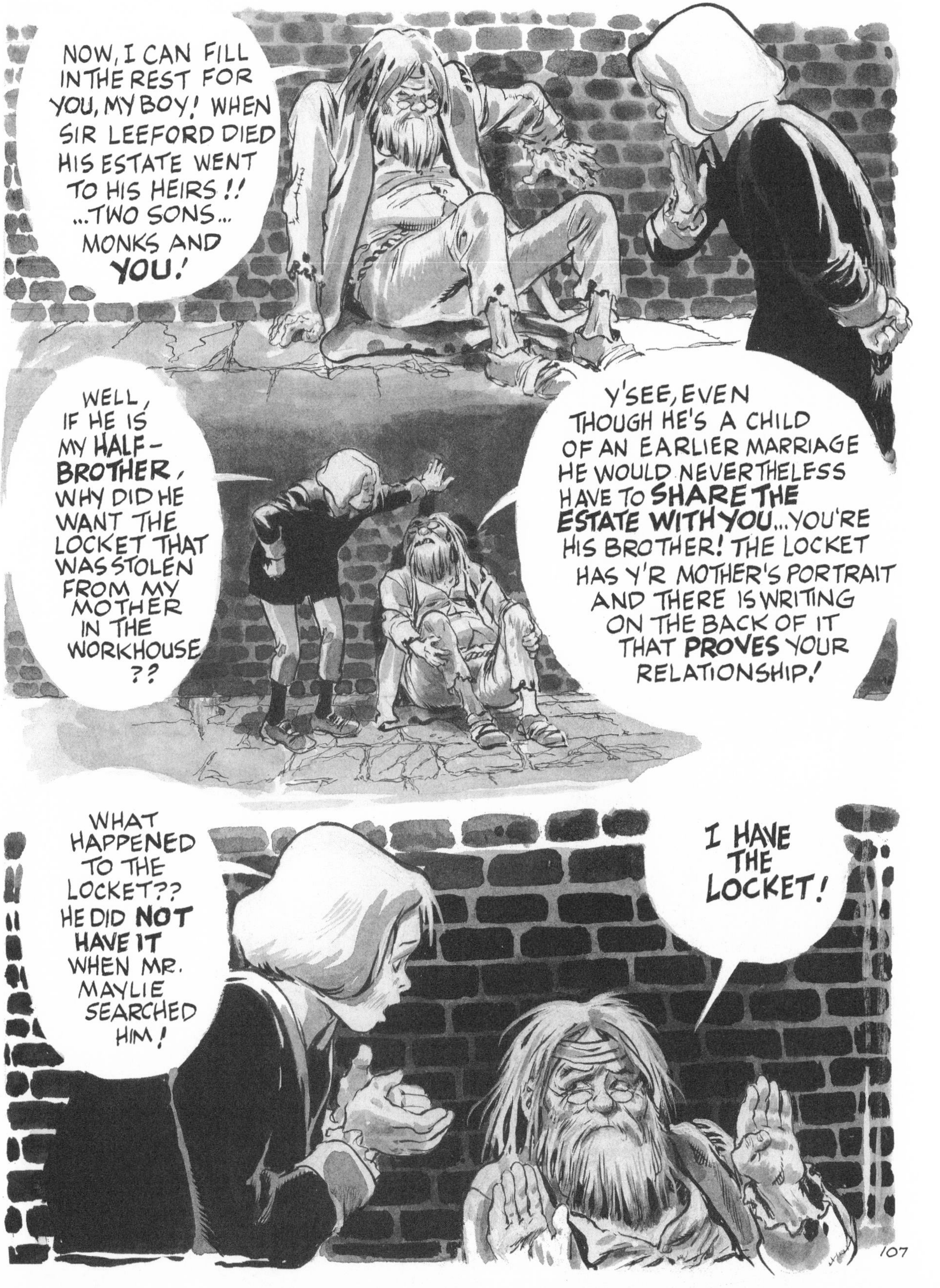

NOW, I CAN FILL IN THE REST FOR YOU, MY BOY! WHEN SIR LEEFORD DIED HIS ESTATE WENT TO HIS HEIRS!! ...TWO SONS... MONKS AND **YOU**!
WELL, IF HE IS MY **HALF-BROTHER**, WHY DID HE WANT THE LOCKET THAT WAS STOLEN FROM MY MOTHER IN THE WORKHOUSE??
Y'SEE, EVEN THOUGH HE'S A CHILD OF AN EARLIER MARRIAGE HE WOULD NEVERTHELESS HAVE TO **SHARE THE ESTATE WITH YOU**... YOU'RE HIS BROTHER! THE LOCKET HAS Y'R MOTHER'S PORTRAIT AND THERE IS WRITING ON THE BACK OF IT THAT **PROVES** YOUR RELATIONSHIP!
WHAT HAPPENED TO THE LOCKET?? HE DID **NOT HAVE IT** WHEN MR. MAYLIE SEARCHED HIM!
I HAVE THE LOCKET!

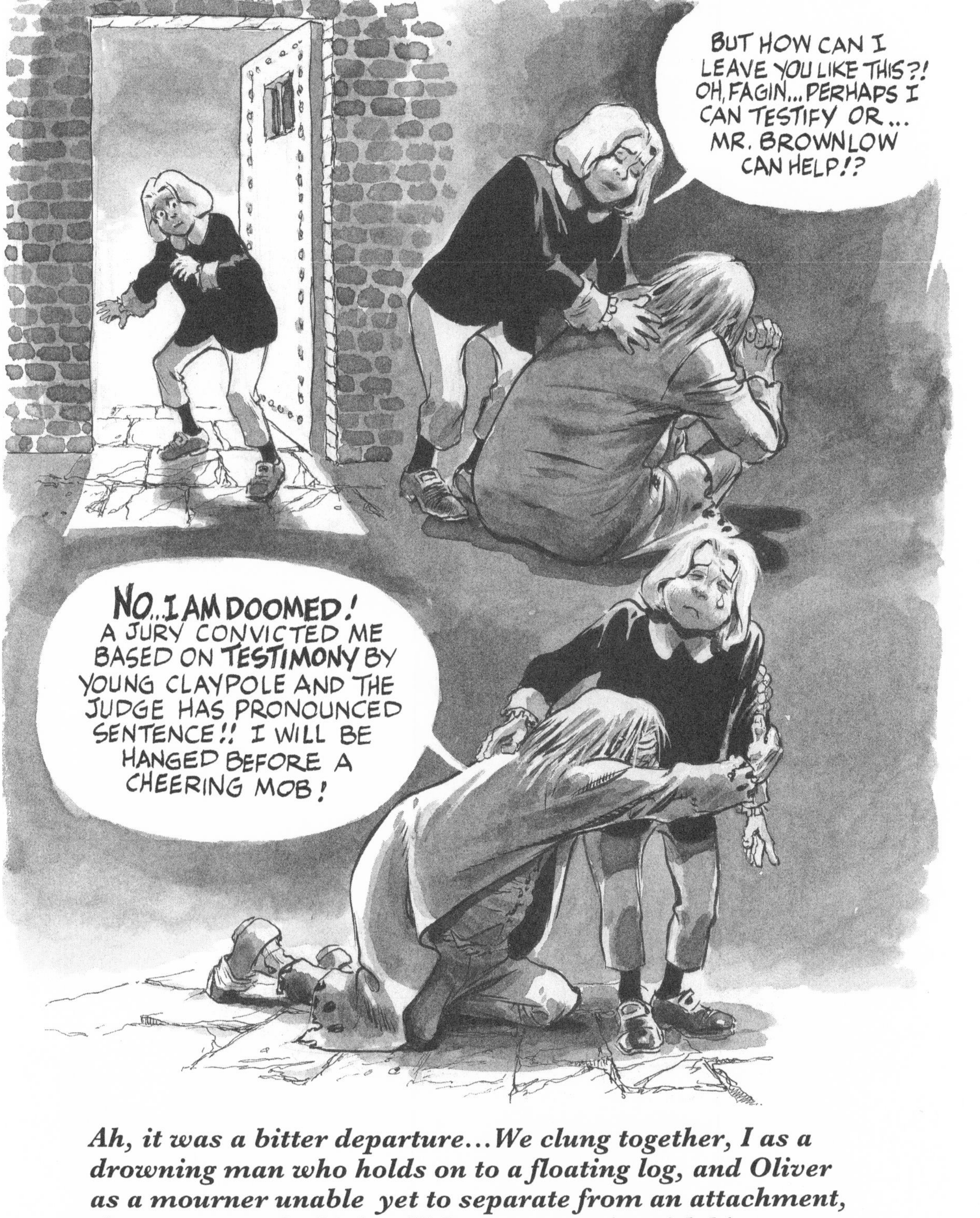
BUT HOW CAN I LEAVE YOU LIKE THIS?! OH, FAGIN...PERHAPS I CAN TESTIFY OR... MR. BROWNLOW CAN HELP!?
NO..I AM DOOMED! A JURY CONVICTED ME BASED ON TESTIMONY BY YOUNG CLAYPOLE AND THE JUDGE HAS PRONOUNCED SENTENCE!! I WILL BE HANGED BEFORE A CHEERING MOB!

Ah, it was a bitter departure...We clung together, I as a drowning man who holds on to a floating log, and Oliver as a mourner unable yet to separate from an attachment, the memory of which will forever remain with him. Finally the boy gathered control of his emotions enough so he could disengage.

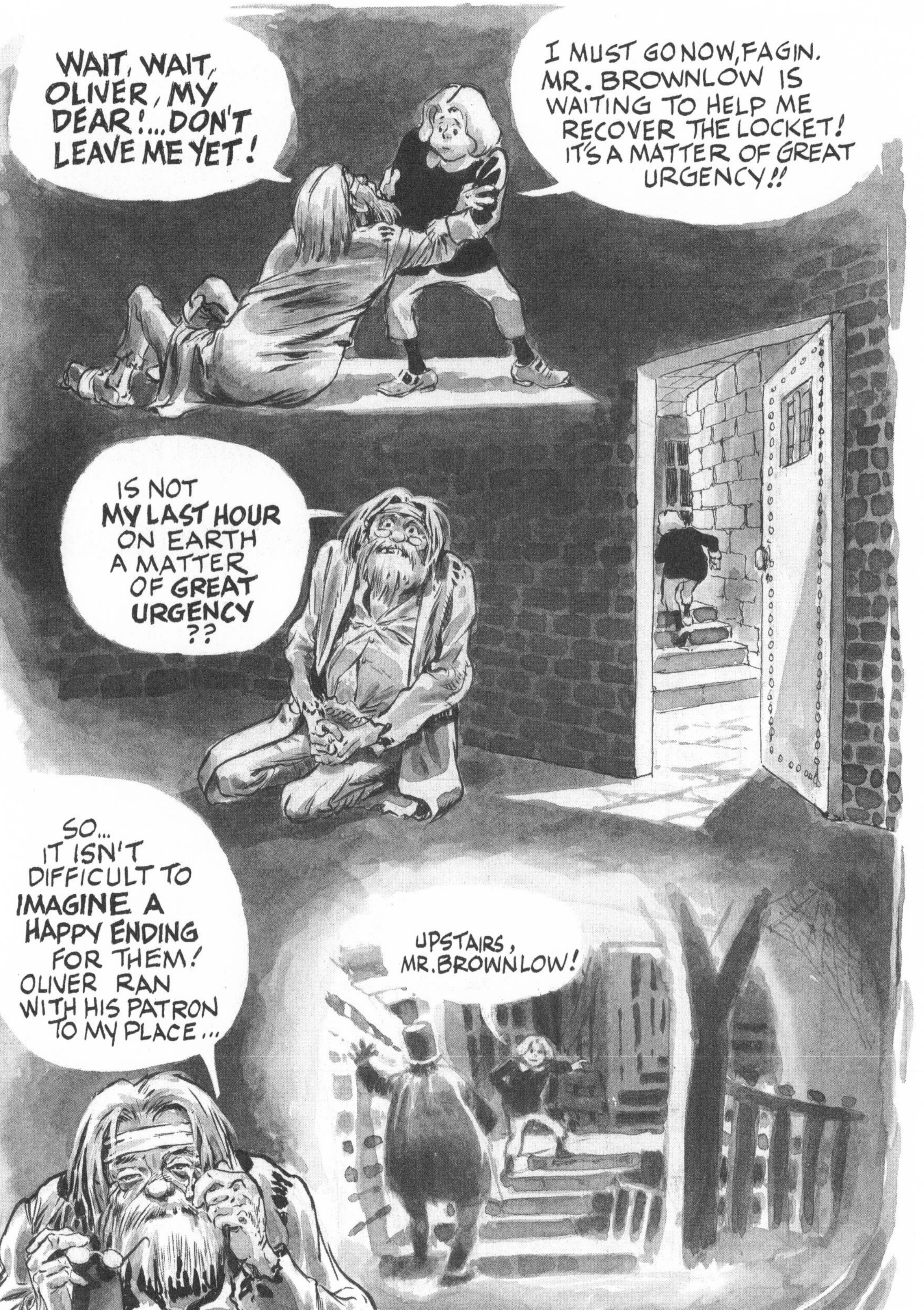
WAIT, WAIT, OLIVER, MY DEAR!... DON'T LEAVE ME YET!
I MUST GO NOW, FAGIN. MR. BROWNLOW IS WAITING TO HELP ME RECOVER THE LOCKET! IT'S A MATTER OF GREAT URGENCY!!
IS NOT MY LAST HOUR ON EARTH A MATTER OF GREAT URGENCY ??
SO... IT ISN'T DIFFICULT TO IMAGINE A HAPPY ENDING FOR THEM! OLIVER RAN WITH HIS PATRON TO MY PLACE...
UPSTAIRS, MR. BROWNLOW!

113

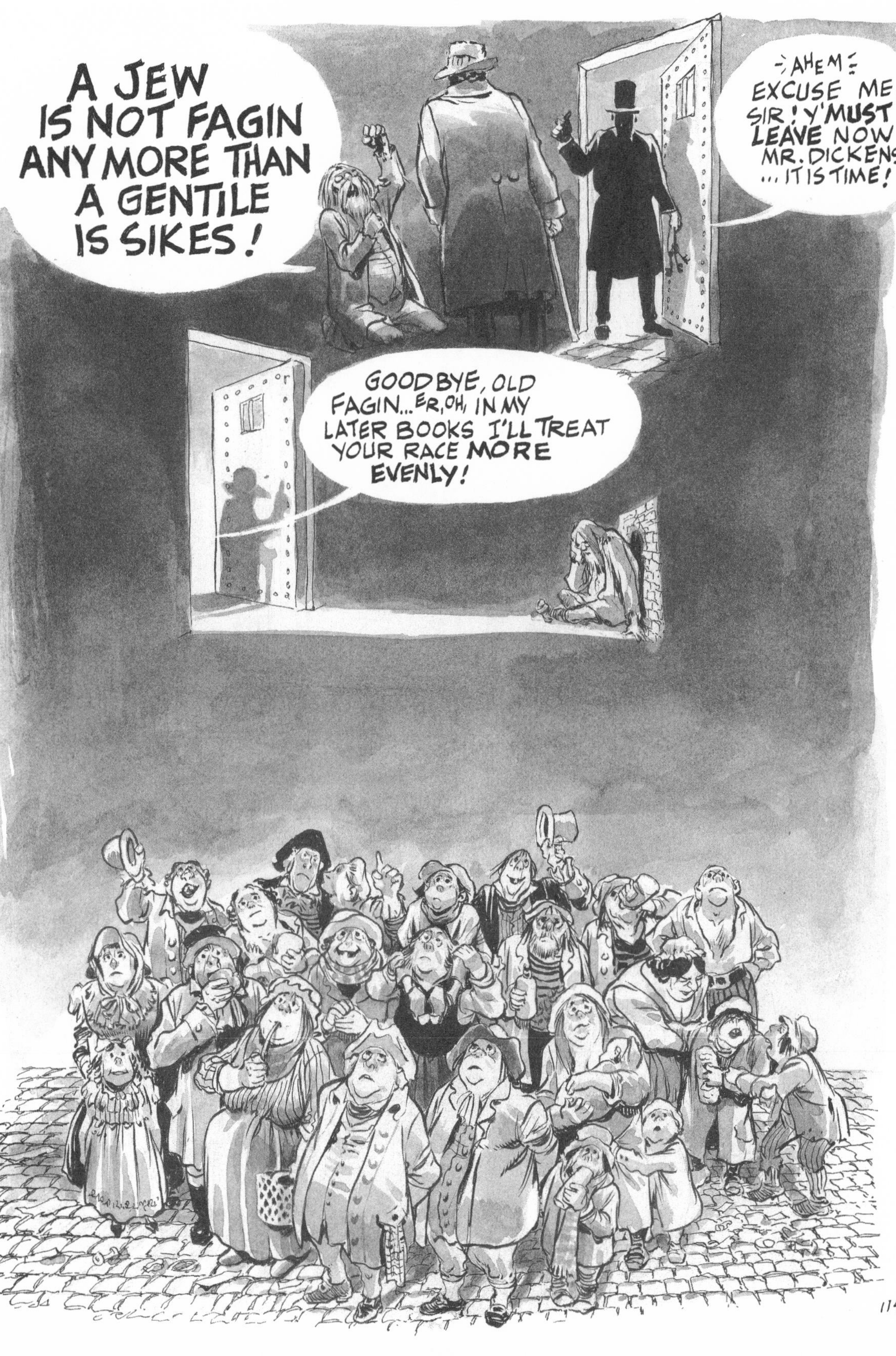
A JEW IS NOT FAGIN ANY MORE THAN A GENTILE IS SIKES!
AHEM EXCUSE ME, SIR! Y'MUST LEAVE NOW MR. DICKENS, ... IT IS TIME!
GOODBYE, OLD FAGIN... ER, OH, IN MY LATER BOOKS I'LL TREAT YOUR RACE MORE EVENLY!

EPILOGUE

Fagin was hanged and buried ignominiously in a pauper's grave, together with others that fate had demeaned.

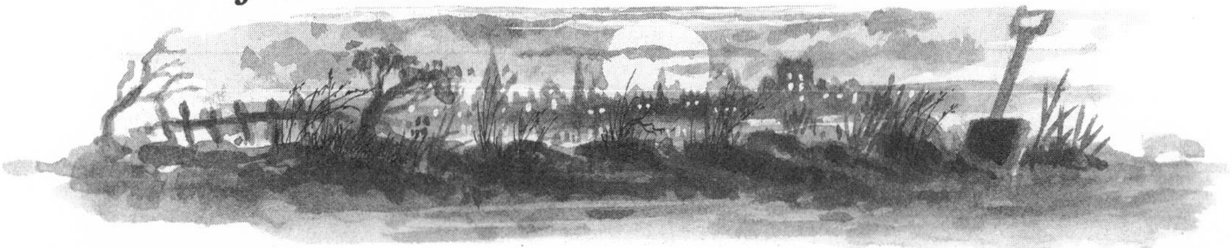

The young lad Oliver was adopted by Mr. Brownlow. He became a successful barrister who at last found out about a turning point in Fagin's life and his legacy.

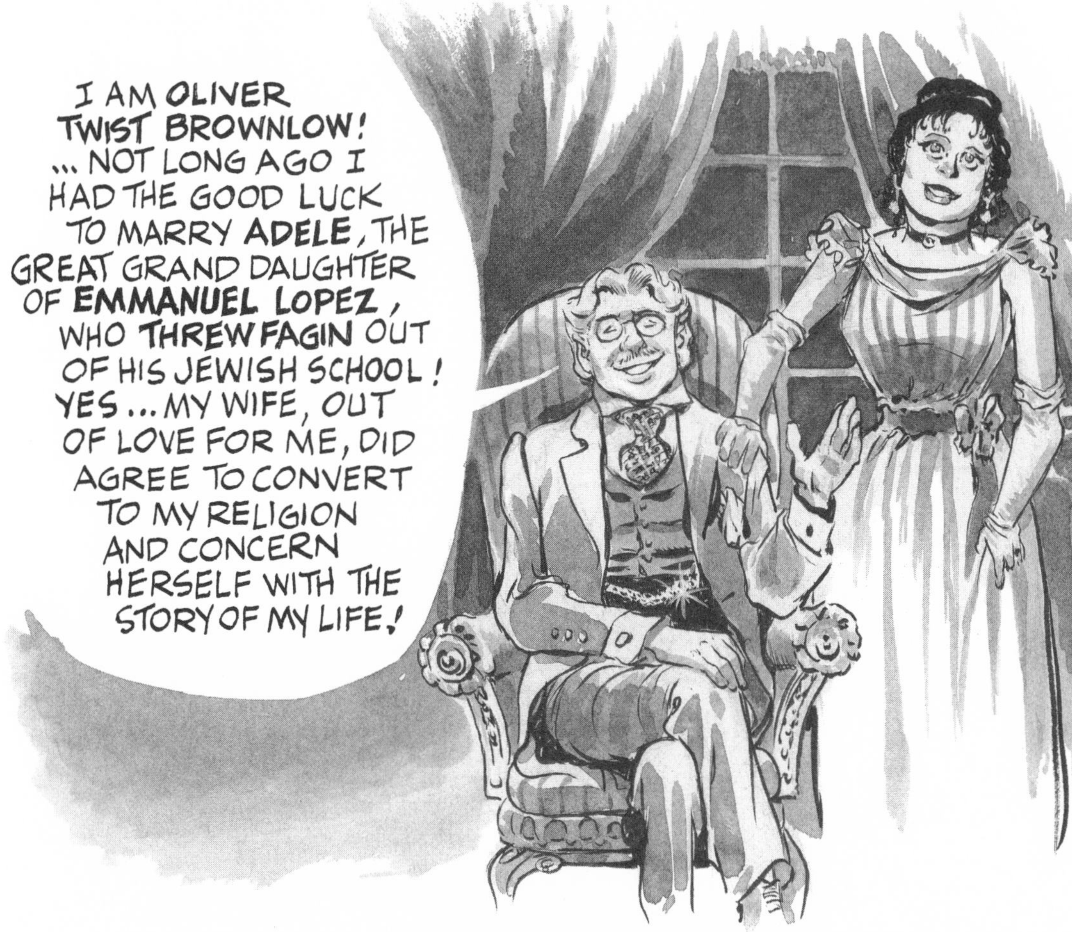
I AM OLIVER TWIST BROWNLOW! ... NOT LONG AGO I HAD THE GOOD LUCK TO MARRY ADELE, THE GREAT GRAND DAUGHTER OF EMMANUEL LOPEZ, WHO THREW FAGIN OUT OF HIS JEWISH SCHOOL! YES ... MY WIFE, OUT OF LOVE FOR ME, DID AGREE TO CONVERT TO MY RELIGION AND CONCERN HERSELF WITH THE STORY OF MY LIFE!

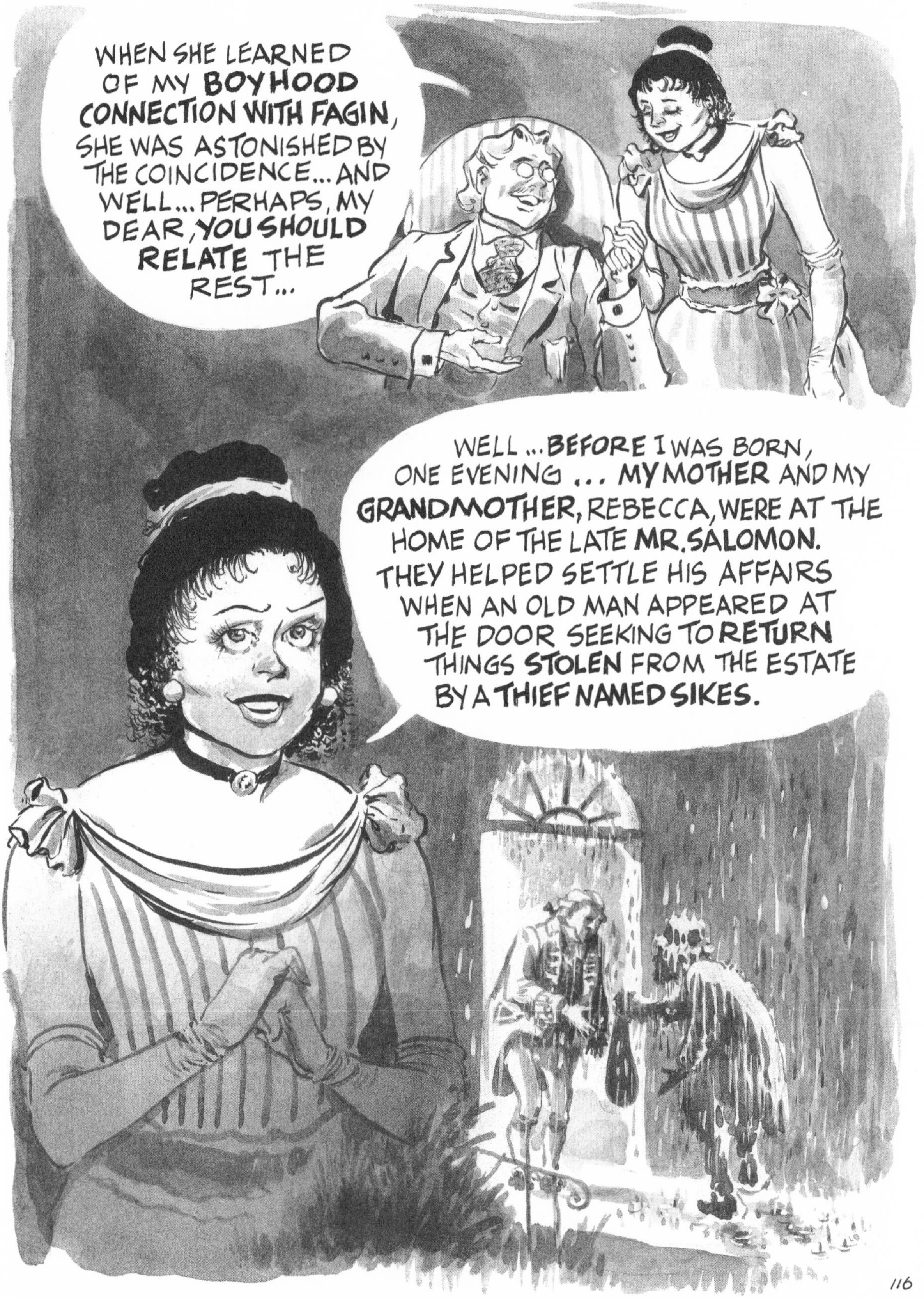
WHEN SHE LEARNED OF MY BOYHOOD CONNECTION WITH FAGIN, SHE WAS ASTONISHED BY THE COINCIDENCE... AND WELL... PERHAPS, MY DEAR, YOU SHOULD RELATE THE REST...
WELL ... BEFORE I WAS BORN, ONE EVENING ... MY MOTHER AND MY GRANDMOTHER, REBECCA, WERE AT THE HOME OF THE LATE MR. SALOMON. THEY HELPED SETTLE HIS AFFAIRS WHEN AN OLD MAN APPEARED AT THE DOOR SEEKING TO RETURN THINGS STOLEN FROM THE ESTATE BY A THIEF NAMED SIKES.

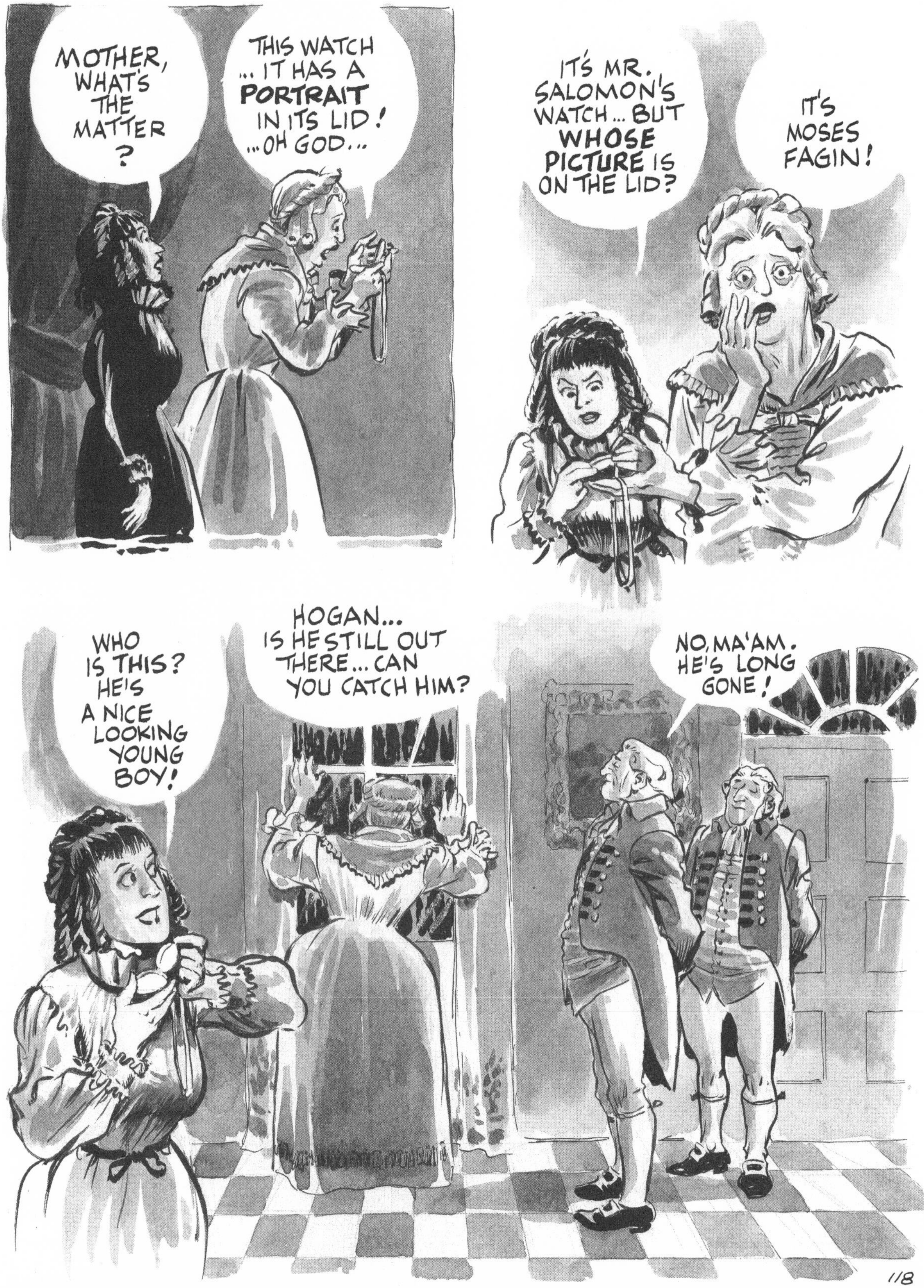
MOTHER, WHAT'S THE MATTER ?
THIS WATCH ... IT HAS A **PORTRAIT** IN ITS LID ! ...OH GOD...
IT'S MR. SALOMON'S WATCH ... BUT **WHOSE PICTURE** IS ON THE LID?
IT'S MOSES FAGIN !
WHO IS **THIS**? HE'S A NICE LOOKING YOUNG BOY!
HOGAN... IS HE STILL OUT THERE... CAN YOU CATCH HIM?
NO, MA'AM. HE'S LONG GONE !

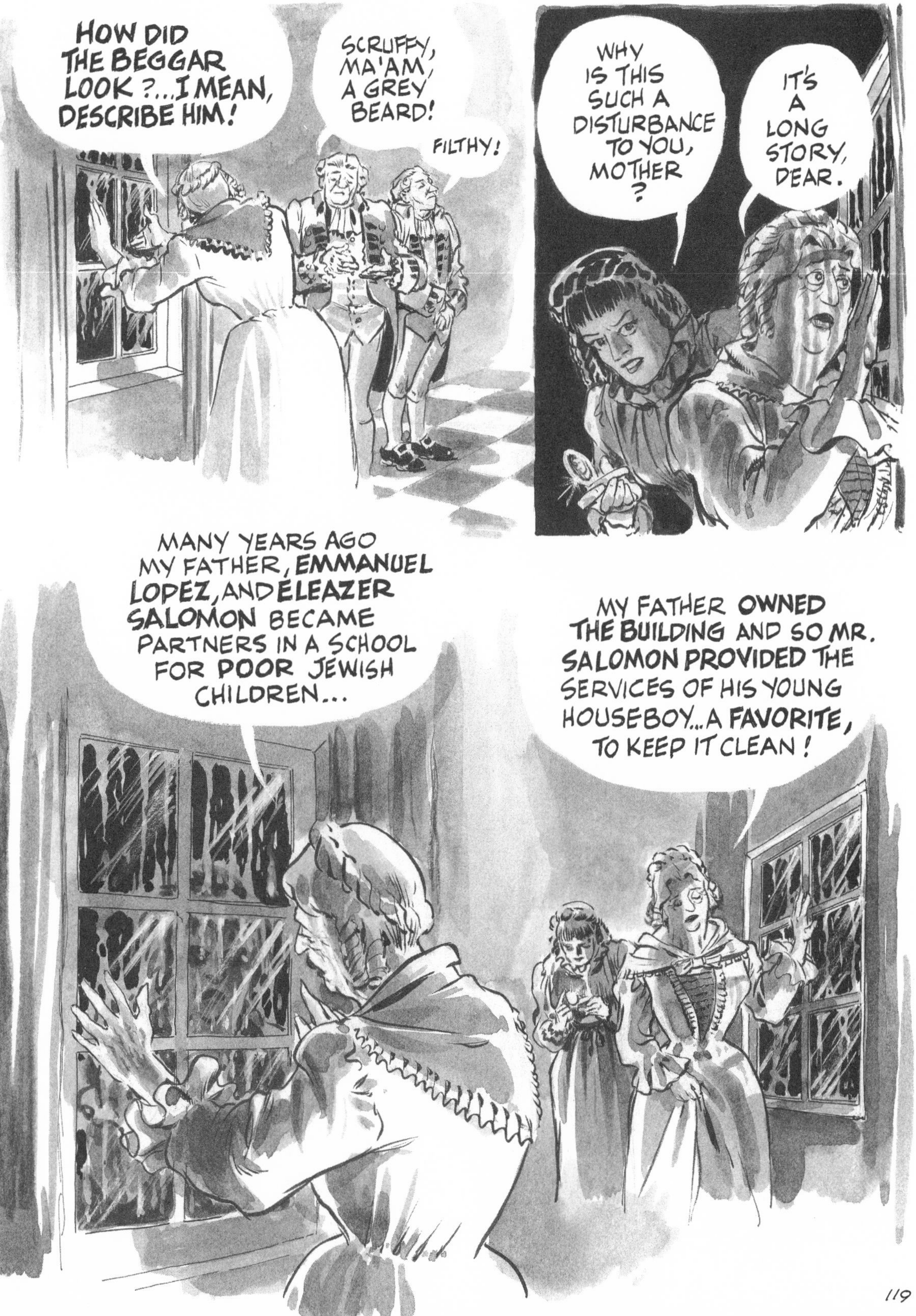
HOW DID THE BEGGAR LOOK ?...I MEAN, DESCRIBE HIM!
SCRUFFY, MA'AM, A GREY BEARD!
FILTHY!
WHY IS THIS SUCH A DISTURBANCE TO YOU, MOTHER ?
IT'S A LONG STORY, DEAR.
MANY YEARS AGO MY FATHER, EMMANUEL LOPEZ, AND ELEAZER SALOMON BECAME PARTNERS IN A SCHOOL FOR POOR JEWISH CHILDREN...
MY FATHER OWNED THE BUILDING AND SO MR. SALOMON PROVIDED THE SERVICES OF HIS YOUNG HOUSEBOY...A FAVORITE, TO KEEP IT CLEAN!

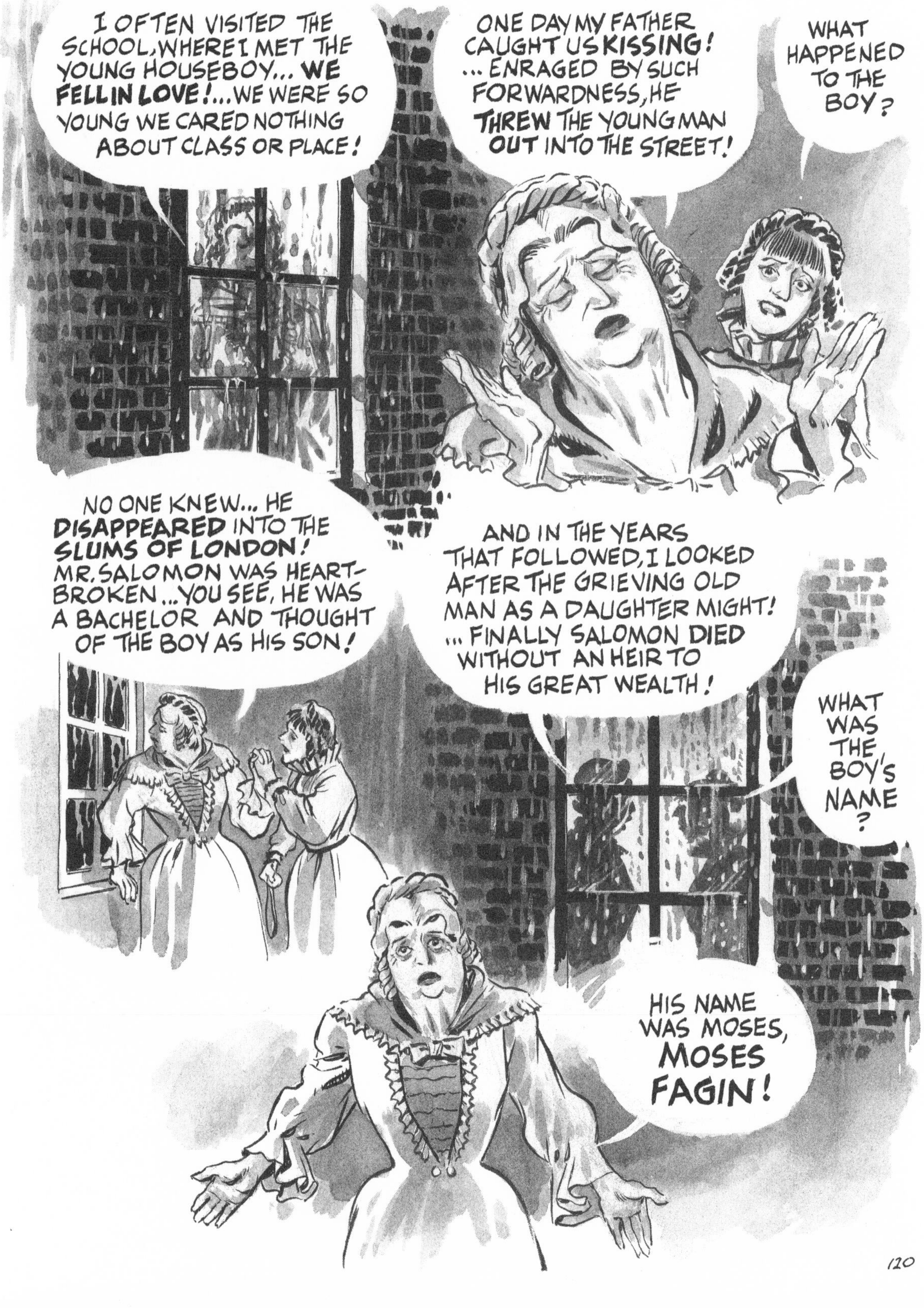
I OFTEN VISITED THE SCHOOL, WHERE I MET THE YOUNG HOUSEBOY... **WE FELL IN LOVE!**... WE WERE SO YOUNG WE CARED NOTHING ABOUT CLASS OR PLACE!
ONE DAY MY FATHER CAUGHT US **KISSING!** ... ENRAGED BY SUCH FORWARDNESS, HE **THREW** THE YOUNG MAN **OUT** INTO THE STREET!
WHAT HAPPENED TO THE BOY?
NO ONE KNEW... HE **DISAPPEARED** INTO THE **SLUMS OF LONDON!** MR. SALOMON WAS HEART-BROKEN ...YOU SEE, HE WAS A BACHELOR AND THOUGHT OF THE BOY AS HIS SON!
AND IN THE YEARS THAT FOLLOWED, I LOOKED AFTER THE GRIEVING OLD MAN AS A DAUGHTER MIGHT! ... FINALLY SALOMON **DIED** WITHOUT AN HEIR TO HIS GREAT WEALTH!
WHAT WAS THE BOY'S NAME?
HIS NAME WAS MOSES, **MOSES FAGIN!**

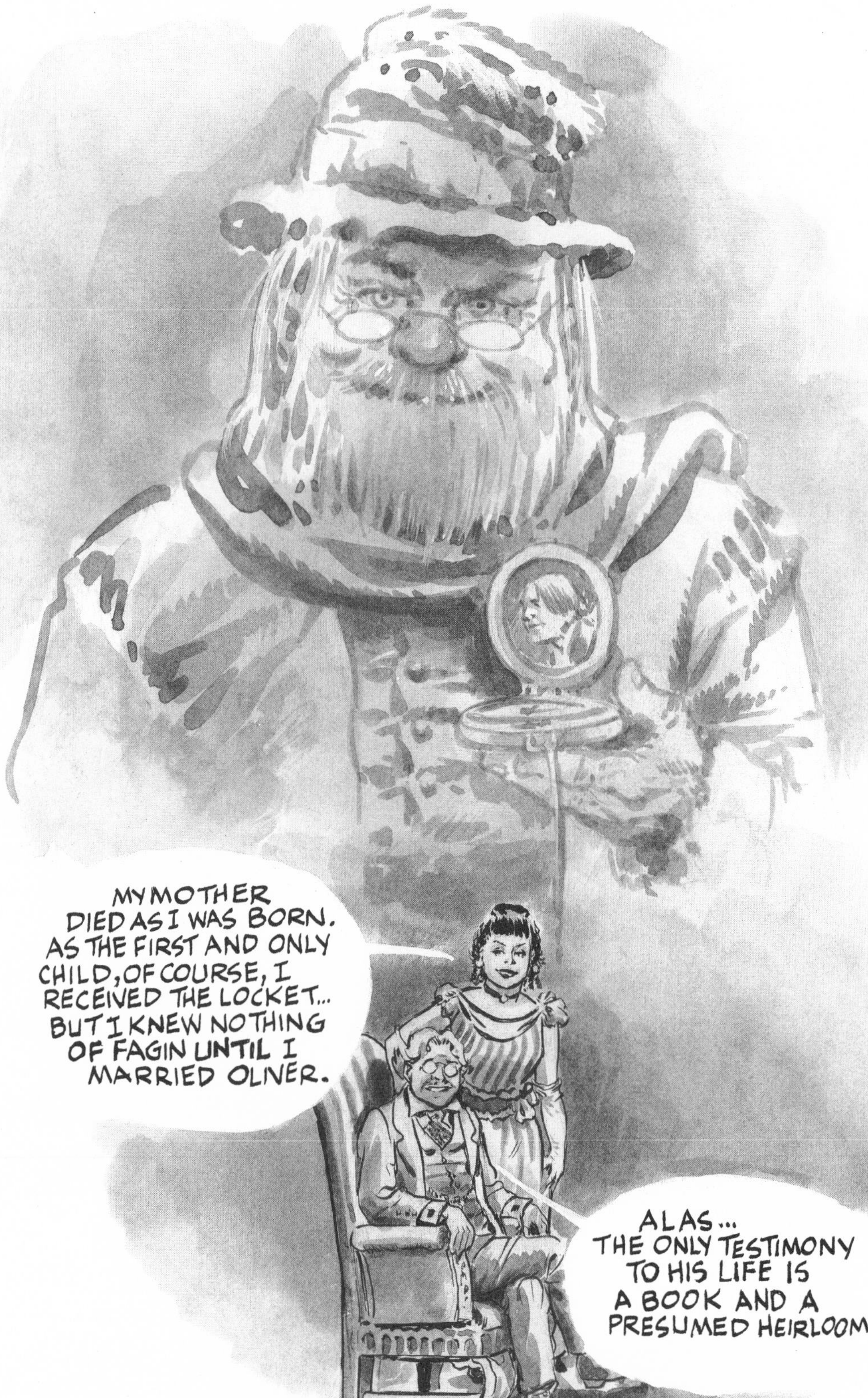
MY MOTHER DIED AS I WAS BORN. AS THE FIRST AND ONLY CHILD, OF COURSE, I RECEIVED THE LOCKET... BUT I KNEW NOTHING OF FAGIN UNTIL I MARRIED OLIVER.
ALAS... THE ONLY TESTIMONY TO HIS LIFE IS A BOOK AND A PRESUMED HEIRLOOM!

Afterword

Throughout history, certain fictional characters in our literature have achieved an illusion of reality due to their popularity. In the main, they became enduring stereotypes and influenced social judgment. Shylock the Jew and Sherlock Holmes the detective are classic examples.

Fagin, created by Charles Dickens in *Oliver Twist*, ultimately became one such "profile" of a Jew that embedded itself in popular culture and prejudice. In truth, the author never intended to defame the Jewish people, but by referring to Fagin as "the Jew" throughout the book he abetted the prejudice against them. Over the years, *Oliver Twist* became a staple of juvenile literature, and the stereotype was perpetuated.

Despite his treatment of Fagin, Charles Dickens maintained that he was not an anti-Semite. He did use anti-Jewish epithets and offhand remarks in his letters and conversation, which were common in the language of the era. Dickens once referred to Richard Benteley, his (Gentile) English publisher, as

"a thundering old Jew." However, in books such as *A Child's History of England*, he deems "cruel and inexcusable" the persecution and expulsion of Jews by Edward I in 1290. Later, he condemned the well-known Thomas Carlyle's aversion to Jews. In a speech to the Westminster Jewish Free School in 1854, Dickens proclaimed, "I do my part in the assertion of their [Jews'] civil rights. . . . I have expressed strong abhorrence of their persecution in old time."

The following segments from Dickens's foreword to the third edition of *Oliver Twist* in 1841 indicate his intentions by explaining his use of Fagin for the role and by implication justifying his use of the label "Jew" to describe him.

The greater part of this tale was originally published in a magazine. When I completed it and put it forth in its present form three years ago, I fully expected it would be objected to on some very high moral grounds in some very high moral quarters.

The result did not fail to prove the justice of my anticipations.

It is, it seems, a very coarse and shocking circumstance, that some of the characters in these pages are chosen from the most criminal and degraded of London's population; that Sikes is a thief and Fagin a receiver of stolen goods; that the boys are pick-pockets and the girl is a prostitute.

It appeared to me that to draw a knot of such associates in crime as really do exist; to paint them in all their wretchedness, in all the squalid poverty of their lives; to show them as they really are, forever skulking uneasily through the dirtiest paths of life, with the great, black, ghastly gallows closing up their prospects, turn them where they may; it appeared to me that to do this, would be to attempt something which was greatly needed and which would be a service to society. And therefore I did it as best I could.

Further, after receiving a letter of complaint from Mrs. Eliza Davis, the wife of a Jewish banker, about twenty years later, Dickens tried to eliminate most of the frequent references to Fagin as a Jew in an 1867 edition of *Oliver Twist*. This, however, was too late, for the earlier and well-distributed popular editions still in use today contain the earlier version that uses "Jew" to refer to Fagin.

Nonetheless, I believe that Dickens's stated intention to describe the conditions of the time places the burden of reportorial accuracy upon him. It has always troubled me that Fagin "the Jew" never got fair treatment, and I challenge Charles Dickens and his illustrator, George Cruikshank, for their description and delineation of Fagin as a classic stereotypical Jew. I believe this depiction was based on ill-considered evidence, imitation, and popular ignorance. Cartoonists certainly understand how easy it is to rely on a common image in the visual language to portray a character, but like the mistakes of illustrators before him, Cruikshank's misuse of a necessary staple in portraying Fagin, one that was so common to contemporary publications, is a contribution to further reprehensible stereotyping of Jews by bigots throughout history.

The Jewish community of London around 1800 consisted of two main groups, the Sephardim and the Ashkenazim. The Sephardim originally came from Portugal and Spain to settle in England after fleeing the Spanish Inquisition. Because they were mostly educated, they were able to achieve an acceptable position in the English community. England was attractive to Jews because it was then one of the more liberal societies, with some religious tolerance and an accessible legal system. The Sephardim assimilated easily and for the most part became professionals, tradesmen, and financiers. Their numbers increased over the years with the arrival of others who had also fled Spain but had sought refuge in Holland. The growth of a lively trade between London and Amsterdam led to an increase in Jewish immigration.

Until about 1700, the Sephardim were the dominant Jewish population in England, but the "lower class" who arrived during the eighteenth century were mostly Ashkenazim. They came from Germany and

Middle Europe, where they had lived in small villages until driven out by intolerance, repression, and pogroms. Rural life and peasant culture had rendered them less educated and cruder in their ways. As a result, when they arrived in London they had difficulty assimilating. Like all new, poor immigrant arrivals throughout history, they clung to old ghetto habits and social behavior. Impoverished and illiterate, they took up marginal occupations in the grim-ier quarters of London. It is reasonable to assume that Fagin came from such origins.

In my opinion, the limning of Jews by illustrators of Dickens's time was most likely inaccurate with regard to Fagin's appearance. Because of their Eastern European origins, Ashkenazic Jews likely had features that had come to resemble the German physiognomy. There were many blond Jews, as a result of rapes that occurred during pogroms. However, the popular illustrations of Jews, including Cruikshank's, were based on the appearance of the Sephardim, whose features when they arrived were sharper, with dark hair and complexions, the result of their four-hundred-year sojourn among the Latin and Mediterranean peoples. The careless disregard of this demography and its impact on cultural acceptance made it necessary to reintroduce Fagin at long last.

The lithograph prints and etchings that were popular in England in the eighteenth century provided the public with satirical commentary on social life of the day. They were sold, sometimes even by Jewish peddlers, on the streets of English cities, in print shops, and in book stalls. These were generally collected in albums or hung in dens, libraries, or workplaces.

In Charles Dickens's time, the most popular creators of these prints included Thomas Rowlandson, Henry Wigstead, George Woodward, Isaac Cruikshank (father of George Cruikshank, who illustrated *Oliver Twist*), and James Gilray. Like the great English artist Hogarth before them, they enjoyed considerable professional stature and popular fame. It was their delineations that contributed to the perpetuation of the negative stereotype of Jews and that provide a record of the public perceptions of that time.

In America during the twentieth century, this genre of illustration and cartoon appeared in newspapers, humor magazines, and family publications that catered to the public taste. Because of this country's large immigrant population the ethnic caricatures were less vitriolic but persisted nevertheless. The influential political drawings by Thomas Nast and fellow political cartoonists that dwelt on the stereotypes of corrupt politicos were successors to their English forerunners. The more social observations of Charles Dana Gibson and James Montgomery Flagg used depictions that mostly avoided exaggerated ethnic characterization.

I include below several examples of prints and illustrations from that period, which demonstrate the limning of Jews by the eighteenth-century illustrators who were most influential at that time.

My version of Fagin is, I believe, a more truthful stereotype.

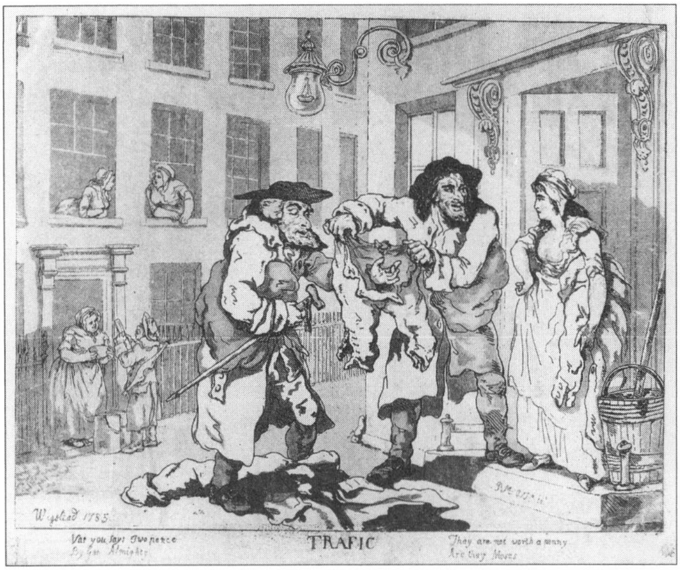
Wigstead 1785
Vat you says Two pence
By God Almighty
TRAFIC
They are not worth a penny
Are they Moses

An aquatint etching by Henry Wigstead (1785) showing two Jewish old-clothes dealers in London buying clothes from a domestic. The title, "Trafic," is accompanied by dialogue.

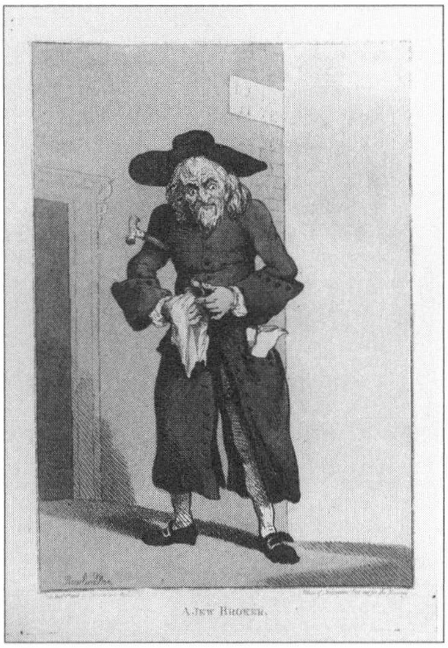
A JEW BROKER.

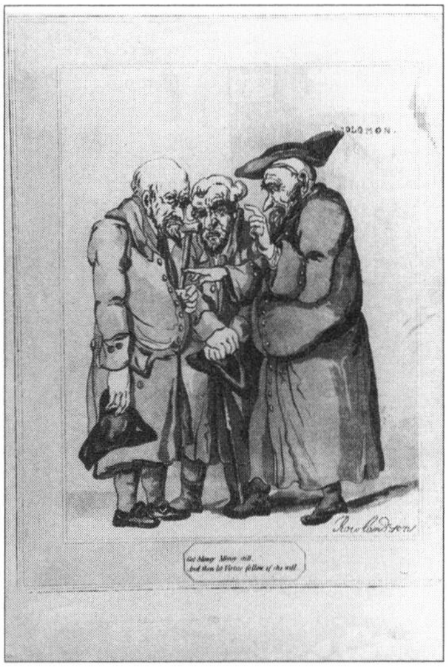
Rowlandson

Two etchings by Thomas Rowlandson (1808) in which Jews are shown as typical of their trade. Rowlandson was a very popular cartoonist of the time.

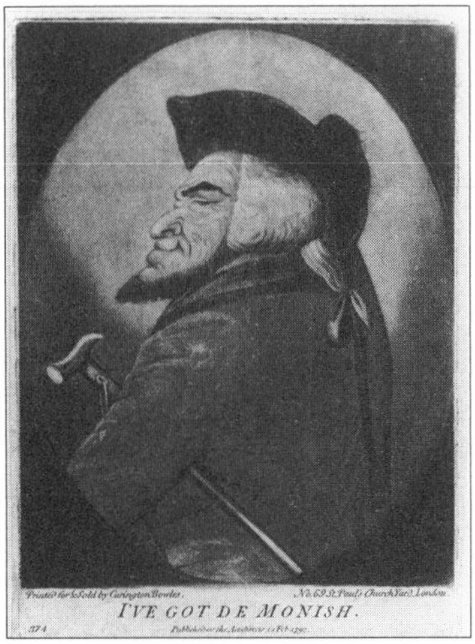
I'VE GOT DE MONISH.

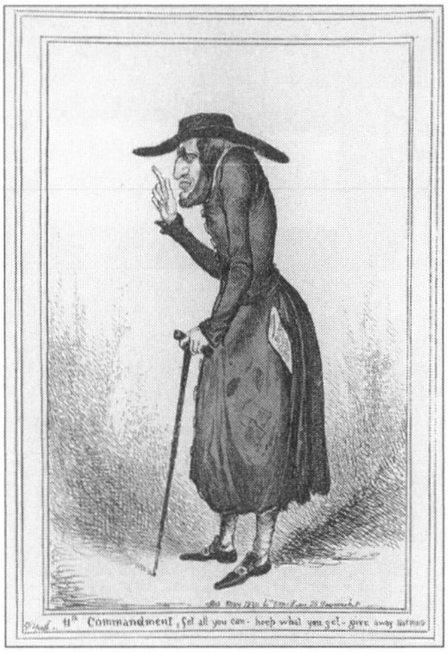
11th Commandment, get all you can - keep what you get - give away nothing

These two published prints, "I've Got de Monish" (circa 1792) and "Commandment, get all you can" (circa 1830), are examples of popular images that were widely sold in London. They helped create the accepted public stereotype of a Jew.

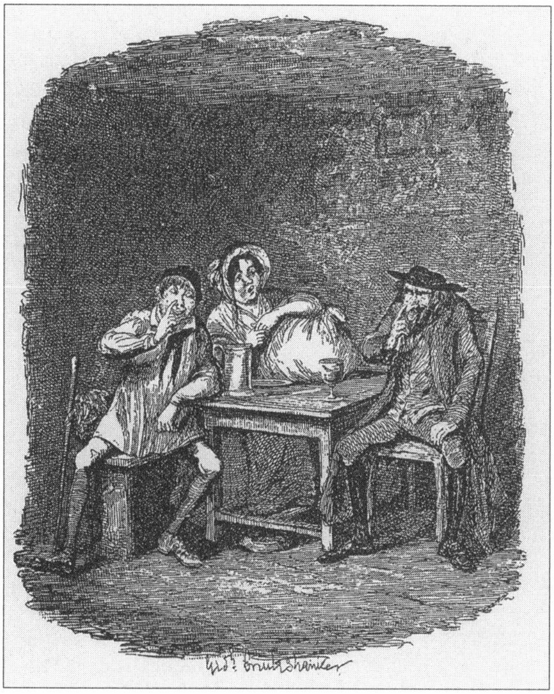

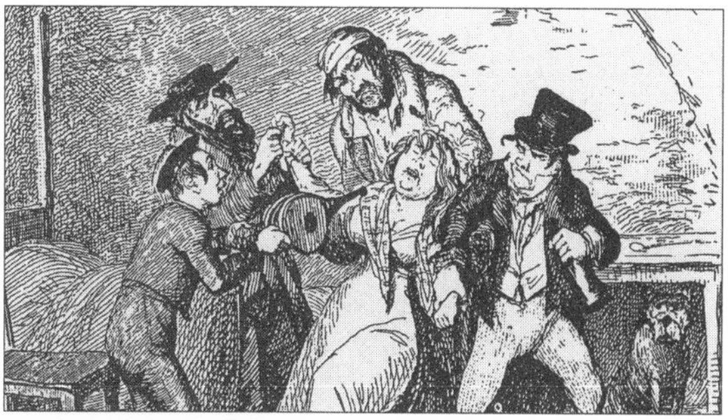

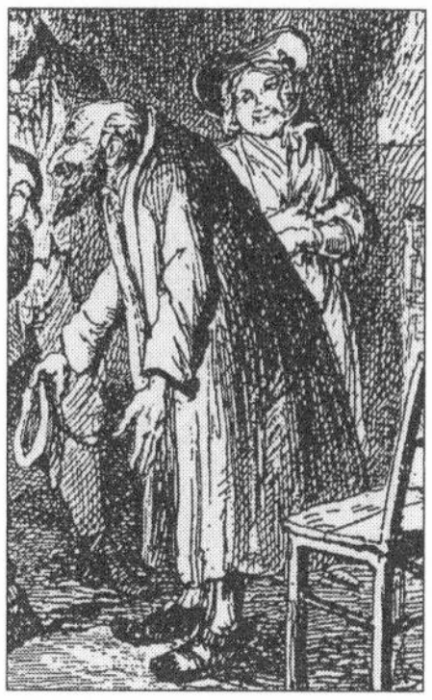

In Cruikshank's version of Fagin, he shows a "Sephardic" physiognomy. My version of Fagin is based on the more Germanic face, which I believe is more truthful.

"Money Lenders"

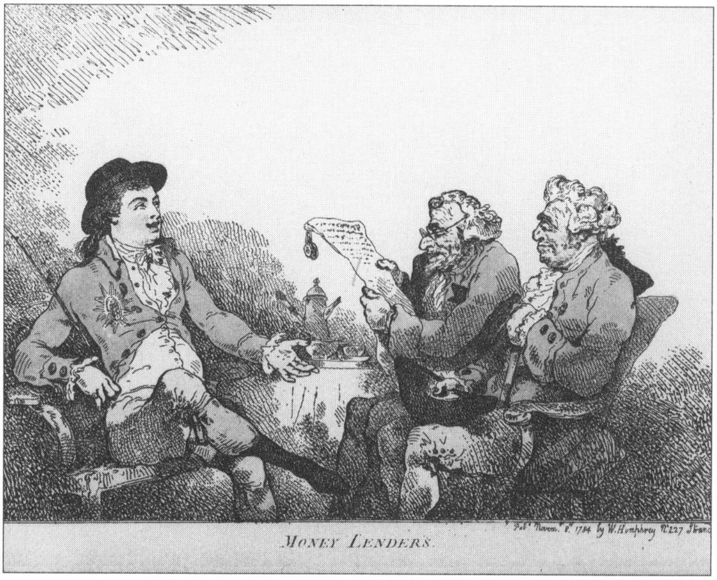
MONEY LENDERS.

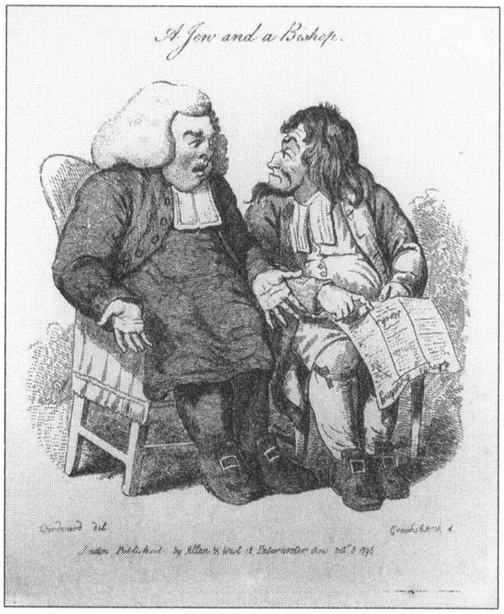
A Jew and a Bishop.

Isaac Cruikshank (left) and Thomas Rowlandson (above) continually characterized Jews as having physiognomies different from Gentiles.

"A Jew and a Bishop"

Sources

The Jews of Georgian England, 1714–1830: Tradition and Change in a Liberal Society by Todd M. Endelman (Ann Arbor: The University of Michigan Press, 1999)

The Jews in the History of England, 1485–1850 by David S. Katz (Oxford: Clarendon Press, 1994)

The Jew as Other: A Century of English Caricature 1730–1830. An Exhibition by the Jewish Theological Seminary of America. April 6–July 31, 1995

Oxford Reader's Companion to Dickens, edited by Paul Schlicke (Oxford: Oxford University Press, 1999)